GETTING THERE

Also by Diana Wells

We Have a Dream
African-American Visions of Freedom

GETTING THERE

The Movement Toward Gender Equality

Compiled by Diana Wells

Carroll & Graf Publishers/Richard Gallen
New York

Collection and preface copyright © 1994 by Diana Wells

The permissions listed on pages v to vii constitute an extension
of this copyright page.

First Carroll & Graf/Richard Gallen edition 1994

Carroll & Graf Publishers, Inc.
260 Fifth Avenue
New York, NY 10001

Library of Congress Cataloging-in-Publication Data

Getting there : the movement toward gender equality / compiled by
   Diana Wells.—1st Carroll & Graf/Richard Gallen ed.
      p. cm.
   ISBN 0-7867-0014-9 : $11.95
   1. Feminism—United States. I. Wells, Diana. II. Title :
Gender equality.
HQ1421.G48   1994
305.42'0973—dc20   93-23501
                                                        CIP

Manufactured in the United States of America.

Acknowledgments

The Publisher greatly acknowledges the following for permission to reprint from previously published material:

Beacon Press for "Claims to Motherhood: Custody Disputes and Maternal Strategies" by Ellen Lewin from *Uncertain Terms* by Faye Ginsburg and Ann Lowenhaupt Tsing. Copyright © 1990 by Faye Ginsburg and Ann Lowenhaupt Tsing; and for the excerpt from *The Woman in the Body: A Cultural Analysis of Reproduction* by Emily Martin. Copyright © 1987 by Emily Martin.

Charlotte Sheedy Literary Agency, Inc., for the excerpt from *The Cancer Journals* by Audre Lorde, published by Aunt Lute Books. Copyright © 1980 by Audre Lorde.

Crown Publishers, Inc., for the excerpt from *Backlash* by Susan Faludi. Copyright © 1991 by Susan Faludi.

Grove/Atlantic Monthly Press for "Is Gender Necessary?" from *Dancing at the Edge of the World: Thoughts on Words, Women, Places* by Ursula K. Le Guin. Copyright © 1989 by Ursula K. Le Guin.

Hartcourt Brace & Company for "Womanist" from *In Search of Our Mothers' Gardens: Womanist Prose*. Copyright © 1983 by Alice Walker.

Harvard University Press for "Sexual Politics of the First Amendment" from *Feminism Unmodified: Discourses on Life and Law* by Catharine A. MacKinnon. Copyright © 1987 by the President and Fellows of Harvard College.

Ms. magazine for "Why a Woman's Medical Specialty" by Karen Johnson and Charlea Massion, Copyright © 1991 by *Ms.* magazine;

"From Carmita Wood to Anita Hill" by Susan Brownmiller and Dolores Alexander, Copyright © 1992 by *Ms.* magazine; "The State of NOW: A Presidential (and Personal) Report" by Patricia Ireland Copyright © 1992 by *Ms.* magazine; "What's Good for the Race?" by Marcia Ann Gillespie, Copyright © 1993 by *Ms.* magazine.

The Nation Company, Inc., for "Who Was Lynched" by Nell Irvin Painter from *The Nation* magazine, Copyright © 1991 by The Nation Company, Inc.; and "Marooned on Gilligan's Island: Are Women Morally Superior to Men?" by Katha Pollitt, from *The Nation* magazine, Copyright © 1993 by The Nation Company, Inc.

The New York Times Company for "The Glass Half Empty," by Anna Quindlen from *The New York Times.* Copyright © 1990 by The New York Times Company.

Plenum Publishing Corporation for "Abortion and the Meaning of Life" by Kristin Luker from *Abortion: Understanding Differences* by Sidney Callahan and Daniel Callahan. Copyright © 1984 by The Hastings Center Institute of Society, Ethics and the Life Sciences.

The Putnam Publishing Group for the excerpt from *The Feminization of America* by Elinor Lenz and Barbara Myerhoff. Copyright © 1985 by Elinor Lenz and Barbara Myerhoff.

Regents of the University of California and the University of California Press for the excerpts from *Hard Choices: How Women Decide About Work, Career and Motherhood* by Kathleen Gerson, Copyright © 1985 by The Regents of the University of California; and from *Bananas, Beaches and Bases: Making Feminist Sense of International Politics* by Cynthia Enloe, Copyright © 1989 by Cynthia Enloe.

Gloria Steinem for "Creating Jobs We *Can't* Be Fired From" from *Ms.* magazine, Copyright © 1992 by *Ms.* magazine; and "Life After Backlash: Our Women in Washington" from *Ms.* magazine, Copyright © 1993 by *Ms.* magazine.

Viking Penguin, a division of Penguin Books USA, Inc., for "The Cultural Cover-up," from *The Second Shift: Working Parents and the Revolution at Home* by Arlie Hochschild with Ann Machung, Copyright © 1989 by Arlie Hochschild; and "Mixed Messages," from *On Her Own: Growing Up in the Shadow of the American Dream* by Ruth Sidel, Copyright © 1990 by Ruth Sidel.

W. W. Norton, Inc., for "The Politics of Silence" from *The Word of a Woman: Feminist Dispatches, 1968–1991* by Robin Morgan. Copyright © 1992, 1989 by Robin Morgan.

W. W. Norton, Inc., and Carolyn G. Heilbrun for the excerpt from *Writing a Woman's Life* by Carolyn G. Heilbrun. Copyright © 1988 by Carolyn G. Heilbrun.

W. W. Norton, Inc., and Adrienne Rich for the excerpt from *Of Woman Born: Motherhood as Experience and Institution* by Adrienne Rich. Copyright © 1986, 1976 by W. W. Norton & Company.

Yale Journal of Law and Feminism for "Theory as Liberatory Practice" by bell hooks from *The Yale Journal of Law and Feminism,* Vol. 4, No. 1, pp.1–12.

Contents

II
The Call to Action

Preface

This anthology of speeches and essays represents the work of nearly thirty contemporary American feminists. It by no means offers a comprehensive survey of feminism in the United States today; nor was it intended to—the body of feminist literature is far too extensive to be accommodated by any single volume. Rather it provides a sampling of feminist work in such disparate fields as medicine, literature, law and politics. What makes these writings feminist in orientation is not only that they focus upon and analyze subjects that concern women but also that they attempt to provide insight as to why and how the historical processes they examine affect women differently than men.

The essays in this collection discuss a broad range of issues—health care, portrayals of women in the media, international politics, abortion—at the same time that they define our need both to reimagine gender roles and to reinvent the institutions that have historically assigned us these roles. The call for equality in these selections is a call for equality of opportunity that neither expects nor intends women to behave exactly like men. An equality of opportunity, they argue, should be made available to all women as it should be to all men.

Gender inequality is fundamentally linked to the inequality Americans suffer based on race, class and sexual preference. An effective movement for gender equality, then, inevitably does more than address women's rights; it necessarily addresses the rights of all Americans. From involvement in the international women's movement and through the activism of third world women in the movement at home,

American feminists have gained a heightened awareness of and sensitivity to the inequities based on color and class.

Historically, the women's movement in the United States falls into three phases. The suffragist movement from roughly 1815–1825 marks the first wave of American feminism. Second-wave feminism, which addressed primarily the issues of white middle-class women, dates from the late 1960s and 1970s. The 1980s brought us what has been called the third wave in feminism: a women's movement that answers the class- and race-based critiques against second-wave feminism and attempts to embrace all women in its political agenda. The movement for gender equality stands at the center of that agenda, and the women in this volume stand among its most avid spokespeople in the 1990s.

The anthology is divided into two sections. The first section, titled "Setting the Record Straight," presents articles and essays that reinterpret and challenge our received notions of womanhood in medical textbooks, the institution of mothering, the ideal of the American Dream, the culture of racism and the application of the First Amendment. These notions are reinterpreted from a gendered perspective that shows how social attitudes and cultural expectations affect men and women differently. From this perspective we can begin to see possibilities for change. Reinterpretation can, therefore, be seen as a first and necessary step in the making of a political act.

In "The Call to Action," the second section of the book, the authors target issues for change and set forth their prescriptions for the changes they deem necessary in the way we think and act. They show us how to move from studying the problem to doing something about it. They describe how far we've come and where we need yet to go. They delineate for us how to effect needed policy changes and, most importantly, how to refrain from silence and inaction.

Several people deserve my thanks for their help in putting this anthology together. I thank Richard Gallen for providing me the opportunity to review the movement and compile this volume. I thank LeeRay Costa and Peter Skutches for assisting, advising and ushering me through the process. I also want to thank Constance Sutton for her insight into how to understand the historical and political processes that have shaped our society and for the inspiration that her political commitment to change provides. Thanks are also due to Deb, Lucy, Paul, Ritu—for being there.

This book is dedicated to my mother, whose intelligence, wit, commitment, compassion and pragmatism are a source of unending inspiration.

—D.W.

I

Setting the Record Straight

Alice Walker

---

from *In Search of Our Mothers' Gardens*
Womanist Prose
"Womanist"

Critically acclaimed novelist, essayist, short story writer and poet Alice Walker is perhaps best known for the Pulitzer Prize-winning novel *The Color Purple*.

Womanist 1. From *womanish*. (Opp. of "girlish," i.e., frivolous, irresponsible, not serious.) A black feminist or feminist of color. From the black folk expression of mothers to female children, "You acting womanish," i.e., like a woman. Usually referring to outrageous, audacious, courageous or *willful* behavior. Wanting to know more and in greater depth than is considered "good" for one. Interested in grown-up doings. Acting grown up. Being grown up. Interchangeable with another black folk expression: "You trying to be grown." Responsible. In charge. *Serious.*

2. *Also:* A woman who loves other women, sexually and/or nonsexually. Appreciates and prefers women's culture, women's emotional flexibility (values tears as natural counterbalance of laughter), and women's strength. Sometimes loves individual men, sexually and/or nonsexually. Committed to survival and wholeness of entire people, male *and* female. Not a separatist, except periodically, for health. Traditionally universalist, as in: "Mama, why are we brown, pink, and yellow, and our cousins are white, beige, and black?" Ans.: "Well, you know the colored race is just like a flower garden, with every color flower represented." Traditionally capable, as in: "Mama, I'm walking to Canada and I'm taking you and a bunch of other slaves with me." Reply: "It wouldn't be the first time."

3. Loves music. Loves dance. Loves the moon. *Loves* the Spirit. Loves love and food and roundness. Loves struggle. *Loves* the Folk. Loves herself. *Regardless.*

4. Womanist is to feminist as purple to lavender.

Susan Faludi

---

from *Backlash: The Undeclared War Against Women*
"Blame It on Feminism"

In this introduction to her best-selling book, writer and reporter Susan Faludi traces backlash against women as a recurrent theme in American history. She is the recipient of a Knight Fellowship at Stanford University.

To be a woman in America at the close of the twentieth century—what good fortune. That's what we keep hearing, anyway. The barricades have fallen, politicians assure us. Women have "made it," Madison Avenue cheers. Women's fight for equality has "largely been won," *Time* magazine announces. Enroll at any university, join any law firm, apply for credit at any bank. Women have so many opportunities now, corporate leaders say, that we don't really need equal opportunity policies. Women are so equal now, lawmakers say, that we no longer need an Equal Rights Amendment. Women have "so much," former President Ronald Reagan says, that the White House no longer needs to appoint them to higher office. Even American Express ads are saluting a woman's freedom to charge it. At last, women have received their full citizenship papers.

And yet . . .

Behind this celebration of the American woman's victory, behind the news, cheerfully and endlessly repeated, that the struggle for women's rights is won, another message flashes. You may be free and equal now, it says to women, but you have never been more miserable.

This bulletin of despair is posted everywhere—at the newsstand, on the TV set, at the movies, in advertisements and doctors' offices and academic journals. Professional women are suffering "burnout" and succumbing to an "infertility epidemic." Single women are grieving from a "man shortage." The *New York Times* reports: Childless women are "depressed and confused" and their ranks are swelling. *Newsweek* says: Unwed women are "hysterical" and crumbling under a "profound crisis of confidence." The health advice manuals inform: High-powered career women are stricken with unprecedented outbreaks of "stress-induced disorders," hair loss, bad nerves, alcoholism, and even heart attacks. The psychology books advise: Independent women's loneliness represents "a major mental health problem today." Even founding feminist Betty Friedan has

6

been spreading the word: she warns that women now suffer from a new identity crisis and "new 'problems that have no name.'"

How can American women be in so much trouble at the same time that they are supposed to be so blessed? If the status of women has never been higher, why is their emotional state so low? If women get what they asked for, what could possibly be the matter now?

The prevailing wisdom of the past decade has supported one, and only one, answer to this riddle: it must be all that equality that's causing all that pain. Women are unhappy precisely *because* they are free. Women are enslaved by their own liberation. They have grabbed at the gold ring of independence, only to miss the one ring that really matters. They have gained control of their fertility, only to destroy it. They have pursued their own professional dreams—and lost out on the greatest female adventure. The women's movement, as we are told time and again, has proved women's own worst enemy.

"In dispensing its spoils, women's liberation has given my generation high incomes, our own cigarette, the option of single parenthood, rape crisis centers, personal lines of credit, free love, and female gynecologists," Mona Charen, a young law student, writes in the *National Review,* in an article titled "The Feminist Mistake." "In return it has effectively robbed us of one thing upon which the happiness of most women rests—men." The *National Review* is a conservative publication, but such charges against the women's movement are not confined to its pages. "Our generation was the human sacrifice" to the women's movement, *Los Angeles Times* feature writer Elizabeth Mehren contends in a *Time* cover story. Baby-boom women like her, she says, have been duped by feminism: "We believed the rhetoric." In *Newsweek,* writer Kay Ebeling dubs feminism "the Great Experiment That Failed" and asserts "women in my generation, its perpetrators, are the casualties." Even the beauty magazines are saying it: *Harper's Bazaar* accuses the women's movement of having "lost us [women] ground instead of gaining it."

In the last decade, publications from the *New York Times* to *Vanity Fair* to the *Nation* have issued a steady stream of indictments against the women's movement, with such headlines as WHEN FEMINISM FAILED or THE AWFUL TRUTH ABOUT WOMEN'S LIB. They hold the campaign for women's equality responsible for nearly every woe besetting women, from mental depression to meager savings accounts, from teenage suicides to eating disorders to bad complexions. The "Today" show says women's liberation is to blame for bag ladies.

A guest columnist in the *Baltimore Sun* even proposes that feminists produced the rise in slasher movies. By making the "violence" of abortion more acceptable, the author reasons, women's rights activists made it all right to show graphic murders on screen.

At the same time, other outlets of popular culture have been forging the same connection: in Hollywood films, of which *Fatal Attraction* is only the most famous, emancipated women with condominiums of their own slink wild-eyed between bare walls, paying for their liberty with an empty bed, a barren womb. "My biological clock is ticking so loud it keeps me awake at night," Sally Field cries in the film *Surrender,* as, in an all too common transformation in the cinema of the eighties, an actress who once played scrappy working heroines is now showcased groveling for a groom. In prime-time television shows, from "thirtysomething" to "Family Man," single, professional, and feminist women are humiliated, turned into harpies, or hit by nervous breakdowns; the wise ones recant their independent ways by the closing sequence. In popular novels, from Gail Parent's *A Sign of the Eighties* to Stephen King's *Misery,* unwed women shrink to sniveling spinsters or inflate to fire-breathing she-devils; renouncing all aspirations but marriage, they beg for wedding bands from strangers or swing axes at reluctant bachelors. We "blew it by waiting," a typically remorseful careerist sobs in Freda Bright's *Singular Women*; she and her sister professionals are "condemned to be childless forever." Even Erica Jong's high-flying independent heroine literally crashes by the end of the decade, as the author supplants *Fear of Flying*'s saucy Isadora Wing, a symbol of female sexual emancipation in the seventies, with an embittered careerist-turned-recoverting-"co-dependent" in *Any Woman's Blues*—a book that is intended, as the narrator bluntly states, "to demonstrate what a dead end the so-called sexual revolution had become, and how desperate so-called free women were in the last few years of our decadent epoch."

Popular psychology manuals peddle the same diagnosis for contemporary female distress. "Feminism, having promised her a stronger sense of her own identity, has given her little more than an identity *crisis,*" the best-selling advice manual *Being a Woman* asserts. The authors of the era's self-help classic *Smart Women/Foolish Choices* proclaim that women's distress was "an unfortunate consequence of feminism," because "it created a myth among women that the apex of self-realization could be achieved only through autonomy, independence, and career."

In the Reagan and Bush years, government officials have needed no prompting to endorse this thesis. Reagan spokeswoman Faith Whittlesey declared feminism a "straitjacket" for women, in the White House's only policy speech on the status of the American female population—titled "Radical Feminism in Retreat." Law enforcement officers and judges, too, have pointed a damning finger at feminism, claiming that they can chart a path from rising female independence to rising female pathology. As a California sheriff explained it to the press, "Women are enjoying a lot more freedom now, and as a result, they are committing more crimes." The U.S. Attorney General's Commission on Pornography even proposed that women's professional advancement might be responsible for rising rape rates. With more women in college and at work now, the commission members reasoned in their report, women just have more opportunities to be raped.

Some academics have signed on to the consensus, too—and they are the "experts" who have enjoyed the highest profiles on the media circuit. On network news and talk shows, they have advised millions of women that feminism has condemned them to "a lesser life." Legal scholars have railed against "the equality trap." Sociologists have claimed that "feminist-inspired" legislative reforms have stripped women of special "protections." Economists have argued that well-paid working women have created "a less stable American family." And demographers, with greatest fanfare, have legitimated the prevailing wisdom with so-called neutral data on sex ratios and fertility trends; they say they actually have the numbers to prove that equality doesn't mix with marriage and motherhood.

Finally, some "liberated" women themselves have joined the lamentations. In confessional accounts, works that invariably receive a hearty greeting from the publishing industry, "recovering Superwomen" tell all. In *The Cost of Loving: Women and the New Fear of Intimacy,* Megan Marshall, a Harvard-pedigreed writer, asserts that the feminist "Myth of Independence" has turned her generation into unloved and unhappy fast-trackers, "dehumanized" by careers and "uncertain of their gender identity." Other diaries of mad Superwomen charge that "the hard-core feminist viewpoint," as one of them puts it, has relegated educated executive achievers to solitary nights of frozen dinners and closet drinking. The triumph of equality, they report, has merely given women hives, stomach cramps, eye-twitching disorders, even comas.

But what "equality" are all these authorities talking about?

If American women are so equal, why do they represent two-thirds of all poor adults? Why are more than 80 percent of full-time working women making less than $20,000 a year, nearly double the male rate? Why are they still far more likely than men to live in poor housing and receive no health insurance, and twice as likely to draw no pension? Why does the average working woman's salary still lag as far behind the average man's as it did twenty years ago? Why does the average female college graduate today earn less than a man with no more than a high school diploma (just as she did in the fifties)—and why does the average female high school graduate today earn less than a male high school dropout? Why do American women, in fact, face the worst gender-based pay gap in the developed world?

If women have "made it," then why are nearly 80 percent of working women still stuck in traditional "female" jobs—as secretaries, administrative "support" workers and salesclerks? And, conversely, why are they less than 8 percent of all federal and state judges, less than 6 percent of all law partners, and less than one half of 1 percent of top corporate managers? Why are there only three female state governors, two female U.S. senators, and two Fortune 500 chief executives? Why are only nineteen of the four thousand corporate officers and directors women—and why do more than half the boards of Fortune companies still lack even one female member?

If women "have it all," then why don't they have the most basic requirements to achieve equality in the work force? Unlike virtually all other industrialized nations, the U.S. government still has no family-leave and child care programs—and more than 99 percent of American private employers don't offer child care either. Though business leaders say they are aware of and deplore sex discrimination, corporate America has yet to make an honest effort toward eradicating it. In a 1990 national poll of chief executives at Fortune 1000 companies, more than 80 percent acknowledged that discrimination impedes female employees' progress—yet, less than 1 percent of these same companies regarded *remedying* sex discrimination as a goal that their personnel departments should pursue. In fact, when the companies' human resource officers were asked to rate their department's priorities, women's advancement ranked last.

If women are so "free," why are their reproductive freedoms in greater jeopardy today than a decade earlier? Why do women who want to postpone childbearing now have fewer options than ten years ago? The availability of different forms of contraception has declined, research for new birth control has virtually halted, new laws restricting abortion—or even *information* about abortion—for young and poor women have been passed, and the U.S. Supreme Court has shown little ardor in defending the right it granted in 1973.

Nor is women's struggle for equal education over; as a 1989 study found, three-fourths of all high schools still violate the federal law banning sex discrimination in education. In colleges, undergraduate women receive only 70 percent of the aid undergraduate men get in grants and work-study jobs—and women's sports programs receive a pittance compared with men's. A review of state equal-education laws in the late eighties found that only thirteen states had adopted the minimum provisions required by the federal Title IX law—and only seven states had anti-discrimination regulations that covered all education levels.

Nor do women enjoy equality in their own homes, where they still shoulder 70 percent of the household duties—and the only major change in the last fifteen years is that now middle-class men *think* they do more around the house. (In fact, a national poll finds the ranks of women saying their husbands share equally in child care shrunk to 31 percent in 1987 from 40 percent three years earlier.) Furthermore, in thirty states, it is still generally legal for husbands to rape their wives; and only ten states have laws mandating arrest for domestic violence—even though battering was the leading cause of injury of women in the late eighties. Women who have no other option but to flee find that isn't much of an alternative either. Federal funding for battered women's shelters has been withheld and one third of the 1 million battered women who seek emergency shelter each year can find none. Blows from men contributed far more to the rising numbers of "bag ladies" than the ill effects of feminism. In the eighties, almost half of all homeless women (the fastest growing segment of the homeless) were refugees of domestic violence.

The word may be that women have been "liberated," but women themselves seem to feel otherwise. Repeatedly in national surveys, majorities of women say they are still far from equality. Nearly 70 percent of women polled by the *New York Times* in 1989 said the movement for women's rights had only just begun. Most women in the 1990 Virginia Slims opinion poll agreed with the statement that conditions for their sex in American society had improved "a little, not a lot." In poll after poll in the decade, overwhelming majorities of women said they needed equal pay and equal pay opportunities, they needed an Equal Rights Amendment, they needed the right to an abortion without government interference, they needed a federal law guaranteeing maternity leave, they needed decent child care services. They have none of these. So how exactly have we "won" the war for women's rights?

Seen against this background, the much ballyhooed claim that feminism is responsible for making women miserable becomes absurd—and irrelevant. . . . [T]he afflictions ascribed to feminism are all myths. From "the man shortage" to "the infertility epidemic" to "female burnout" to "toxic day care," these so-called female crises have had their origins not in the actual conditions of women's lives but rather in a closed system that starts and ends in the media, popular culture, and advertising—an endless feedback loop that perpetuates and exaggerates its own false images of womanhood.

Women themselves don't single out the women's movement as the source of their misery. To the contrary, in national surveys 75 to 95 percent of women credit the feminist campaign with *improving* their lives, and a similar proportion say that the women's movement should keep pushing for change. Less than 8 percent think the women's movement might have actually made their lot worse.

What actually is troubling the American female population, then? If the many ponderers of the Woman Question really wanted to know, they might have asked their subjects. In public opinion surveys, women consistently rank their own *inequality,* at work and at home, among their most urgent concerns. Over and over, women complain to pollsters about a lack of economic, not marital, opportunities; they protest that working men, not working women, fail to spend time in the nursery and the kitchen. The Roper Organization's survey analysts find that men's opposition to equality is "a major cause of resentment and stress" and "a major irritant for most women today." It is justice for their gender, not wedding rings and bassinets, that women believe to be in desperately short supply. When the *New York Times* polled women in 1989 about "the most important problem facing women today," job discrimination was the overwhelming winner; none of the crises the media and popular culture had so assiduously promoted even made the charts. In the 1990 Virginia Slims poll, women were most upset by their lack of money, followed by the refusal of their men to shoulder child care and domestic duties. By contrast, when the women were asked where the quest for a husband or the desire to hold a "less pressured" job or to stay at home ranked on their list of concerns, they placed them at the bottom.

As the last decade ran its course, women's unhappiness with inequality only mounted. In national polls, the ranks of women protesting discriminatory treatment in business, political, and personal life climbed sharply. The proportion of women complaining of unequal employment opportunities jumped more than ten points from the seventies, and the number of women complaining of unequal barriers to job advancement climbed even higher. By the end of the decade, 80 percent to 95 percent of women said they suffered from job discrimination and unequal pay. Sex discrimination charges filed with the Equal Employment Opportunity Commission rose nearly 25 percent in the Reagan years, and charges of general harassment directed at working women climbed 208 percent. In the decade, complaints of sexual harassment jumped 70 percent. At home, a much increased proportion of women complained to pollsters of male mistreatment, unequal relationships, and male efforts to, in the words of the Virginia Slims poll, "keep women down." The share of women in the Roper surveys who agreed that men were "basically kind, gentle, and thoughtful" fell from almost 70 percent in 1970 to 50 percent in 1990. And outside their homes, women felt more threatened, too: in the 1990 Virginia Slims poll, 72 percent of women said they felt "more afraid and uneasy on the streets today" than they did a few years ago. Lest this be attributed only to a general rise in criminal activity, by contrast only 49 percent of men felt this way.

While the women's movement has certainly made women more cognizant of their own inequality, the rising chorus of female protest shouldn't be written off as feminist-induced "oversensitivity." The monitors that serve to track slippage in women's status have been working overtime since the early eighties. Government and private surveys are showing that women's already vast representation in the lowliest occupations is rising, their tiny presence in higher-paying trade and craft jobs stalled or backsliding, their minuscule representation in upper management posts stagnant or falling, and their pay dropping in the very occupations where they have made the most "progress." The status of women lowest on the income ladder has plunged most perilously; government budget cuts in the first four years of the Reagan administration alone pushed nearly 2 million female-headed families and nearly 5 million women below the poverty line. And the prime target of government rollbacks has been one sex only: one-third of the Reagan budget cuts, for example, came out of programs that predominantly serve women—even more extraordinary when one considers that all these programs combined represent only 10 percent of the federal budget.

The alarms aren't just going off in the work force. In national politics, the already small numbers of women in both elective posts and political appointments fell during the eighties. In private life, the average amount that a divorced man paid in child support fell by about 25 percent from the late seventies to the mid-eighties (to a mere $140 a month). Domestic-violence shelters recorded a more than 100 percent increase in the numbers of women taking refuge in their quarters between 1983 and 1987. And government records chronicled a spectacular rise in sexual violence against women. Reported rapes more than doubled from the early seventies—at nearly twice the rate of all other violent crimes and four times the overall crime rate in the United States. While the homicide rate declined, sex-related murders rose 160 percent between 1976 and 1984. And these murders weren't simply the random, impersonal by-product of a violent society; at least one-third of the women were killed by their husbands or boyfriends, and the majority of that group were murdered just after declaring their independence in the most intimate manner—by filing for divorce and leaving home.

By the end of the decade, women were starting to tell pollsters that they feared their sex's social status was once again beginning to slip. They believed they were facing an "erosion of respect," as the 1990 Virginia Slims poll summed up the sentiment. After years in which an increasing percentage of women had said their status had improved from a decade earlier, the proportion suddenly shrunk by 5 percent in the last half of the eighties, the Roper Organization reported. And it fell most sharply among women in their thirties—the age group most targeted by the media and advertisers—dropping about ten percentage points between 1985 and 1990.

Some women began to piece the picture together. In the 1989 *New York Times* poll, more than half of black women and one-fourth of white women put it into words. They told pollsters they believed men were now trying to retract the gains women had made in the last twenty years. "I wanted more autonomy," was how one woman, a thirty-seven-year-old nurse, put it. And her estranged husband "wanted to take it away."

The truth is that the last decade has seen a powerful counterassault on women's rights, a backlash, an attempt to retract the handful of small and hard-won victories that the feminist movement did manage to win for women. This counterassault is largely insidious: in a kind of pop-culture version of the Big Lie, it stands the truth boldly on its head and proclaims that the very steps that have elevated women's position have actually led to their downfall.

The backlash is at once sophisticated and banal, deceptively "progressive" and proudly backward. It deploys both the "new" findings of "scientific research" and the dime-store moralism of yesteryear; it turns into media sound bites both the glib pronouncements of pop-psych trend-watchers and the frenzied rhetoric of New Right preachers. The backlash had succeeded in framing virtually the whole issue of women's rights in its own language. Just as Reaganism shifted political discourse far to the right and demonized liberalism, so the backlash convinced the public that women's "liberation" was the true contemporary American scourge—the source of an endless laundry list of personal, social, and economic problems.

But what has made women unhappy in the last decade is not their "equality"—which they don't yet have—but the rising pressure to halt, and even reverse, women's quest for that equality. The "man shortage" and the "infertility epidemic" are not the price of liberation; in fact, they do not even exist. But these chimeras are the chisels of a society-wide backlash. They are part of a relentless whittling-down process—much of it amounting to outright propaganda—that has served to stir women's private anxieties and break their political wills. Identifying feminism as women's enemy only furthers the ends of a backlash against women's equality, simultaneously deflecting attention from the backlash's central role and recruiting women to attack their own cause.

Some social observers may well ask whether the current pressures on women actually constitute a backlash—or just a continuation of American society's long-standing resistance to women's rights. Certainly hostility to female independence has always been with us. But if fear and loathing of feminism is a sort of perpetual viral condition in our culture, it is not always in an acute stage; its symptoms subside and resurface periodically. And it is these episodes of resurgence, such as the one we face now, that can accurately be termed ''backlashes'' to women's advancement. If we trace these occurrences in American history (as we will do in a later chapter), we find such flare-ups are hardly random; they have always been triggered by the perception—accurate or not—that women are making great strides. These outbreaks are backlashes because they have always arisen in reaction to women's ''progress,'' caused not simply by a bedrock of misogyny but by the specific efforts of contemporary women to improve their status, efforts that have been interpreted time and again by men—especially men grappling with real threats to their economic and social well-being on other fronts—as spelling their own masculine doom.

The most recent round of backlash first surfaced in the late seventies on the fringes, among the evangelical right. By the early eighties, the fundamentalist ideology had shouldered its way into the White House. By the mid-eighties, as resistance to women's rights acquired political and social acceptability, it passed into the popular culture. And in every case, the timing coincided with signs that women were believed to be on the verge of breakthrough.

Just when women's quest for equal rights seemed closest to achieving its objectives, the backlash struck it down. Just when a ''gender gap'' at the voting booth surfaced in 1980, and women in politics began to talk of capitalizing on it, the Republican party elevated Ronald Reagan and both political parties began to shunt women's rights off their platforms. Just when support for feminism and the Equal Rights Amendment reached a record high in 1981, the amendment was defeated the following year. Just when women were starting to mobilize against battering and sexual assaults, the federal government stalled funding for battered-women's programs, defeated bills to fund shelters, and shut down its Office of Domestic Violence—only two years after opening it in 1979. Just when record numbers of younger women were supporting feminist goals in the mid-eighties (more of them, in fact, than older women) and a majority of all women were calling themselves feminists, the media declared the advent of a younger ''postfeminist generation'' that supposedly reviled the women's movement. Just when women racked up their largest percentage ever supporting the right to abortion, the U.S. Supreme Court moved toward reconsidering it.

In other words, the anti-feminist backlash has been set off not by women's achievement of full equality but by the increased possibility that they might win it. It is a preemptive strike that stops women long before they reach the finish line. "A backlash may be an indication that women really have had an effect," feminist psychiatrist Dr. Jean Baker Miller has written, "but backlashes occur when advances have been small, before changes are sufficient to help many people. . . . It is almost as if the leaders of backlashes use the fear of change as a threat before major change has occurred." In the last decade, some women did make substantial advances before the backlash hit, but millions of others were left behind, stranded. Some women now enjoy the right to legal abortion—but not the forty-four million women, from the indigent to the military work force, who depend on the federal government for their medical care. Some women can now walk into high-paying professional careers—but not the more than nineteen million still in the typing pools or behind the department store sales counters. (Contrary to popular myth about the "have-it-all" baby-boom women, the largest percentage of women in this generation remain typists and clerks.)

As the backlash has gathered force, it has cut off the few from the many—and the few women who have advanced seek to prove, as a social survival tactic, that they aren't so interested in advancement after all. Some of them parade their defection from the woman's movement, while their working-class peers founder and cling to the splintered remains of the feminist cause. While a very few affluent and celebrity women who are showcased in news articles boast about having "found my niche as Mrs. Andy Mill" and going home to "bake bread," the many working-class women appeal for their economic rights—flocking to unions in record numbers, striking on their own for pay equity and establishing their own fledgling groups for working women's rights. In 1986, while 41 percent of upper-income women were claiming in the Gallup poll that they were not feminists, only 26 percent of low-income women were making the same claim.

Women's advances and retreats are generally described in military terms: battles won, battles lost, points and territory gained and surrendered. The metaphor of combat is not without its merits in this context and, clearly, the same sort of martial accounting and vocabulary is already surfacing here. But by imagining the conflict as two battalions neatly arrayed on either side of the line, we miss the entangled nature, the locked embrace, of a "war" between women and the male culture they inhabit. We miss the reactive nature of a backlash, which, by definition, can exist only in response to another force.

In times when feminism is at a low ebb, women assume the reactive role—privately and most often covertly struggling to assert themselves against the dominant cultural tide. But when feminism itself becomes the tide, the opposition doesn't simply go along with the reversal: it digs in its heels, brandishes its fists, builds walls and dams. And its resistance creates countercurrents and treacherous undertows.

The force and furor of the backlash churn beneath the surface, largely invisible to the public eye. On occasion in the last decade, they have burst into view. We have seen New Right politicians condemn women's independence, antiabortion protesters firebomb women's clinics, fundamentalist preachers damn feminists as "whores" and "witches." Other signs of the backlash's wrath, by their sheer brutality, can push their way into public consciousness for a time— the sharp increase in rape, for example, or the rise in pornography that depicts extreme violence against women.

More subtle indicators in popular culture may receive momentary, and often bemused, media notice, then quickly slip from social awareness: A report, for instance, that the image of women on prime-time TV shows has suddenly degenerated. A survey of mystery fiction finding the numbers of female characters tortured and mutilated mysteriously multiplying. The puzzling news that, as one commentator put it, "So many hit songs have the B-word [bitch] to refer to women that some rap music seems to be veering toward rape music." The ascendancy of virulently misogynist comics like Andrew Dice Clay—who called women "pigs" and "sluts" and strutted in films in which women were beaten, tortured, and blown up—or radio hosts like Rush Limbaugh, whose broadsides against "femi-Nazi" feminists made his syndicated program the most popular radio talk show in the nation. Or word that in 1987, the American Women in Radio & Television couldn't award its annual prize for ads that feature women positively: it could find no ad that qualified.

These phenomena are all related, but that doesn't mean they are somehow coordinated. The backlash is not a conspiracy, with a council dispatching agents from some central control room, nor are the people who serve its ends often aware of their role; some even consider themselves feminists. For the most part, its workings are encoded and internalized, diffuse and chameleonic. Not all of the manifestations of the backlash are of equal weight or significance either; some are mere ephemera, generated by a culture machine that is always scrounging for a "fresh" angle. Taken as a whole, however, these codes and cajolings, these whispers and threats and myths, move overwhelmingly in one direction: they try to push women back into their "acceptable" roles—whether as Daddy's girl or fluttery romantic, active nester or passive love object.

Although the backlash is not an organized movement, that doesn't make it any less destructive. In fact, the lack of orchestration, the absence of a single string-puller, only makes it harder to see—and perhaps more effective. A backlash against women's rights succeeds to the degree that it appears *not* to be political, that it appears not to be a struggle at all. It is most powerful when it goes private, when it lodges inside a woman's mind and turns her vision inward, until she imagines the pressure is all in her head, until she begins to enforce the backlash, too—on herself.

In the last decade, the backlash has moved through the culture's secret chambers, traveling through passageways of flattery and fear. Along the way, it has adopted disguises: a mask of mild derision or the painted face of deep "concern." Its lips profess pity for any woman who won't fit the mold, while it tries to clamp the mold around her ears. It pursues a divide-and-conquer strategy: single versus married women, working women versus homemakers, middle- versus working-class. It manipulates a system of rewards and punishments, elevating women who follow its rules, isolating those who don't. The backlash remarkets old myths about women as new facts and ignores all appeals to reason. Cornered, it denies its own existence, points an accusatory finger at feminism, and burrows deeper underground.

Backlash happens to be the title of a 1947 Hollywood movie in which a man frames his wife for a murder he's committed. The backlash against women's rights works in much the same way: its rhetoric charges feminists with all the crimes it perpetrates. The backlash line blames the women's movement for the "feminization of poverty"—while the backlash's own instigators in Washington pushed through the budget cuts that helped impoverish millions of women, fought pay equity proposals, and undermined equal opportunity laws. The backlash line claims the women's movement cares nothing for children's rights—while its own representatives in the capital and state legislatures have blocked one bill after another to improve child care, slashed billions of dollars in federal aid for children, and relaxed state licensing standards for day care centers. The backlash line accuses the women's movement of creating a generation of unhappy single and childless women—but its purveyors in the media are the ones guilty of making single and childless women feel like circus freaks.

To blame feminism for women's "lesser life" is to miss entirely the point of feminism, which is to win women a wider range of experience. Feminism remains a pretty simple concept, despite repeated—and enormously effective—efforts to dress it up in greasepaint and turn its proponents into gargoyles. As Rebecca West wrote sardonically in 1913, "I myself have never been able to find out precisely what feminism is: I only know that people call me a feminist whenever I express sentiments that differentiate me from a doormat."

The meaning of the word "feminist" has not really changed since it first appeared in a book review in the *Athenaeum* of April 27, 1895, describing a woman who "has in her the capacity of fighting her way back to independence." It is the basic proposition that, as Nora put it in Ibsen's *A Doll's House* a century ago, "Before everything else I'm a human being." It is the simply worded sign hoisted by a little girl in the 1970 Women's Strike for Equality: I AM NOT A BARBIE DOLL. Feminism asks the world to recognize at long last that women aren't decorative ornaments, worthy vessels, members of a "special-interest group." They are half (in fact, now more than half) of the national population, and just as deserving of rights and opportunities, just as capable of participating in the world's events, as the other half. Feminism's agenda is basic: It asks that women not be forced to "choose" between public justice and private happiness. It asks that women be free to define themselves—instead of having their identity defined for them, time and again, by their culture and their men.

The fact that these are still such incendiary notions should tell us that American women have a way to go before they enter the promised land of equality.

Notes

6   *Women's fight for* . . . : Nancy Gibbs, "The Dreams of Youth," *Time,* Special Issue: "Women: The Road Ahead," Fall 1990, p. 12.

6   *Women have "so much"* . . . : Eleanor Smeal, *Why and How Women Will Elect the Next President* (New York: Harper & Row, 1984) p. 56.

6   *The New York Times reports* . . . : Georgia Dullea, "Women Reconsider Childbearing Over 30," *New York Times,* Feb. 25, 1982, p. C1.

6   *Newsweek says: Unwed women* . . . : Eloise Salholz, "The Marriage Crunch," *Newsweek,* June 2, 1986, p. 55.

6   *The health advice manuals* . . . : See, for example, Dr. Herbert J. Freudenberger and Gail North, *Women's Burnout* (New York: Viking Penguin, 1985); Marjorie Hansen Shaevitz, *The Superwoman Syndrome* (New York: Warner Books, 1984); Harriet Braiker, *The Type E Woman* (New York: Dodd, Mead, 1986); Donald Morse and M. Lawrence Furst, *Women Under Stress* (New York: Van Nostrand Reinhold Co., 1982); Georgia Witkin-Lanoil, *The Female Stress Syndrome* (New York: Newmarket Press, 1984).

6   *The psychology books* . . . : Dr. Stephen and Susan Price, *No More Lonely Nights: Overcoming the Hidden Fears That Keep You from Getting Married* (New York: G.P. Putnam's Sons, 1988) p. 19.

6   *Even founding feminist Betty Friedan* . . . : Betty Friedan, *The Second Stage* (New York: Summit Books, 1981) p. 9.

7   *"In dispensing its spoils . . ."*: Mona Charen, "The Feminist Mistake," *National Review,* March 23, 1984, p. 24.

7   *"Our generation was the human sacrifice . . ."*: Claudia Wallis, "Women Face the '90s," *Time,* Dec. 4, 1989, p. 82.

7   *In Newsweek, writer* . . . : Kay Ebeling, "The Failure of Feminism," *Newsweek,* Nov. 19, 1990, p. 9.

7   *Even the beauty magazines* . . . : Marilyn Webb, "His Fault Divorce," *Harper's Bazaar,* Aug. 1988, p. 156.

7   *In the last decade* . . . : Mary Anne Dolan, "When Feminism Failed," *The New York Times Magazine,* June 26, 1988, p. 21; Erica Jong, "The Awful Truth About Women's Liberation," *Vanity Fair,* April 1986, p. 92.

7   *The "Today" show* . . . : Jane Birnbaum, "The Dark Side of Women's Liberation," *Los Angeles Herald Examiner,* May 24, 1986.

8   *A guest columnist* . . . : Robert J. Hooper, "Slasher Movies Owe Success to Abortion" (originally printed in the *Baltimore Sun*), *Minneapolis Star Tribune,* Feb. 1, 1990, p. 17A.

8   In popular novels ...: Gail Parent, *A Sign of the Eighties* (New York: G.P. Putnam's Sons, 1987); Stephen King, *Misery* (New York: Viking, 1987).

8   We "blew it by ...": Freda Bright, *Singular Women* (New York: Bantam Books, 1988) p. 12.

8   Even Erica Jong's ...: Erica Jong, *Any Woman's Blues* (New York: Harper & Row, 1989) pp. 2–3. A new generation of young "post-feminist" female writers, such as Mary Gaitskill and Susan Minot, also produced a bumper crop of grim-faced unwed heroines. These passive and masochistic "girls" wandered the city, zombie-like; they came alive and took action only in seeking out male abuse. For a good analysis of this genre, see James Wolcott, "The Good-Bad Girls," *Vanity Fair,* Dec. 1988, p. 43.

8   "Feminism, having promised her ...": Dr. Toni Grant, *Being a Woman: Fulfilling Your Femininity and Finding Love* (New York: Random House, 1988) p. 25.

8   The authors of ...: Dr. Connell Cowan and Dr. Melvyn Kinder, *Smart Women/Foolish Choices* (New York: New American Library, 1985) p. 16.

9   Reagan spokeswoman Faith ...: Faith Whittlesey, "Radical Feminism in Retreat," Dec. 8, 1984, speech at the Center for the Study of the Presidency, 15th Annual Leadership Conference, St. Louis, Mo., p. 7.

9   As a California sheriff ...: Don Martinez, "More Women Ending Up in Prisons," *San Francisco Examiner,* Sept. 4, 1990, p. A1. Judges have blamed women's increasing economic independence for increasing *male* crime, too: "What do we do [about crowded prisons]?" Texas District Judge John McKellips asked, rhetorically. "Well, we can start in our homes. Mothers can stay home and raise their children during the formative years." See "For the Record," *Ms.,* May 1988, p. 69.

9   The U.S. Attorney General's ...: Attorney General's Commission on Pornography. Final Report, July 1986, p. 144. The commissioner's report goes on to undermine its own logic, conceding that since women raped by acquaintances are the least likely to report the crime, it might be difficult to attribute a rise in reported rape rates to them, after all.

9   On network news ...: Sylvia Ann Hewlett, *A Lesser Life: The Myth of Women's Liberation in America* (New York: William Morrow, 1986).

9   Legal scholars have ...: Mary Ann Mason, *The Equality Trap* (New York: Simon and Schuster, 1988).

9   Economists have argued ...: James P. Smith and Michael Ward, "Women in the Labor Market and in the Family," *The Journal of Economic Perspectives,* Winter 1989, 3, no. 1: 9–23.

9   In *The Cost of Loving* ...: Megan Marshall, *The Cost of Loving: Women and the New Fear of Intimacy* (New York: G.P. Putnam's Sons, 1984) p. 218.

9   Other diaries of ...: Hilary Cosell, *Woman on a Seesaw: The Ups and Downs of Making It* (New York: G.P. Putnam's Sons, 1985); Deborah Fallows, *A Mother's Work* (Boston: Houghton Mifflin, 1985); Carol Orsborn, *Enough is Enough* (New York: Pocket Books, 1986); Susan Bakos, *This Wasn't Supposed to Happen* (New York: Continuum, 1985). Even when the women aren't really renouncing their liberation, their publishers promote the texts as if they were. Mary Kay Blakely's *Wake Me When It's Over* (New York: Random House, 1989), an account of the author's diabetes-induced coma, is billed on the dust jacket as "a chilling memoir in which a working supermom exceeds her limit and discovers the thin line between sanity and lunacy and between life and death."

10   If American women are so equal ...: "Money, Income and Poverty Status in the U.S.," 1989, Current Population Reports, U.S. Bureau of the Census, Department of Commerce, Series P-60, #168.

10   Why are more than 80 percent ...: Margaret W. Newton, "Women and Pension Coverage," *The American Woman 1988–89: A Status Report,* ed. by Sara E. Rix (New York: W.W. Norton & Co., 1989) p. 268.

10   Why are they still ...: Cushing N. Dolbeare and Anne J. Stone, "Women and Affordable Housing," *The American Woman 1990–91: A Status Report,* ed. by Sara E. Rix (W.W. Norton & Co., 1990) p. 106; Newton, "Pension Coverage,"

p. 268; "1990 Profile," 9 to 5/National Association of Working Women; Salaried and Professional Women's Commission Report, 1989, p. 2.

10   Why does the average . . . : "Briefing Paper on the Wage Gap," National Committee on Pay Equity, p. 3; "Average Earnings of Year-Round, Full-Time Workers by Sex and Educational Attainment," 1987, U.S. Bureau of the Census, February 1989, cited in *The American Woman 1990–91*, p. 392.

10   If women have "made it," then . . . : Susanna Downie, "Decade of Achievement, 1977–1987," The National Women's Conference Center, May 1988, p. 35; statistics from 9 to 5/National Association of Working Women.

10   And, conversely, . . . : Statistics from Women's Research & Education Institute, U.S. Bureau of the Census, U.S. Bureau of Labor Statistics, Catalyst, Center for the American Woman and Politics. See also *The American Woman 1990–91*, p. 359; Deborah L. Rhode, "Perspectives on Professional Women," *Stanford Law Review*, 40, no. 5 (May 1988): 1178–79; Anne Jardim and Margaret Hennig, "The Last Barrier," *Working Woman*, Nov. 1990, p. 130; Jaclyn Fierman, "Why Women Still Don't Hit the Top," *Fortune*, July 30, 1990, p. 40.

10   Unlike virtually . . . : "1990 Profile," 9 to 5/National Association of Working Women; Bureau of Labor Statistics, 1987 survey of nation's employers. See also "Who Gives and Who Gets," *American Demographics,* May 1988, p. 16; "Children and Families: Public Policies and Outcomes, A Fact Sheet of International Comparisons," U.S. House of Representatives, Select Committee on Children, Youth and Families.

10   In a 1990 national poll . . . : "Women in Corporate Management," national poll of Fortune 1000 companies by Catalyst, 1990.

11   Why do women who want . . . : Data from Alan Guttmacher Institute.

11   Nor is women's struggle for equal education . . . : *The American Woman 1990–91,* p. 63; "Feminization of Power Campaign Extends to the Campus," Eleanor Smeal Report, 6, no. 1, Aug. 31, 1988; Project on Equal Education Rights, National Organization for Women's Legal Defense and Education Fund, 1987.

11   Nor do women . . . : Rhode, "Professional Women," p. 1183; Mark Clements Research Inc.'s Annual Study of Women's Attitudes, 1987; Arlie Hochschild, *The Second Shift: Working Parents and the Revolution at Home* (New York: Viking, 1989), p. 227. In fact, Hochschild's twelve-year survey, from 1976 to 1988, found that the men who said they were helping tended to be the ones who did the least.

11   Furthermore, in three-fourths of the states . . . : Statistics from National Center on Women and Family Law, 1987; National Woman Abuse Prevention Project; Cynthia Diehm and Margo Ross, "Battered Women," *The American Woman 1988–89,* p. 292.

11   Federal funding . . . : "Unlocking the Door: An Action Program for Meeting the Housing Needs of Women," Women and Housing Task Force, 1988, National Low-Income Housing Coalition, pp. 6, 8.

11   In the eighties, almost half of all homeless . . . : Katha Pollitt, "Georgie Porgie Is a Bully," *Time,* Fall 1990, Special Issue, p. 24. A survey in New York City found as many as 40 percent of all homeless people are battered women: "Understanding Domestic Violence Fact Sheets," National Woman Abuse Prevention Project.

11   Nearly 70 percent . . . : E.J. Dionne, Jr., "Struggle for Work and Family Fueling Women's Movement," *New York Times,* Aug. 22, 1989, p. A1. The Yankelovich Clancy Shulman poll (Oct. 23–25, 1989, for *Time*/CNN) and the 1990 Virginia Slims Opinion Poll (The Roper Organization Inc., 1990) found similarly large majorities of women who said that they needed a strong women's movement to keep pushing for change.

11   Most women in the . . . : The 1990 Virginia Slims Opinion Poll, The Roper Organization Inc., pp. 8, 18.

12   In poll after . . . : The Louis Harris poll, 1984, found 64 percent of women wanted the Equal Rights Amendment and 65 percent favored affirmative action. Similar results emerged from the national *Woman's Day* poll (Feb. 17, 1984) by *Woman's Day* and Wellesley College Center for Research on Women, which emphasized

middle-American conventional women (80 percent were mothers and 30 percent were full-time homemakers). The *Woman's Day* poll found a majority of women, from all economic classes, seeking a wide range of women's rights. For instance, 68 percent of the women said they wanted the ERA, 79 percent supported a woman's right to choose an abortion, and 61 percent favored a federally subsidized national child-care program. Mark Clements Research Inc.'s Annual Study of Women's Attitudes found in 1987 that 87 percent of women wanted a federal law guaranteeing maternity leave and about 94 percent said that more child care should be available. (In addition, 86 percent wanted a federal law enforcing the payment of child support.) The Louis Harris Poll found 80 percent of women calling for the creation of more day-care centers. See *The Eleanor Smeal Report,* June 28, 1984, p. 3; Warren T. Brookes, "Day Care: Is It a Real Crisis or a War Over Political Turf?" *San Francisco Chronicle,* April 27, 1988, p. 6; Louis Harris, *Inside America* (New York: Vintage Books, 1987), p. 96.

12   To the contrary . . . : In the 1989 *Time*/CNN poll, 94 percent of women polled said the movement made them more independent; 82 percent said it is still improving women's lives. Only 8 percent said it may have made their lives worse. A 1986 *Newsweek* Gallup poll found that 56 percent of women identified themselves as "feminists," and only 4 percent described themselves as "anti-feminists."

12   In public opinion . . . : In the Annual Study of Women's Attitudes (1988, Mark Clements Research), when women were asked, "What makes you angry?" they picked three items as their top concerns: poverty, crime, and their own inequality. In the 1989 *New York Times* Poll, when women were asked what was the most important problem facing women today, job inequality ranked first.

12   The Roper Organization's . . . : Bickley Townsend and Kathleen O'Neil, "American Women Get Mad," *American Demographics,* Aug. 1990, p. 26.

12   When the *New York Times* . . . : Dionne, "Struggle for Work and Family," p. A14.

13   In the 1990 . . . : 1990 Virginia Slims Opinion Poll, pp. 29–30, 32.

13   In national polls . . . : Data from Roper Organization and Louis Harris polls. The 1990 Roper survey found most women reporting that things had "gotten worse" in the home and that men were more eager "to keep women down"; See 1990 Virginia Slims Opinion Poll, pp. 18, 21, 54. The Gallup Organization polls charted an 8 percent increase in job discrimination complaints from women between 1975 and 1982. Mark Clements Research's 1987 Women's Views Survey (commissioned by *Glamour* magazine) found that on the matter of women's inequality, "more women feel there is a problem today." Reports of wage discrimination, the survey noted, had jumped from 76 percent in 1982 to 85 percent in 1988. (See "How Women's Minds Have Changed in the Last Five Years," *Glamour,* Jan. 1987, p. 168.) The annual surveys by Mark Clements Research also find huge and increasing majorities of women complaining of unequal treatment in hiring, advancement, and opportunities in both corporate and political life. (In 1987, only 30 percent of women believed they got equal treatment with men when being considered for financial credit.) A *Time* 1989 poll found 94 percent of women complaining of unequal pay, 82 percent of job discrimination.

13   Sex discrimination charges . . . : Statistics from U.S. Equal Employment Opportunity Commission, "National Database: Charge Receipt Listing," 1982–88; "Sexual Harassment," 1981–89.

13   At home, a much increased . . . : Townsend and O'Neil, "American Women Get Mad," p. 28.

13   And outside their . . . : 1990 Virginia Slims Opinion Poll, p. 38.

13   Government and private surveys . . . : Economic trends from U.S. Bureau of Labor Statistics, U.S. Equal Employment Opportunity Commission, Office of Federal Contract Compliance, National Committee on Pay Equity, National Commission on Working Women. . . .

14   The status of women . . . : In the first six years of the Reagan administration, $50 billion was cut from these social programs, while at the same time defense spending rose $142 billion. See "Inequality of Sacrifice: The Impact of the Reagan Budget on Women," Coalition on Women and the Budget, Washington, D.C., 1986, pp.

5, 7; Sara E. Rix and Anne J. Stone, "Reductions and Realities: How the Federal Budget Affects Women," Women's Research and Education Institute, Washington, D.C., 1983, pp. 4–5.

14　In national politics . . . : Data from Center for the American Woman and Politics, Eagleton Institute of Politics. . . .

14　In private life, the average . . . .: Philip Robins, "Why Are Child Support Award Amounts Declining?" June 1989, Institute for Research on Poverty Discussion Paper No. 885–89, pp. 6–7.

14　Domestic-violence shelters . . . : "Unlocking the Door," p. 8.

14　Reported rapes more than . . . : Statistics are from the U.S. Department of Justice's Bureau of Justice Statistics, the Sourcebook of Criminal Justice Statistics, 1984, p. 380; Uniform Crime Reports, FBI, "Crime in the United States," 1986; "Sexual Assault: An Overview," National Victims Resource Center, Nov. 1987, p. 1. While rape rates between 1960 and 1970 rose 95 percent, this increase—unlike that of the eighties—was part of a 126 percent increase in violent crime in that era. (Crime statisticians have widely rejected the argument that the increase in the eighties might simply be the result of an increasing tendency for women to report sexual assaults. The National Crime Survey found no significant change in the percentage of rapes reported to police in the periods between 1973–77 and 1978–82.) Scattered indicators suggest a sharp rise in the rate of rapes committed by young men, too. Between 1983 and 1987, rape arrests of boys under eighteen years old rose 15 percent. In New York City between 1987 and 1989, according to data from the district attorney's office, rape arrests of boys under the age of thirteen rose 200 percent. In Alaska, according to the state Division of Youth and Family Services, sexual abuse and assaults from young men increased ninefold in the course of the eighties, the fastest growing juvenile problem in the state. See Larry Campbell, "Sexually Abusive Juveniles," *Anchorage Daily News,* Jan. 9, 1981, p. 1.

14　They believed they were facing . . . : 1990 Virginia Slims Opinion Poll, p. 16.

14　In the 1989 *New York Times* . . . : Lisa Belkin, "Bars to Equality of Sexes Seen as Eroding, Slowly," *New York Times,* Aug. 20, 1989, p. 16.

16　Just when women . . . : "Inequality of Sacrifice," p. 23.

16　Just when record numbers . . . : A 1986 Gallup poll conducted for *Newsweek* found a majority of women described themselves as feminists and only 4 percent said they were "anti-feminists." While large majorities of women throughout the eighties kept on favoring the full feminist agenda (from the ERA to legal abortion), the proportion of women who were willing publicly to call themselves feminists dropped off suddenly in the late eighties, after the mass media declared feminism the "F-word." By 1989, only one in three women were calling themselves feminists in the polls. Nonetheless, the pattern of younger women espousing the most pro-feminist sentiments continued throughout the decade. In the 1989 Yankelovich poll for *Time*/CNN, for example, 76 percent of women in their teens and 71 percent of women in their twenties said they believed feminists spoke for the average American woman, compared with 59 percent of women in their thirties. Asked the same question about the National Organization for Women, the gap appeared again: 83 percent of women in their teens and 72 percent of women in their twenties said NOW was in touch with the average woman, compared with 65 percent of women in their thirties. See Downie, "Decade of Achievement," p. 1; 1986 Gallup/*Newsweek* poll; 1989 Yankelovich/*Time*/CNN poll.

17　"A backlash may be an indication that . . ." : Dr. Jean Baker Miller, *Toward a New Psychology of Women* (Boston: Beacon Press, 1976) pp. xv–xvi.

17　Some women now . . . : Kate Michelman, "20 Years Defending Choice, 1969–1988," National Abortion Rights Action League, p. 4.

17　Some women can now . . . : "Employment and Earnings," Current Population Survey, Table 22, Bureau of Labor Statistics, U.S. Department of Labor.

17　(Contrary to popular myth . . .) : Cheryl Russell, *100 Predictions for the Baby Boom* (New York: Plenum Press, 1987), p. 64.

17　While a very few . . . : "A New Kind of Love Match," *Newsweek,* Sept. 4, 1989,

p. 73; Barbara Hetzer, "Superwoman Goes Home," *Fortune,* Aug. 18, 1986, p. 20; "Facts on Working Women," Aug. 1989, Women's Bureau, U.S. Department of Labor, no. 89-2; and data from the Coalition of Labor Union Women and Amalgamated Clothing and Textile Workers Union. The surge of women joining unions in the late eighties was so great that it single-handedly halted the ten-year decline in union membership. Black women joined unions at the greatest rate. Women led strikes around the country, from the Yale University administrative staff to the Daughters of Mother Jones in Virginia (who were instrumental in the Pittston coal labor battle) to the Delta Pride catfish plant processors in Mississippi (where women organized the largest strike by black workers ever in the state, lodging a protest against a plant that paid its mostly female employees poverty wages, punished them if they skinned less than 24,000 fish a day, and limited them to six timed bathroom breaks a week). See Tony Freemantle, "Weary Strikers Hold Out in Battle of Pay Principle," *Houston Chronicle,* Dec. 2, 1990, p. 1A; Peter T. Kilborn, "Labor Fight on a Catfish 'Plantation,' " *The News and Observer,* Dec. 16, 1990, p. J2.

17   In 1986, while ... : 1986 Gallup Poll; Barbara Ehrenreich, "The Next Wave," *Ms.,* July/August 1987, p. 166; Sarah Harder, "Flourishing in the Mainstream: The U.S. Women's Movement Today," *The American Woman 1990–91,* p. 281. Also see 1989 Yankelovich Poll: 71 percent of black women said feminists have been helpful to women, compared with 61 percent of white women. A 1987 poll by the National Women's Conference Commission found that 65 percent of black women called themselves feminists, compared with 56 percent of white women.

18   Other signs of ... : For increase in violent pornography, see, for example, April 1986 study in the Attorney General's Commission on Pornography, Final Report, pp. 1402–3.

18   More subtle indicators ... : Sally Steenland, "Women Out of View: An Analysis of Female Characters on 1987–88 TV Programs," National Commission on Working Women, November 1987. Mystery fiction survey was conducted by Sisters In Crime and presented at the 1988 Mystery Writers of America conference; additional information comes from personal interview in May 1988 with the group's director, mystery writer Sara Paretsky. On popular music: Alice Kahn, "Macho—the Second Wave," *San Francisco Chronicle,* Sept. 16, 1990, Sunday Punch section, p. 2. On Andrew Dice Clay: Craig MacInnis, "Comedians Only a Mother Could Love," *Toronto Star,* May 20, 1990, p. C6; Valerie Scher, "Clay's Idea of a Punch Line Is a Belch After a Beer," *San Diego Union and Tribune,* Aug. 17, 1990, p. C1. On Rush Limbaugh: Dave Matheny, "Morning Rush Is a Gas," *San Francisco Examiner,* Jan. 2, 1991, p. C1. On American Women in Radio & TV: Betsy Sharkey, "The Invisible Woman," *Adweek,* July 6, 1987, p. 4.

19   The backlash line claims ... : Data from Children's Defense Fund. See also Ellen Wojahm, "Who's Minding the Kids?" *Savvy,* Oct. 1987, p. 16; "Child Care: The Time is Now," Children's Defense Fund, 1987, pp. 8–10.

20   "I myself ..." : Rebecca West, *The Clarion,* Nov. 14, 1913, cited in Cheris Kramarae and Paula A. Treichler, *A Feminist Dictionary* (London: Pandora Press, 1985) p. 160.

20   The meaning of the word "feminist" ... : *The Feminist Papers: From Adams to de Beauvoir,* ed. by Alice S. Rossi (New York: Bantam Books, 1973) p. xiii. For discussion of historical origins of term feminism, see Karen Offen, "Defining Feminism: A Comparative Historical Approach," in *Signs: Journal of Women in Culture and Society,* 1988, 14, no. 1, pp. 119–57.

20   I AM NOT A BARBIE DOLL ... : Carol Hymowitz and Michaele Weissman, *A History of Women in America* (New York: Bantam Books, 1978) p. 341.

Susan Brownmiller and Dolores Alexander

"From Carmita Wood to Anita Hill"

Susan Brownmiller, author of *Against Our Will: Men, Women and Rape,* and journalist Dolores Alexander examine a 1970 sexual harassement case in Ithaca, New York, which defined the issue that Anita Hill brought into focus for all Americans in 1992.

Professor Anita Hill's testimony last October at the Senate Judiciary Committee hearing may have been some people's first exposure to the legal concept of sexual harassment on the job, but the issue had been named and developed in the mid 1970s.

The women's movement was full blown by the time Lin Farley, a twenty-nine-year-old activist, was teaching an experimental course on women and work at Cornell University in 1974. During a consciousness-raising session with her class, students talked about disturbing behavior they had been subjected to on summer jobs; in all the cases, the women had been forced off the job by these unwanted advances.

Coincidentally, Carmita Wood, a forty-four-year-old administrative assistant, walked out of the office of a Cornell physicist after becoming physically ill from the stress of fending off his advances. When Ms. Wood filed for unemployment compensation in Ithaca, New York, claiming it wasn't her fault she had quit her job, the nascent movement acquired its first heroine, as well as a clear delineation of a problem as endemic as the abuse itself. The credibility of an office worker, a mother of four, was pitted against the reputation of an eminent scientist whose status was—and remains—so lofty that to this day his name has not appeared in accounts of her case.

Farley and two Cornell colleagues, Susan Meyer and Karen Sauvigné, found a lawyer for Wood and brainstormed to invent a name for their newly identified issue: "sexual harassment." The young feminists and their complainant proceeded to hold a movement-style speakout (a technique that had been used effectively to articulate the issues of abortion and rape) in a community center in Ithaca in May 1975. A questionnaire collected after the meeting showed that an astonishing number of women had firsthand experience to contribute.

Eleanor Holmes Norton, then chair of the New York City Commission on Human Rights, was conducting hearings on women and work that year. Farley came to testify, half expecting to be laughed out of the hearing room. "The titillation value of sexual harassment was always obvious,'' Farley recalls. ''But Norton treated the issue with dignity and great seriousness.'' Norton, who had won her activist spurs in the civil rights movement, was to put her understanding of sexual harassment to good use during her later tenure in Washington, D.C., as head of the Equal Employment Opportunity Commission (EEOC). But we are moving ahead of our history.

Reporter Enid Nemy covered the Human Rights Commission hearings for the *New York Times.* Her story, ''Women Begin to Speak Out Against Sexual Harassment at Work,'' appeared in the *Times* on August 19, 1975, and was syndicated nationally, to a tidal wave of response from women across the country.

Sauvigné and Meyer set up the Working Women's Institute in New York City as a clearing house for inquiries, and to develop a data bank with an eye toward public policy. Wood lost her case; the unemployment insurance appeals board ruled her reasons for quitting were personal. Lin Farley's breakthrough book, *Sexual Shakedown: The Sexual Harassment of Women on the Job,* was published by McGraw-Hill in 1978—after twenty-seven rejections. ''I thought my book would change the workplace,'' Farley says. ''It is now out of print.''

Things had begun to percolate on the legal front. Working with a large map and color-coded pushpins, Sauvigné and Meyer matched up complainants with volunteer lawyers and crisis counselors. Initially, aggrieved women sought redress by filing claims for unemployment insurance after they'd quit their jobs under duress, or by bringing their complaints to local human rights commissions. Ultimately the most important means of redress became the EEOC, the federal agency charged with investigating and mediating discrimination cases under Title VII of the 1964 Civil Rights Act. (The inclusion of sex discrimination in the 1964 act had been introduced at the last minute in an attempt to defeat the bill.)

By 1977, three cases argued at the appellate level (*Barnes* vs. *Costle; Miller* vs. *Bank of America; Tomkins* vs. *Public Service Electric & Gas*) had established a harassed woman's right, under Title VII, to sue the corporate entity that employed her. ''A few individual women stuck their necks out,'' says Nadine Taub, the court-appointed attorney for Adrienne Tomkins against the New Jersey utilities company.

The Tomkins case, in particular, made it clear that the courts would no longer view harassment as a personal frolic, but as sex discrimination for which the employer might be held responsible. A young woman named Catharine MacKinnon had followed these cases with avid interest while a law student at Yale; later she published an impassioned, if somewhat obfuscating, treatise, *Sexual Harassment of Working Women,* in 1979.

Job-threatening though it was, sexual harassment remained on a back burner of the public conscience, as life-threatening issues—rape, battery, child abuse, and the ongoing pro-choice battle—continued to dominate feminist activity and media attention.

"We felt so alone out there," remembers Freada Klein, whose Boston area advocacy group was called the Alliance Against Sexual Coercion. "There was a *Redbook* survey in 1976 and a *Ms.* speakout and cover story in 1977. That was all." Peggy Crull, director of research for the New York City Commission on Human Rights, recalls that by the close of the decade, however, "every women's magazine had run a piece."

Slowly and quietly, case law broadened the definition of unlawful harassment. As women entered the work force in greater numbers, committing themselves not only to jobs but to careers, new cases went beyond those situations in which a boss suggested sex to a subordinate as a quid pro quo for keeping her job or getting a promotion. A court decision in Minnesota established that coworker harassment was as inimical to working conditions as harassment by a boss. A New York decision held that a receptionist could not be required to wear revealing clothes that brought her unwanted attention.

Meanwhile, a clerk-typist named Karen Nussbaum was pursuing her own mission to organize women office workers through a national network she called 9 to 5. An old friend from the antiwar movement, Jane Fonda, visited her headquarters in Cleveland with the idea of making a movie about underpaid and unappreciated secretaries in a large U.S. corporation.

9 to 5, produced by Fonda's IPC Films, and starring Fonda, Lily Tomlin, and Dolly Parton, was released in 1980, with Parton playing the plucky secretary who fends off her lecherous boss. The loopy movie, a commercial success, used broad comedic strokes to highlight the woman's perspective.

In the waning days of the Carter administration, when Eleanor Holmes Norton was chair of the EEOC, she seized the initiative by issuing a set of federal guidelines on sexual harassment. The guidelines, a single-page memorandum issued on November 10, 1980, as Norton's tenure was running out, stated with admirable brevity that sexual activity as a condition of employment or promotion was a violation of Title VII. The creation of an intimidating, hostile, or offensive working environment was also a violation. Verbal abuse alone was deemed sufficient to create a hostile workplace. The guidelines encouraged corporations to write their own memoranda and inform employees of appropriate means of redress.

Guidelines are interpretations of existing statutes and do not have the full authority of law. But in 1981 (while Anita Hill was working for Clarence Thomas at the Department of Education), the EEOC was required to defend itself in *Bundy* vs. *Jackson,* said the former EEOC general counsel Leroy D. Clark. The District of Columbia circuit court ruled in favor of Sandra Bundy, a corrections department employee, and accepted the EEOC's guidelines as law, holding that Title VII could be violated even if a woman remained on the job.

Employers who were caught off guard were in for another surprise. During that same first year of the Reagan administration, the Merit Systems Protection Board, a regulatory agency that seldom makes news, released the results of a random survey of 20,100 federal employees. The findings revealed that a staggering 42 percent of the government's female workers had experienced an incident of sexual harassment on the job in the previous two years. "It was the first decent methodological study," says Freada Klein, who served as an adviser. "They did it again in 1988 and came up with the same figures."

It took the U.S. Supreme Court until 1986 to affirm unanimously, in *Meritor Savings Bank* vs. *Vinson,* that sexual harassment even without economic harm was unlawful discrimination, although the court drew back in some measure from employer liability in hostile-environment cases.

Five years later, Anita Hill's testimony to fourteen white male senators, and the merciless attacks on her credibility, echoed the agonies of her predecessors from Carmita Wood to Mechelle Vinson, who came forward at the risk of ridicule to tell about an abuse of power by a favored, institutionally protected, high-status male.

Detractors of the feminist role in social change have sought to create the impression that sexual harassment is yet another nefarious plot cooked up by an elite white movement to serve middle-class professionals. As it happens, veterans of the battle have been struck time and again by the fact that the plaintiffs in most of the landmark cases, brave women every one, have been working-class and African-

American: Paulette Barnes, payroll clerk; Margaret Miller, proofing machine operator; Diane Williams, Justice Department employee; Rebekah Barnett, shop clerk; Mechelle Vinson, bank teller trainee.

We collected many speculations as to why black women have led this fight, but the last word goes to Eleanor Holmes Norton, who said, succinctly, "With black women's historic understanding of slavery and rape, it's not surprising to me."

Ruth Sidel

from *On Her Own: Growing Up in
the Shadow of the American Dream*
"Mixed Messages"

Television, advertising, movies and newspapers continue
to barrage young American women with negative and often
contradictory images of themselves. In this excerpt Ruth
Sidel, Professor of Sociology at Hunter College in New York
City, analyzes the obstructive effects of the media's mixed
messages on young women in search of role models.

Love the mansion. But do I really want to be mayor?
Woman speaking on the telephone
in a Diane Von Furstenberg
advertisement

She comes out every evening in a different sexy dress—some with ruffles, some strapless, some with sequins or lace, some short, some long, provocative yet somehow sweet, but all ultra-feminine, the old-fashioned way. And she's always smiling, smiling and clapping. Not applauding—clapping. She's Vanna White, recognizable by millions of Americans. She walks, she pirouettes, she models jewelry and furs, and she turns letters. She is the "girl" of the fifties, the Barbie doll come alive on our television screens six times a week—in some cities twice a day, six times a week.

And then there is Bonnie Blair. Lean and determined, she skated into our consciousness in her peach-and-gray body suit, which was neither masculine nor feminine but was made to help her do the job. When she realized she had set a world-record time of 39.10 seconds and had won the gold medal in the 500-meter speed-skating race at the 1988 Winter Olympic games, she threw her arms up and her head back in a thrilling moment of accomplishment and exultation.

Two images of women: the woman who is and the woman who does; the woman who is exhibited and exhibits herself as a commodity and the woman who because of skill and hard work is valued for her accomplishments. This duality of images of woman is all around us: on the one hand, the women lawyers and M.B.A.s in their suits, carrying briefcases, the perfect wife/mother/professional of the television sitcoms, the oh-so-successful women jumping, leaping, running in action shots about the pages of fashion magazines; and on the other hand, the women featured in the *Sports Illustrated* "swimsuit issue," the socialites on the women's pages in the latest designer clothes, and the nude women provocatively displayed in the pages of *Playboy* and *Penthouse*.

What are our young women to fathom from these disparate images? What are the messages we send them in our popular culture with every advertisement, every song, every film, and every sitcom? What are we telling them about our expectations of their future roles in society?

There is no doubt that woman as success story has been a major theme of the 1980s: women in law, women in medicine, women in banking, even women on Wall Street—but also women employees who have a clever idea for the firm and are promoted to vice-president, and homemakers who have a clever idea and become successful entrepreneurs. Above all, there is the image of the professional woman who, combining hard work and commitment, "makes it" in the world of work.

In magazines, in the "style" sections of newspapers, and on television she is often portrayed—this prototype, this model of how to do it all, be it all, and have it all—as outgoing, attractive, personable, bright, and "assertive" but surely not too "aggressive." She is likely to be in her thirties; she exercises, has a snappy executive wardrobe, flies all over the country or the world with relative ease, is comfortable eating alone in upscale restaurants, and, while never pushy, certainly does not allow the maître d' to give her a table in front of the kitchen.

If she is married, her husband is comradely, egalitarian, "supportive," and "does his share" at home. If there are children, they are smiling and happy and she is involved with them, too. Despite her often hectic schedule, she makes time for their plays and recitals, and the family gets away for companionable weekends together—often skiing. Above all, she is confident, fulfilled—and she can even whip up a quick, elegant dinner for eight when necessary. She's a woman for our time.

But despite the number of women in the work force and the number who are the primary breadwinners and caretakers of their families, the role of sex object is by no means obsolete. The objectification of women is still all around us. Beauty pageants remain a booming business for the sponsors, the participants, and the media. The onlookers are in a real sense participants as well. While some of us may scoff and mock this archaic vestige of another era, an estimated 55 million Americans—75 percent of them women—tune in each year to watch the Miss America Pageant. Many yearn, sometimes against their will, to look just like the contestants, and feel any deviation must be due to personal failure. "If only I dieted enough and exercised enough," the fantasy goes, "I could [should] look like that, too." If we doubt that these women are models for how millions of Americans would like to look, we need only examine the statistics on diseases such as anorexia nervosa and bulimia ("women's diseases," virtually unknown in the male population but particularly prevalent among women in their late teens and early twenties) to realize that women are tyrannized by the desire to be thin. A recent study reported in the journal *Pediatrics* found that by the age of seven girls come to believe that thin is beautiful. By adolescence most girls think they are fatter than they really are; according to the physician who conducted the study, "One young girl broke into tears when her mother asked her to go for a swim. The girl said she'd look too fat in a swimsuit, when in fact her weight was normal for her height."

And, of course, it is not just the Miss America Pageant but the Miss Universe, Miss USA, Miss Teen USA, and all the state and local pageants that feed into the grand finales. That amounts to a lot of young women in bathing suits walking up and down a lot of runways and being judged, for the most part, on how they look. In 1987, for example, some eighty thousand women vied for the title of Miss America in local and state contests. No matter how well they juggle or sing or play "Malagüeña" on the accordion, we all know that it is their measurements and pretty faces and how well they turn that are really being judged. And the message is not lost on the young women who are watching and trying to figure out who they are, what they want to be, and how they will get there. According to clinical psychologist Dr. Susan Schenkel, the Miss America competition is "the contemporary embodiment of the traditional fairy tale: it's like magic elevating you to success. Because most of us are exposed to these images at a very young age, they remain a visceral part of us, no matter how much we may resist them intellectually." Dr. Rita Freedman, author of *Beauty Bound,* a book about images of women's beauty, states, "Physical attractiveness is still a major source of women's power and they tune into these shows to find out what an attractive female is supposed to look like. They want to know how to package themselves."

To "win," it may even be necessary to transform not only one's body but also one's ethnic image. The 1988 Miss California, Marlise Ricardos, tried three times to win the title. It was only after she changed her hair color from brunet to blond and wore blue contact lenses when she competed that she became entitled to represent California in the 1988 Miss America contest in Atlantic City. As journalist Anne Taylor Fleming had observed, "She's the ultimate self-made competitor, a chemically "sun-streaked" miss who rid herself of both pounds and ethnic identity to please pageant judges."

Women are also told in a variety of ways that although many of them may be executives on the way up, they must also still be warm, expressive, and frivolous, perhaps more concerned about what they wear than about the next corporate merger. An excellent example of this double message is an engaging Smirnoff vodka advertisement that shows three young, upwardly mobile women having drinks (all with vodka, presumably) while laughing, gesturing in typically feminine ways, and admiring a pair of red, sling-back, spike-heel shoes. The message the ad seems to be giving is, "You're working women now, you're out for a drink without a man, you're 'liberated,' but we know that underneath all that you're still into feelings and fashion."

This ad at least presumes by their clothes that these are working women out for a relaxing, good time. A far more disturbing example of advertising that seems to be urging a retreat from feminism is the Diane Von Furstenberg ad in the *New York Times* special section *Fashions of the Times* in February 1988. A woman is sitting on a chair talking on the telephone, one shoe kicked off, her fashionably short skirt halfway up her thigh. She says, "Love the mansion. But do I really want to be mayor?" The next page shows her with a tall stack of packages wrapped in a way that indicates they are from fashionable shops, and gives the answer: "No, there are better ways of having it all—and for a lot less!" What are the implications of this incredible ad? That the only reason women are interested in being mayor is to live in the mansion? That they are not really interested in power and substance and hard work? How is our woman in the advertisement going to get the "mansion" and all those consumer goods? There is certainly no indication that she plans to go into law, banking, or medicine instead of politics. Is the implication really that she is going to get them through a man, that she would rather marry the mayor than be one? In 1988? What is going on?

Recent fashion trends have surely indicated that there has been substantial backlash in reaction to the women's movement and to the changing nature of women's roles over the past twenty-five years. In 1987, just about the time that women's wages reached the all-time pinnacle of 65 percent of men's wages, fashion took an abrupt turn—many would say backwards. The stylish look moved from relatively simple clothes with shoulder pads, a modified dress-for-success look, to plunging necklines, bare shoulders, "waistlines snugly fitted, and skirts ... rounded in an egg shape, tightly draped, or flared and poufed with myriad petticoats." Tops are "translucent if not transparent," dresses often "look like lingerie, with slip tops and lacy edges." And everywhere the short skirt. Skirts two, three, and four inches above the knee in the board room, the courtroom, and the operating room? Skirts above the knee to sell insurance and real estate or to do the taxes of a Fortune 500 company? Are women really going to get pay equity or run for the House of Representatives in a plunging neckline and a draped skirt? Why did we see "the most seductive, feminine-looking clothes since the days of Napoleon I's Empire" in the late 1980s? Did we try to go too far too fast? Is this the backlash to all those career women of the past decade? One designer said that women in his clothes will look "like little dolls"; one analyst has termed it "bimbo chic." These clothes, which hark back to the fifties but are far more provocative, are clearly not for the aspiring CEO or the nurse's aide. To their credit, millions of American women rejected these extreme styles and simply stopped buying for the period of time when that was all that was available. While the shortest skirts have all but disappeared, many clothes still end an inch or two above the knee, giving women a little-girl look hardly compatible with positions of power and respect in a society in which the dark blue suit is the ultimate badge of authority.

There is, moreover, the stereotypic look of the prostitute about some of the clothes and poses in many contemporary advertisements: black net stockings; see-through black lace; women draped over chairs, waiting to be used. The most flagrant advertisements showing woman-as-erotic-object and man-as-powerful-manipulator are those for Guess jeans. These ads, which appear in a variety of women's and general-interest magazines, are frequently several pages long, as though they are telling a story. The man is older, perhaps in his fifties, sinister looking, with dark glasses; the women are young, intense, and often partially nude. In one picture a woman, nude above the waist, her skirt pulled up to show black net stockings, sits on the man's lap. There is a table nearby indicating that they have had dinner and possibly a good deal of wine. In another picture in the series, a young woman is leaning over him as though she is about to mount him. He has a faint smile, almost a sneer, on his face. He is calling the shots; she is there to amuse him, to service him. The final picture shows a young woman, in her late teens or early twenties, dressed only in what looks to be a black leotard and a jean jacket (jean jackets can be worn anywhere!), kneeling at his feet. We know he is rich, because the door to the room is in dark-grained wood with a handsome brass handle. She looks up at him inquiringly, obediently. Is she about to perform fellatio? Is he going to beat her, whip her? There is certainly a sadomasochistic tone to this series of advertisements. At the very least, we are seeing the "ritualization of subordination," as sociologist Erving Goffman has termed it, which is often manifested by "lowering oneself physically in some form . . . of prostration." There is no doubt in these ads who is in charge.

Yet another series of advertisements for Guess jeans is centered on the toreador theme. The women are again young, in provocative clothes, and are either waiting for the great man to appear or swooning, almost literally, against a poster of the handsome bullfighter. On the opposite page the toreador is shown in action: on a horse, the adoring multitudes all around, fighting the bull, and finally walking off in glory to resounding cheers. It is no accident that Guess jeans uses the most macho of all male images—the bullfighter—and pictures women as flimsily dressed, yearning, passive, carried away by desire. These advertisements seem targeted to the adolescent young woman. Is it the ad agencies' view that adolescents are "turned on" by pictures of submissive women and dominant men, by implied sadomasochism? There is certainly evidence that sadomasochism sells in the culture at large; much of the content in sex shops and sex magazines and the incredible amount of violence in films and on television attest to the pervasiveness of the themes of cruelty and pain. Sociologist Lynn Chancer has, in fact, suggested that sadomasochistic relationships are deeply imbedded in many aspects of American culture, particularly those that involve male-female interaction.

These are not the only ads in which women are portrayed as being "carried away," either literally or figuratively. In magazine after magazine, in image after image, women are literally being carried by men, leaning on men, being helped down from a height of two feet, or figuratively being carried away by emotion. When men and women are portrayed together, men are invariably solid citizens, responsible, dependable, in charge, busy; women are emoting, leaning, giddy, carried away—clearly not the persons you would choose to perform your neurosurgery, to handle your money, or even to care for your child.

While many designers have retreated from the extreme clothes of 1987, in part because women refused to buy what one observer called "a new boffo outrage each season," women are still often portrayed as little girls, seductive, passive, dependent, and, above all, beautiful and thin, with knock-'em-dead figures. After twenty-five years of the women's movement, is it how we look that is really important after all?

Women's magazines are key transmitters of values, attitudes, information, and the latest consensus about appropriate behavior. They help to socialize young women into their adult roles and enable more mature women to stay *au courant* with norms, expectations, and style. In a period of rapidly changing expectations, they have played a crucial role in molding women's attitudes toward work, toward family life, and toward themselves.

In an effort to understand the messages young women are receiving, fourteen women's magazines for March 1988 were systematically examined for content, for the ways in which women were portrayed, and for the values and norms that were both subtly and directly communicated. The magazines, chosen for their appeal to a broad spectrum of women by age, class, and interest, were *Seventeen, Mademoiselle, Glamour, Cosmopolitan, Harper's Bazaar, Vogue, Ladies' Home Journal, Working Mother, New Women, Self, Working Woman, Savvy, Ms.,* and *Essence.* All of the magazines focused, in varying degrees, on beauty tips, hair, fashion, fitness, health, food (both nutrition and recipes), and work. Virtually everyone pictured is clearly middle class; several magazines (*Vogue, Savvy,* and *Harper's Bazaar*) are upper middle class in tone, with an emphasis on upper-class lifestyle. A few of the magazines openly disparage the lower middle and working classes: a comic strip in *Seventeen* indicates that any high-school student foolish enough to invite a guy who works in an auto muffler shop to the school prom will find that he is no better than a prehuman ape, and *Mademoiselle* cautions women who want to move up the career ladder not to "leave the ratty little sweater on the chair just like the secretary does." Among the hundreds of features, viewpoints, articles, occasional fiction, advice, and how-to columns, there was not one instance of members of the working class being depicted in a positive light.

The overall message, transmitted both explicitly and implicitly, is

"You can be all you want to be." You can be fit, thin, and trim; you can have a good job, be upwardly mobile, and invest your money wisely; you can wear stunning suits in your march toward success or slinky, sexy, almost childlike clothes, if you prefer; you can have an attractive, no-fuss hairstyle and blend just the right, ever-flattering makeup; you can have great (albeit safe) sex and know just what to do when *he* cannot perform; and, above all, you really *can* have it all—a warm, close family life and lucrative, pleasurable work. You really *can* have both love and success. It may mean starting your own business at home, but there are all those success stories to serve as models: Mrs. Fields, who has made millions on her chocolate-chip cookies and looks gorgeous too; the woman from Virginia who does $1 million worth of business annually making flags and is about to license national franchises; or the woman from Scottsdale, Arizona, who delivers teddy bears as special-occasion gifts the way FTD sells flowers and currently owns two stores, twenty-three franchises, and has annual sales of $1.5 million. What could be easier? And all that is involved are skills that women already have! Women are being told that they can use traditional female skills and make a fortune without ever leaving the kitchen or the sewing machine. The implication is that the fulfillment of the American Dream can be simply one clever idea or marketing strategy away.

Different magazines appeal, of course, to different constituencies: in March 1988, *Seventeen* features prom gowns and many advertisements for sanitary products; *Working Mother* had numerous articles on parenting and homemaking; *Vogue* and *Harper's Bazaar* showed the trendiest and most expensive clothes; and *Essence* dealt, for the most part, with issues particularly relevant to black women. But the overall message is that "working women" are "on the way up," that "you're headed for the top," and that you can "be your own boss."

Not only can you remake your career but you can also remake your looks. The "makeover" (frequently called the "five-minute makeover") is ubiquitous and offers the promise of instant results. Often using "ordinary" people, neither models nor film stars, the makeover is meant to show us all how much more appealing and contemporary we can look by the ever-changing standards of beauty. Are we to have accented lips or accented eyes? Slightly unmanageable long hair or a trim, stylish short cut? Must we still diet until we are reed slim, or is it once again fashionable to look voluptuous? If you do not look like the models and celebrities smiling on every page, you are not exercising properly, eating the correct food, getting the right haircut, using the appropriate gel or mousse; or perhaps you need cosmetic surgery—liposuction, eyelid surgery, nose alteration, or breast enlargement or reduction. The magazines often feature pro and con articles about cosmetic surgery, but the bottom line is that it is yet another legitimate weapon, currently very much in vogue, in women's endless struggle toward a more attractive face and body.

"Older" women are frequently exhorted by women's magazines to be beautiful, fit, and above all, youthful. While the positive aspects of the emphasis on midlife beauty and fitness are that women in their forties, fifties, sixties, and beyond often see themselves today as vibrant, sexually attractive and truly in the prime of life, there are negative aspects as well. Columnist Ellen Goodman points out that the women who are currently held up as paragons

> raise the threshold of self-hate faster than the age span. . . . Those of us who failed to look like Brooke Shields at seventeen can now fail to look like Victoria Principal at thirty-three and like Linda Evans at forty-one and like Sophia Loren at fifty. When Gloria Steinem turned fifty . . . she updated her famous line from forty. She said, "This is what fifty looks like." With due apologies to the cult of midlife beauty, allow me two words: "Not necessarily."

And what is so sad, and in some sense shameful, is that a broad spectrum of businesses and advertisers are playing on that self-hatred in their unending quest to sell products and services. It is the combination of self-hatred and "willful suspension of disbelief" that leads women, over and over, to those cosmetics counters, health spas, and plastic surgeons. Maybe we can come just a little closer to what they tell us we should look like. . . .

Even *Ms.* promised that "whatever it is we want, we can succeed." Despite the opening paragraph of the editor's essay, which suggests that all women might not choose the stressful life of a "corporate or government job," the ultimate message is that whatever we do choose, "we can succeed." The *Essence* editor's column gave the same message: that although there are powerful forces "arrayed against us—racism, sexism, poverty, homelessness, illiteracy, poor health"—black women must reach for the sky, saying "I can!" The message is that changing our lives is fundamentally within our control: "If you're living below your standard, get busy devising a plan to improve your life. If your work is a bore, renew your attitude. . . .Surround yourself with positive people who encourage you. . . . Each of us must become an active participant in empowering ourselves and our people. Only the single-minded succeed."

To their credit, *Essence* and *Ms.* were the only magazines that suggested that the well-being of the individual is at all connected with the well-being of the larger group and made a point of urging their readers to work toward "empowering ourselves and our people."

Are women's magazines the Horatio Alger novels of our time? Part of their mission is to help women cope with a rapidly changing society. From the "tips" on hair, fashion, and makeup to the reviews of books, films, and drama and the longer, often thoughtful, articles on health, sexual mores, or work options, they put women in touch with current attitudes, norms, and expectations. And at the same time they reaffirm the American Dream: by telling women repeatedly that they can, if they work hard enough, exercise long enough, eat correctly, and dress fashionably, achieve their dreams, these powerful agents of socialization are reinforcing the ideology that in America the individual can indeed make of herself whatever she chooses. Since there is rarely a suggestion that opportunity is related to economic, political, or social factors beyond the control of the individual, if a woman does not succeed after all these how-tos, perhaps she has no one to blame but herself. Moreover, the constant emphasis on celebrities, on stars, on those who have succeeded beyond most people's wildest dreams serves to reinforce the message.

Some of the magazines deal explicitly with the American Dream and extend it beyond the individual to the family unit. With the March 1988 issue, *Ms.* began a new series titled "Tracking the Dream." In the series the magazine plans to explore "how families are faring in the late 1980s." For their first family they chose a young couple with two small children who live in a small town in Pennsylvania. In this era of divorce, single-parent families, step-families, urban alienation, and the "new poor," *Ms.* chose a family straight out of Norman Rockwell's America. The husband works repairing furnaces; his wife is a full-time homemaker. They live in the same community in which they were raised, with their extended family all around, able and willing to help one another. Their two children are "blond, curly-haired, blue-eyed, and have the [family's] famous . . . dimples." They are a Shirley Temple, "Leave It to Beaver," "Father Knows Best" family come to life.

Although their 1987 income was $29,565, just the U.S. median family income, "they have acquired a home [traditional Dutch colonial] of which they are rightfully proud, they eat well, and they enjoy life." They have a swimming pool in the back and swings in the basement playroom. They don't buy on credit; nor, by the way, do they vote. The husband does not want his wife to work and expects his daughters to live the same life as their mother. *Ms.* admits that this family is representative of only 6 percent of all Americans—those who "still live in families with a working father, a homemaker mother, and dependent children." And if we factor in living in small-town America with a readily available family support system, they are typical of an even smaller percentage of the American population.

Why, then, would *Ms.* choose such an old-fashioned, atypical family for their first "documentary portrait of American families today" and then portray their lifestyle in such glowing terms? Do the *Ms.* editors think that we want to believe in this traditional image of the United States, where men are men and women are women and children have dimples and grandparents are there to help out? Do they think that reaffirming our image of an America straight out of the Frank Capra film *It's a Wonderful Life* will woo more traditional women to the *Ms.* readership? But of course in selling themselves they are selling an ideology; they are reinforcing a largely outdated image of America that has clear implications for the formulation of social policy. *Ms.* is clearly sending a message that self-reliance, mutual aid, the importance of the extended family and traditional family roles are alive and well in the United States in the late 1980s. With families like this, why would we need job training programs, day care, or a comprehensive family policy? Did they choose this particular family in order to reaffirm that old American Dream; to say to the faint of heart, the disbelievers, the urban cynics, "You see, it can still be done"? If it had been put onto videotape, the entire piece could have been a Ronald Reagan campaign commercial.

That same month, March 1988, *Ladies' Home Journal* also ran an article on the American Dream. The lives and finances of four families, each with two children, were described: a black family with an annual income of $28,600, and three white families, one with an income of $43,000, another with an income of $60,000, and the last with an income of $150,000. Each of the families has two parents, and in all but one both parents work. (In the remaining family, the wife plans to return to work within the year, when the younger child enters school full-time.) All of the families own their own homes and various luxury consumer goods—VCRs, stereos, a cabin cruiser, central air conditioning—and one has taken an anniversary trip to Hawaii. The family earning $28,600 says that life is a constant struggle but stresses that they have come a long way from the near-poverty days early in their marriage. The family earning $150,000 is striving for an income of $250,000; the husband states, "Success is being able to work a four-day week and still get what you want." The *Ladies' Home Journal* summarizes, "The American Dream of the good life for all is still very much with us."

In all these magazines, scattered among the hairstyles, the fashion layouts, and the endless advertisements is perhaps the central message: the American Dream is alive and well. If you work hard, believe in yourself, and consume relentlessly, you, too, can be a success in America.

One of the most appealing twists on the "having it all" theme was pictured on the cover and inside the December 1987 *Harper's Bazaar* in an extensive and lavish layout. Amid the holiday glitter, the "festive fantasy" of "blazing gold sequins," "paillettes," and "huge faux gems," actresses Shelley Long and Phylicia Rashad and model Christie Brinkley were pictured in sumptuous designer gowns and jewels while holding their own young children, also dressed in lavish outfits. *Bazaar*'s Christmas issue is not only celebrating gorgeous women who are performers and mothers ("The most popular mom on television, 'The Cosby Show' 's Phylicia Rashad does an equally good job of parenting in reality" and "Nothing expresses the true meaning of this season more clearly than the special glow between mother and child") but is also celebrating the family ("For even in this age of high-tech and high finance, the primal bonds of family—no matter how stretched or strained—remain squarely at the heart of Christmas"). Nothing is sacred in the selling of consumerism—especially at Christmastime. The message is clear: these women truly have it all—money, beauty, fabulous careers, husbands, and beautiful babies. Should the rest of us expect anything less?

Yet another example of the having-it-all-including-baby theme is a Donna Karan advertisement in the August 1988 issue of *Vogue*. The "mother" is lying half on the bed and half on the floor, dressed in a black, scoop-backed bodysuit. She is presumably a professional woman, since she is reading papers concerning shareholders. Strewn around the bedroom are clothes, pocketbooks, shoes, and scads of jewelry. A baby is sitting on the bed, presumably a girl, also "working" with pen and paper, an open notebook nearby. The child is wearing nothing more than a diaper and a necklace—a Donna Karan necklace, one assumes. The message again is clear: it *is* possible to have it all—and, by the way, it is never too early to teach a girl to want pretty things!

If the fashion world and women's magazines are giving us contradictory messages about women's roles and goals in the late 1980s— that women should achieve in the workplace and take greater control of their lives but that they should also look great, feel great, consume ceaselessly, and play the old roles of sex object, dependent woman, and devoted mom—what is television telling us? According to a recent study conducted by the National Commission on Working Women, nearly one million adolescent girls watch prime-time network television programs every night, and many of the programs they watch contain adolescent female characters. The study found that "viewers are likely to see girls with no visible skills, no favorite subjects in school, no discussions about college majors or vocational plans. . . . These images create the impression that one can magically jump from an adolescence of dating and shopping to a well-paid professional career." The report continues by pointing out that "on TV, girls' looks count for more than their brains." Plots focus on shopping, makeup, and dating—girls are often pictured as misfits if they do not have a date on Friday or Saturday night. Adolescent girls outnumber boys on prime time, but boys are usually the center of the action while girls play more passive, subsidiary roles. Furthermore, 94 percent of adolescent girls on TV are middle class or wealthy; very few are working class or poor. In reality, over one-third of teenage girls live in families with incomes under $20,000.

The study does find some positives—intelligent teenagers who are pictured as likable and successful—but they are relatively rare. Far more common are outmoded, insidious stereotypes that suggest that young women are shallow, vain, materialistic—and sometimes the traditional dumb, sexy blonde. On one episode of "Who's the Boss?" "a young practical nurse, depicted as a dim-witted buxom blonde, claims she entered nursing after failing beauty school, where she was undone by the pressure of remembering different shades of nail polish. Unable to wash a dish or run an appliance, she's eager to give Tony, her patient, a sponge bath. 'I'm Doreen the practical nurse,' she purrs. 'I do it all.' "

The depiction of adult women on TV tells us, on the one hand, that working women are very much part of the culture. Women are lawyers ("L.A. Law" and "The Cosby Show"); women are doctors ("Heartbeat"); women are members of the police force ("Cagney and Lacey"); women manage bars ("Cheers"); and they even run funeral homes ("Frank's Place"). Women can be on their own ("The Days and Nights of Molly Dodd," "Designing Women," "Kate and Allie," "Murphy Brown"), can kill as easily as men ("Miami Vice" and assorted other programs), and can find alternatives to the nuclear family ("Designing Women," "The Golden Girls," "Kate and Allie," and even "Beauty and the Beast"). But what we still rarely find on TV are straightforward, intelligent, admirable heroines who are working class (Mary Beth Lacey of "Cagney and Lacey" was a notable exception; and, sad to say, that excellent, human, courageous program was canceled at the end of the 1987–88 season) or poor or even a realistic depiction of what life is really like for working women today. The female lawyers on "L.A. Law" are simply too stunning, too elegant, too affluent; the one featured woman on that program who is a secretary is significantly less attractive and less savvy than the female lawyers and, moreover, was for a significant period of time in love with her womanizing lawyer/boss, who takes her devotion for granted and never quite sees her as a full-fledged person. Even Miss DiPesto, the secretary on "Moonlighting," while she is a marvelously zany and lovable character, is pictured as less than attractive (particularly compared with Cybill Shepherd!), worshiping her bosses, not quite in control of her own life, someone who barely muddles through.

"Nightingales," a program supposedly about nurses, *is* in actuality, according to the managing editor of the *American Journal of Nursing,* about sex. The program, she states, is a "mindless series" which humiliates and ridicules nurses on prime time. It is unlikely to encourage women to go into nursing the way "L.A. Law" has encouraged women to go to law school.

"Roseanne," the hit sitcom of the 1988–89 season, does portray a working-class family. Both parents work, breakfast is appropriately chaotic, the husband helps out around the house, and Roseanne keeps everyone in line with firmness, wisecracks, and a considerable dose of wisdom. While the program sometimes seems to be putting down upper-middle-class pretensions, one wonders if it isn't also an upper-middle-class putdown of the working class. Roseanne solves most daily problems with a combination of clever one-liners and a level of sensitivity unusual on TV sitcoms, but her comments are often so extreme, her delivery so abrupt, and her weight so omnipresent that the program sometimes seems like a parody of working-class life rather than a sympathetic and realistic depiction.

While the viewer at least sees Cagney and Lacey and the female lawyers on "L.A. Law" at work, one rarely sees the four characters on "Designing Women" or Bill Cosby's wife working. These women may indeed work, but it is their home life, their interpersonal life that we are shown. Even in the daytime soap operas, where most women characters today "work as lawyers, surgeons, and journalists and discuss their problems over business lunches or hurried snacks in the hospital cafeteria ... these professional women are rarely shown doing their work. What concerns them most are the problems of their families and friends and their own romantic and sexual adventures." Yet, with all the preoccupation with appearance and sex and romance, the "media's version of feminism" is, fundamentally, that "women can have, and do, it all—without help from men."

And what about all those female social workers, teachers, and firefighters out there? Couldn't they be the heroines of gripping weekly programs? They might even have problems with child care, after-school care, getting enough money together to pay the rent, or worrying about their own elderly, ailing parents. For, while much television programming has responded to the recent changes in the roles of women, both within the workplace and in the home, few programs show the nitty-gritty of daily life. "Thirtysomething" does exactly this but focuses on the upper middle class. "Frank's Place" tried to portray real life for the black working class; but, of course, Frank was a former professor—and the show was canceled after one season.

Perhaps Hope, the central female character on "thirtysomething," tells us something about the current messages women are receiving. It is no coincidence that several young women whom I interviewed used "thirtysomething" as a model for the lives they hoped to lead. According to a 1988 A. C. Nielson report, 43 percent of the eighteen-to-thirty-four-year-old women surveyed watched "thirtysomething," ranking it eleventh out of eighty-one television shows for that age group for the season. During the first season Hope, a Princeton graduate and the mother of a toddler, was at home caring for her daughter and agonizing with her friends about their possible choices and options. At the beginning of the second season, Hope had returned to work part-time, and she and Michael were still agonizing, this time over the timing of a second child. Hope had just begun to mesh her work life with her home life, but Michael was eager for another child. After an episode in which Hope imagined the lives of those who lived in their house during World War II and which focused on the fragility of human life and love, Hope succumbed. During the Christmas/Hanukkah episode, which showed Michael realizing the importance of his religious heritage, Hope announced that she was pregnant. The reaffirmation of traditional values was complete.

If Hope, intelligent, beautiful, thoughtful, upper middle class, married to Michael, sensitive, caring, and loving, cannot effectively integrate work and home, who of us can? When the high-school student from Westchester County tells me she wants to be a lawyer *and* be home to give her children the proverbial "milk and cookies" but that what she *really* wants it to be like Hope and be married to Michael, isn't she saying that she, too, recognizes that she cannot have it all—at least while the children are young? But while on one level she seems to understand the limitations that are built into many women's lives, on another level she has internalized the message that she must succeed, achieve, and be able to stand alone. The media have very effectively played on both sides of women's ambivalence and presented very few models of women—or, rather, families—who have managed to work out the work/family conflict.

While TV is making a gesture at portraying working women, how are men currently being portrayed? For much of the 1970s and early 1980s, the ideal American man as rendered by television was an Alan Alda type, caring, sensitive, able to relate to others' feelings well as to his own. Frank Furillo, the captain on "Hill Street Blues," was perhaps the prototype of the sensitive, aware hero of the past decade. But by the late 1980s the new male on American television is, according to one analysis, "spontaneous, unhesitant, sure. In action drama, his antagonists are unqualifiedly bad, and he disposes of them accordingly, shooting first and getting in touch with his feelings later, if at all. In comedy, he is a womanizer, eager for the easy score." The new heroes are the "super-cool, super-detached detectives" of "Miami Vice," the "lecherous bar proprietor" Sam Malone in "Cheers," and the "unreconstructed chauvinist" David

Addison in "Moonlighting." And even Bill Cosby is the authoritative, all-knowing head-of-household on "The Cosby Show."

Several analysts have seen the changes in male heroes in the mid- and late 1980s as a direct reaction to the feminist movement. Glenn Caron, the original producer of "Moonlighting," has stated, "I very much wanted to see a *man* on television." The message of many recent programs is that for a man to be a *real* man, he must try to "conquer" rather than "relate," be a relentless womanizer, and surely be aggressive, willing to kill at any opportunity. The introspective male hero who sees many sides of an issue and is torn apart by his understanding of individuals and their limitations as well as society and its limitations is being replaced by characters who see issues in starker terms and who believe in individual accountability rather than societal accountability. According to sociologist Amitai Etzioni, "There is a mild reaction to the women's movement. There is some part of the population which wishes men to reassert themselves. You see, the new world turned out to be very complicated. You don't know what relationships are proper, and the world yearns for something simpler."

A few recent TV programs (for example, "Murphy Brown" and "Anything But Love") feature gutsy, risk-taking women and "wimpy" men. As one observer has noted, these programs seem to be "delving into the 'male' side of women and the 'female' side of men." But these efforts are all too rare.

Analyzing films is considerably more difficult than analyzing television programming, in part because of the wide variety of films made for different audiences: the teen film; the action film; the intellectual, arty film; the issue film. All the same, some generalizations are possible. First, there seems to have been a significant retreat from the films of the late 1970s and early 1980s, which regularly featured strong, positive, even heroic female characters: Sally Field in *Norma Rae* (1979) and *Places in the Heart* (1984), Jane Fonda in *The China Syndrome* (1979), Jessica Lange in *Frances* (1982), Meryl Streep in *Silkwood* (1983), Jane Alexander in *Testament* (1983). Over the past few years there have been Sigourney Weaver in *Gorillas in the Mist* (1988), Meryl Streep in *Out of Africa* (1986), and, most notably, Barbara Hershey in *A World Apart* (1988)—a film that features strong, serious, substantive roles for three women, including a black and an eleven-year-old. Nevertheless, heroic roles for women have been in shorter supply.

Today we have the either/or film: *Broadcast News* (1987), the either-professional-success-or-love film in which the heroine (Holly Hunter) is so driven by professional ambition that she confides to her friend and co-worker, "I'm beginning to repel people I'm trying to seduce"; or *The Good Mother* (1988), the either-sex-or-mother-hood film in which the leading character, played by Diane Keaton, is not only without rewarding work but loses both her child and her lover. One must wonder why the novel from which this film was made was so popular. It was seen almost as a fable for our time—that women had better not enjoy sex as much as men do, or they may lose everything.

As the late 1980s was a time of ascendancy of "real men" on television, so it was in films. The movie plot of the "virile lower-class male [who] subdues the haughty lady who is his social or professional superior and who 'needs' to be taken down a peg" is with us once again. In *House of Games* (1987) Lindsay Crouse plays an "uptight psychiatrist and best-selling author who is lured by a seductively sleazy con man (Joe Mantegna) into a high-stakes game that allows her to release her own inhibitions." In *Overboard* (1988) Goldie Hawn is a "brittle heiress" who is "humanized by a carpenter." In *Baby Boom* (1987) Diane Keaton, a yuppie executive, is melted by a "woodsy veterinarian" played by Sam Shepard. As Molly Haskell has stated, "The toughness of the woman in each of these films is often a facade: she gives herself away, but only to a certain kind of man, a man who has little respect for the rules of the power world in which she was raised." These men may be the social inferiors of these women, but they are not intimidated by them, and in fact are really in control.

Female nudity, often for its own sake, is perhaps a signal that "misogyny on film may be far from dead." In the adaptation of Milan Kundera's *The Unbearable Lightness of Being* (1988), the hero, Tomas, often opens a conversation with a woman he has just met by saying, "Take off your clothes"—and many, of course, are only too willing. As Janet Maslin points out, the success of *Blue Velvet* (1986), in which "Isabella Rossellini performed much of her role stark naked, and was violently abused again and again by Dennis Hopper," gave "kinkiness in the art film . . . a new lease on life, and sexism in a serious context was respectable all over again." Today it is far more common than it would have been five to ten years ago for leading American actresses to provide flashes of nudity.

And, of course, no discussion of misogyny in films would be complete without a mention of *Fatal Attraction* (1987). The film may pretend to be concerned with the woman who is used for a weekend fling and then forgotten, but it is really a cautionary tale for both men and women. A central moral of the film is surely that women who play around with other people's husbands and enjoy it are not only driven mad by the experience but will not live to do it again.

While the overt message of much advertising and of many of the articles in women's magazines is that women today should be able to "have it all," in fact, the underlying message of many films and television programs and even advertising is that women actually cannot "have it all." It is the rare woman in films, for example, who really manages to have a satisfying job and a gratifying private life. In several recent films, the professional woman is portrayed as either obsessed with work to the exclusion of love and intimacy or obsessed with a man. When she is obsessed with a man, she not infrequently destroys him or herself as part of the resolution of the conflict.

The obvious exception to this pattern is *Working Girl* (1988), a modern fairy tale starring Melanie Griffith as a working-class secretary from Staten Island who makes it in New York's financial district and gets the man as well. While on the one hand it is a satire of the cutthroat, success-at-any-price norms of Wall Street, it is also a Horatio Alger story for women, a triumph of talent and gutsiness over privilege based on class and gender, a reaffirmation of the American Dream. That we identify with Tess McGill and cheer her on all the way is, I believe, crucial to the success of the film. Tess is played so softly, so sweetly, and so sexily that we never see her as a threat; she is never "aggressive," merely a bit nervy—and in any case, she is entitled to practice one or two deceptions, because her boss, masterfully and oh-so-nastily played by Sigourney Weaver, has tried to steal Tess's big idea. We see her as the quintessential American underdog, deserving and hardworking, proof that the American Dream can still work for all of us.

Mystery novels are yet another example of popular culture tuning in to changes in society, sometimes mirroring those changes and occasionally moving ahead of the culture in terms of the role models they portray. Recently there has been a spate of mysteries in which the sleuth is a woman—not the elderly, wise, quick-witted, all-observant sleuth like Agatha Christie's famed Miss Marple but gutsy, fast-talking, fast-moving women who far more resemble Sam Spade.

Perhaps the most conventional of the women sleuths is Kate Fansler, the central character of the Amanda Cross books. A professor by trade, married, upper middle class, Kate Fansler is in many ways the opposite of the typical loner-detective who lives from case to case on meager earnings and in somewhat dingy surroundings. She and her husband have cocktails before dinner, eat out with intellectual, entertaining friends; and in between professional meetings, semesters, and exam periods, she manages to solve the mysteries and murders that come her way. Fansler is unusual in yet another respect—she has an aura of authority around her. She has the authority of middle age, the authority of status by virtue of her profession, and the authority of class. She doesn't need to earn the respect of others; she already has it.

Maggie Ryan, heroine of P. M. Carlson's novels, is also married; and in *Rehearsal for Murder,* she carries her five-month-old daughter, Sarah, with her as she shuttles on the New York subway between her work as a consulting statistician, her actor-husband's theater, and the various New York City sites relevant to the plot. Woven in and around the plot are the pressures a new baby brings to marriage and the image of a family in which the father does a fair amount of the child care. Through it all, Maggie manages to solve the crime, protect her baby, and maintain an enviable relationship with her husband!

Jemima Shore, the central character of Antonia Fraser's series of British mysteries, is a savvy, attractive, well-known television investigator who often travels among the glamorous and the affluent. A single, independent woman who is clearly in charge of her life, Shore has relationships with men as she chooses and is pictured as being able, for the most part, to take them or leave them.

Anna Lee, also British and the heroine of mysteries by Liza Cody, is far more typical of the modern female sleuth. A private investigator by trade, she is competent, persevering, somewhat cynical, and very good at repairing cars. A loner who must struggle for minimal respect even within the agency in which she works, she typically has her own individual sense of morality. She may bend the truth and the rules to figure out what is going on, but she is loyal and caring with her friends and generally on the side of those who are hurting.

V. I. (Vic) Warshawski, a half-Jewish, part-Italian, part-Polish lawyer turned private investigator, is the central character in Sara Paretsky's Chicago-based mysteries. Typical of this new breed of women detectives, Warshawski is tough, intellectual (she reads Primo Levi in the original Italian), wisecracking, courageous, and has a solid inner sense of self-worth. She has a close circle of female friends (bright, achieving, independent women who are also role models for a new kind of woman) to whom she is extremely loyal and a circle of male characters with whom she holds her own. She provides a key to the character of many of these women when she says that action is what every detective needs. While she spends a fair amount of time mulling things over in a hot bath or drinking Johnnie Walker Black, when action is needed or she is faced with a dangerous, even life-threatening situation, she packs her Smith and Wesson into her tote bag or into the waist of her jeans and forges ahead.

But perhaps Kinsey Millhone is the epitome of this new heroine. The private investigator at the center of Sue Grafton's alphabetical mysteries (*"A" Is for Alibi, "B" Is for Burglar, "C" Is for Corpse,* etc.), she introduces herself:

> My name is Kinsey Millhone. I'm a private investigator, licensed by the state of California, operating a small office in Santa Teresa, which is where I've lived all my thirty-two years. I'm female, self-supporting, single now, having been married and divorced twice. I confess I'm sometimes testy, but for the most part I credit myself with an easygoing disposition, tempered (perhaps) by an exaggerated desire for independence.

Like most of this new breed of sleuth, Millhone lives alone and has definite, very individual habits. Whenever the weather permits, she jogs on the beach at six A.M. because

> I notice the older I get, the more my body seems to soften, like butter left out at room temp. I don't like to watch my ass drop and my thighs spread outward like jodhpurs made of flesh. In the interest of tight-fitting jeans, my standard garb, I jog three miles a day on the bicycle path that winds along the beach front.

She is outspoken, self-reliant, and yet capable of intense empathy. In *"D" Is for Deadbeat,* she attempts to talk a fifteen-year-old out of committing suicide:

> "Tony, listen," I said finally. "What you're talking about is dumb and it doesn't make any sense. Do you have any idea

how crummy life seemed when I was your age? I cried all the time and I felt like shit. I was ugly. I was skinny. I was lonely. I was mad. I never thought I'd pull out of it, but I did. Life is hard. Life hurts. So what? You tough it out. You get through and then you'll feel good again, I swear to God.''

These novels provide an image of women very different from most popular culture. These women are smart, independent, and somehow centered within themselves. They do not need a man in order to feel worthwhile. They have men friends and women friends, and while they are sometimes lonely, they would rather be alone than live with someone they do not respect. Several of these characters have, in fact, walked out on husbands who are pictured as affluent and successful but inferior to them in character and intellect. They are physically fit, capable, and not shy about speaking their minds, even if the language is not always pretty. They sleep with whomever they please and have no regrets in the morning. But, perhaps most important, they are women of both action and compassion.

It is noteworthy that among the various forms of popular culture, mystery novels are almost unique in portraying women who either manage to have both intimacy and professional gratification or who have forsaken traditional family involvement in favor of a more independent, androgynous lifestyle. Why are women pictured so differently in mysteries than they are in films or on television? First, most films and television programs are made to appeal to a wide, general audience, while mysteries have a smaller but devoted audience, most of whom are aware of and committed to the conventions of the genre. Moreover, the typical sleuth, usually male, is traditionally a loner, an outsider, with few ties to family or community. The typical detective, private investigator, or Scotland Yard superintendent stands apart, somewhat outside of society, thereby able to see individuals and groups with greater clarity, to understand complex motivation, to think in unconventional ways about behavior and the extremes to which people can be driven. It is this distance of the loner, the stranger that enables him or her to think more creatively than the person who is tightly connected to one segment of society. Being ''unconnected,'' in a sense, gives the sleuth the freedom to go, literally, where the action is, to keep irregular hours, talk to unusual people in unlikely places, to connect facts and human responses in ways the more conventional among us would never consider. If women are to play the role as effectively as men, they must be willing to take on a similar lifestyle; if we are to believe in them, they must be willing and able to play the role in ways we have come to know so well. It is a ready-made part; what is new is that women are now playing it using their own particular style, strengths, and values, and in doing so they are breaking new ground.

What, then, is popular culture telling young women? The messages are clearly conflicting. The fundamental message seems to be that while women's lives have changed dramatically because so many of them are in the work force, supporting or at the very least helping to support themselves and their families, many other aspects of their lives have changed very little. The message is that women can be successful in the workplace and look the part as well but had better not forget how to be provocative, sexy, dependent; that women are to be in charge of their own lives yet "carried away" either by their own feelings or by men; that women can be it all, have it all, and do it all, but while ability and hard work are important, looks are still crucial. With the right clothes and the right look—in other words, the right packaging—women can market themselves the way any other commodity is marketed and achieve their dreams in both the public and the private sphere.

The messages of television and films are more complex. On the one hand, women can be anything they wish, but on the other, their personal lives, not their work lives, are nearly always predominant. You may be a lawyer, but your private life is what is really important. In much of popular culture the women may wear suits and carry briefcases, but their new roles often seem grafted onto the traditional ones of the past—the sex object, the "caring" person more involved with private than with public concerns, or the individual in search of fulfillment through love. Because American society has not truly accepted the implications of women's new roles and therefore not adapted to those profound changes, most popular culture has not really integrated these changes, either. It is often as though a veneer of pseudofeminism is lightly brushed over the story line but underneath that veneer is the same old message. Issues such as dominance and subservience, autonomy and dependence, and how to truly, realistically mesh career and caring are rarely explored seriously. When they are, conflicts are often resolved through traditional solutions.

Moreover, television's need for a wrap-up of the problem each week (or occasionally after two or more episodes) requires simplistic solutions that are invariably within the control of the individual. Seldom are problems depicted as larger than the individual's or the family unit's capacity for coping; rarely are problems depicted as systemic, originating in the very structure of society. The individual generally finds a solution, a formula for working out the problem or conflict, thereby further strengthening the ideology of individualism, an ideology that states, week after week, that we are indeed in charge of our lives and can make of them what we wish. Women may find it harder to regulate their lives because of their presumed greater need for love and approval or because of their again presumed greater conflicts around doing and caring, but in the long run the illusion of self-determination is generally preserved.

But the message of popular culture is above all that everyone is middle and upper middle class. Women are portrayed as doctors, lawyers, and television stars, rarely as salespeople, secretaries, nurse's aides. And when they are playing working-class roles, they are nearly always objects of derision, of sympathy, or of humor. For young women growing up today, the options as reflected by much of popular culture are upper-middle-class options. You need to have a job with status, dress stunningly, and live well if not magnificently. Other measures of success are rarely portrayed. While little in popular culture tells you how to get there, the implication is that the American Dream is there for those who want to make it a reality.

This narrow definition of success and the media's emphasis on individualism have clearly had an impact on all three groups of young women whom I interviewed. The New American Dreamers have most clearly accepted the upper-middle-class model and adopted it as their own. They sometimes see conflicts down the road but assume, as though they were in a thirty-minute sitcom, that they will work out the problems. The Neotraditionalists have more problems with the ''having it all'' model. While they, too, hope for a comfortable lifestyle, they more clearly reflect the conflicts portrayed by the characters in ''thirtysomething.'' They want to do and to be, but they also want to care and to nurture; and while they accept the ideology that these issues are individual problems to be worked out on an individual basis, they can't quite figure out how to put it all together. The Outsiders are perhaps most poignantly affected by much of popular culture, because they do not see themselves anywhere (except in the occasional film and in much contemporary popular music). Where are the teenagers who have had a baby and now must go it alone? Where are the "burn-outs" who feel they fit in nowhere—not at home, not at school, not in their communities? Where are the poor, the near-poor, and the working class struggling to pay the rent and feed their children? "The Cosby Show" may be an advance in a medium that often ignores or denigrates people of color, but what can this quintessentially "Father Knows Best" upper-middle-class family mean to a single woman with two children living in a welfare hotel? By excluding so many Americans from the images and content of popular culture, the society is clearly reinforcing their feelings of being outside the society while simultaneously holding out the promise of the American Dream. Are working-class blacks supposed to feel that "if Bill Cosby can live like that, so can I"? Does identification with the Huxtable family show the way to millions of low-income black Americans, or does it, rather, deflect the anger they might otherwise feel at being largely outside the system? Does it, in other words, promote an unrealistic identification with an improbable, if not impossible, dream?

By defining success almost solely in terms of status, wealth, and power, we are presenting few realistic options for the vast majority of American women and men. Popular culture, by focusing almost entirely on the lives of the top fifth of the population, reinforces the ideology of the American Dream but implicitly devalues all those who will never achieve it. And when young women describe their dreams for the future—their hopes of affluence, their images of themselves as successful professionals, their conflicts around doing and caring, their belief that they must be able to take care of themselves and solve their problems on an individual basis, or, in some cases, when they speak flatly of their inability to imagine a future at all—we know they have been listening to the mixed messages of much of American popular culture.

Emily Martin

from *The Woman in the Body*
A Cultural Analysis of Reproduction
"Medical Metaphors of Women's Bodies
Menstruation and Menopause"

Science has long claimed its objectivity, but anthropology professor (at Johns Hopkins University) Emily Martin argues otherwise as she surveys the attitudes toward menstruation and menopause historically and in contemporary medical textbooks.

*Lavoisier makes experiments with substances in his labora-
tory and now he concluded that this and that takes place
when there is burning. He does not say that it might happen
otherwise another time. He has got hold of a definite world-
picture—not of course one that he invented: he learned it
as a child. I say world-picture and not hypothesis, because
it is the matter-of-course foundation for his research and as
such also goes unmentioned.*

—Ludwig Wittgenstein
On Certainty

It is difficult to see how our current scientific ideas are infused
by cultural assumptions; it is easier to see how scientific ideas
from the past, ideas that now seem wrong or too simple, might
have been affected by cultural ideas of an earlier time. To lay the
groundwork for a look at contemporary scientific views of menstruation and menopause, I begin with the past.

It was an accepted notion in medical literature from the ancient
Greeks until the late eighteenth century that male and female bodies
were structurally similar. As Nemesius, bishop of Emesa, Syria, in
the fourth century, put it, "women have the same genitals as men,
except that theirs are inside the body and not outside it." Although
increasingly detailed anatomical understanding (such as the discovery
of the nature of the ovaries in the last half of the seventeenth century)
changed the details, medical scholars from Galen in second-century
Greece to Harvey in seventeenth-century Britain all assumed that
women's internal organs were structurally analogous to men's external ones.[1] (See Figures 1–4.)

Although the genders were structurally similar, they were not equal.
For one thing, what could be seen of men's bodies was assumed as the
pattern for what could not be seen of women's. For another, just as
humans as a species possessed more "heat" than other animals, and
hence were considered more perfect, so men possessed more "heat"

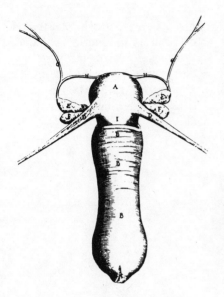

Fig. 1 Vidius's depiction of the uterus and vagina as analogous to the penis and scrotum. (Vidius 1611, Vol. 3. Photo taken from Weindler 1908:140.)

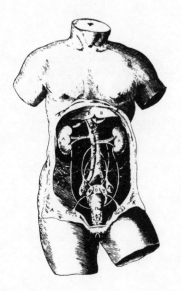

Fig. 2 Vidius's illustration of how the female organs are situated inside the body. (Vidius 1611, Vol. 3. Photo taken from Weindler 1908:139.)

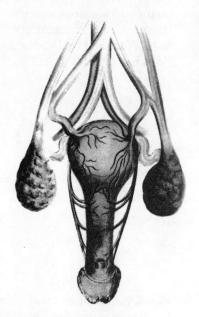

Fig. 3 Georg Bartisch's illustration of phallus-like female reproductive organs. (Attributed by Weindler 1908:141 to Bartisch's *Kunstbuche*, 1575 [MS Dresdens. C. 291]. Photo taken from Weindler 1908, fig. 104b, p. 144.)

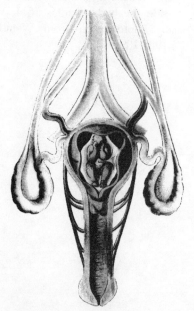

Fig. 4 Bartisch's cross-section of the female organs, showing a fetus inside the uterus. (Attributed by Weindler to Bartisch's *Kunstbuche*, 1575 [MS Dresdens. C. 291]. Photo taken from Weindler 1908, fig. 104b, p. 144.)

than women and hence were considered more perfect. The relative cool-ness of the female prevented her reproductive organs from extruding outside the body but, happily for the species, kept them inside where they provided a protected place for conception and gestation.[2]

During the centuries when male and female bodies were seen as composed of analogous structures, a connected set of metaphors was used to convey how the parts of male and female bodies functioned. These metaphors were dominant in classical medicine and continued to operate through the nineteenth century:

> The body was seen, metaphorically, as a system of dynamic interactions with its environment. Health or disease resulted from a cumulative interaction between constitutional endowment and environmental circumstance. One could not well live with-out food and air and water; one had to live in a particular climate, subject one's body to a particular style of life and work. Each of these factors implied a necessary and continuing physio-logical adjustment. The body was always in a state of becom-ing—and thus always in jeopardy.[3]

Two subsidiary assumptions governed this interaction: first, that "every part of the body was related inevitably and inextricably with every other" and, second, that "the body was seen as a system of intake and outgo—a system which had, necessarily, to remain in balance if the individual were to remain healthy."[4]

Given these assumptions, changes in the relationship of body func-tions occurred constantly throughout life, though more acutely at some times than at others. In Edward Tilt's influential mid-nine-teenth-century account, for example, after the menopause blood that once flowed out of the body as menstruation was then turned into fat:

> Fat accumulates in women after the change of life, as it accu-mulates in animals from whom the ovaries have been removed. The withdrawal of the sexual stimulus from the ganglionic ner-vous system, enables it to turn into fat and self-aggrandisement that blood which might otherwise have perpetuated the race.[5]

During the transition to menopause, or the "dodging time," the blood could not be turned into fat, so it was either discharged as hemorrhage or through other compensating mechanisms, the most important of which was "the flush":

> As for thirty-two years it had been habitual for women to lose about 3 oz. of blood every month, so it would have been indeed singular, if there did not exist some well-continued compensating discharges acting as waste gates to protect the system, until health could be permanently reestablished by striking new balances in the allotment of blood to the various parts ... The flushes determine the perspirations. Both evidence a strong effect of conservative power, and as they constitute the most important and habitual safety-valve of the system at the change of life, it is worth while studying them.[6]

In this account, compensating mechanisms like the "flush" are seen as having the positive function of keeping intake and outgo in balance.

These balancing acts had exact analogues in men. In Hippocrates' view of purification, one that was still current in the seventeenth century,

> women were of a colder and less active disposition than men, so that while men could sweat in order to remove the impurities from their blood, the colder dispositions of women did not allow them to be purified in that way. Females menstruated to rid their bodies of impurities.[7]

Or in another view, expounded by Galen in the second century and still accepted into the eighteenth century, menstruation was the shedding of an excess of blood, a plethora.[8] But what women did through menstruation men could do in other ways, such as by having blood let.[9] In either view of the mechanism of menstruation, the process itself not only had analogues in men, it was seen as inherently health-maintaining. Menstrual blood, to be sure, was often seen as foul and unclean,[10] but the process of excreting it was not intrinsically pathological. In fact, failure to excrete was taken as a sign of disease, and a great variety of remedies existed even into the nineteenth century specifically to reestablish menstrual flow if it stopped.[11]

By 1800, according to Laqueur's important recent study, this long-established tradition that saw male and female bodies as similar both in structure and in function began to come "under devastating attack. Writers of all sorts were determined to base what they insisted were fundamental differences between male and female sexuality, and thus between man and woman, on discoverable biological distinctions."[12] Laqueur argues that this attempt to ground differences between the genders in biology grew out of the crumbling of old ideas about the existing order of politics and society as laid down by the order of nature. In the old ideas, men dominated the public world and the world of morality and order by virtue of their greater perfection, a result of their excess heat. Men and women were arranged in a hierarchy in which they differed by degree of heat. They were not different in kind.[13]

The new liberal claims of Hobbes and Locke in the seventeenth century and the French Revolution were factors that led to a loss of certainty that the social order could be grounded in the natural order. If the social order were merely convention, it could not provide a secure enough basis to hold women and men in their places. But after 1800 the social and biological sciences were brought to the rescue of male superiority. "Scientists in areas of diverse as zoology, embryology, physiology, heredity, anthropology, and psychology had little difficulty in proving that the pattern of male-female relations that characterized the English middle classes was natural, inevitable, and progressive."[14]

The assertion was that men's and women's social roles themselves were grounded in nature, by virtue of the dictates of their bodies. In the words of one nineteenth-century theorist, "the attempt to alter the present relations of the sexes is not a rebellion against some arbitrary law instituted by a despot or a majority—not an attempt to break the yoke of a mere convention; it is a struggle against Nature; a war undertaken to reverse the very conditions under which not man alone, but all mammalian species have reached their present development."[15] The doctrine of the two spheres discussed in the last chapter—men as workers in the public, wage-earning sphere outside the home and women (except for the lower classes) as wives and mothers in the private, domestic sphere of kinship and morality inside the home—replaced the old hierarchy based on body heat.

During the latter part of the nineteenth century, new metaphors that posited fundamental differences between the sexes began to appear. One nineteenth-century biologist, Patrick Geddes, perceived two opposite kinds of processes at the level of the cell: "upbuilding, constructive, synthetic processes,'' summed up as anabolism, and a ''disruptive, descending series of chemical changes,'' summed up as katabolism.[16] The relationship between the two processes was described in frankly economic terms:

> ... The processes of income and expenditure must balance, but only to the usual extent, that expenditure must not altogether outrun income, else the cell's capital of living matter will be lost,—a fate which is often not successfully avoided ... Just as our expenditure and income should balance at the year's end, but may vastly outstrip each other at particular times, so it is with the cell of the body. Income too may continuously preponderate, and we increase in wealth, or similarly, in weight, or in anabolism. Conversely, expenditure may predominate, but business may be prosecuted at a loss; and similarly, we may live on for a while with loss of weight, or in katabolism. This losing game of life is what we call a katabolic habit.[17]

Geddes saw these processes not only at the level of the cell, but also at the level of entire organisms. In the human species, as well as in almost all higher animals, females were predominantly anabolic, males katabolic. (See Figure 5.) Although in the terms of his saving-spending metaphor it is not at all clear whether katabolism would be an asset, when Geddes presents male-female differences, there is no doubt which he thought preferable:

> It is generally true that the males are more active, energetic, eager, passionate, and variable; the females more passive, conservative, sluggish, and stable ... The more active males, with a consequently wider range of experience, may have bigger brains and more intelligence; but the females, especially as mothers, have indubitably a larger and more habitual share of the altruistic emotions. The males being usually stronger, have greater independence and courage; the females excel in constancy of affection and in sympathy.[18]

In Geddes, the doctrine of separate spheres was laid on a foundation of separate and fundamentally different biology in men and women, at the level of the cell. One of the striking contradictions in his account is that he did not carry over the implications of his

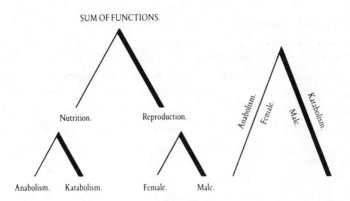

Fig. 5 An illustration accompanying the late nineteenth-century biologist Geddes's account of what he saw as radical physiological distinctions between males and females, the male dominated by active, energetic katabolic functions and the female by passive, conservative anabolic functions. (Geddes 1890:213.)

economic metaphors to his discussion of male-female differences. If he had, females might have come off as wisely conserving their energy and never spending beyond their means, males as in the "losing game of life," letting expenditures outrun income.

Geddes may have failed to draw the logical conclusions from his metaphor, but we have to acknowledge that metaphors were never meant to be logical. Other nineteenth-century writers developed metaphors in exactly opposite directions: women spent and men saved. The Rev. John Todd saw women as voracious spenders in the marketplace, and so consumers of all that a man could earn. If unchecked, a woman would ruin a man, by her own extravagant spending, by her demands on him to spend, or, in another realm, by her excessive demands on him for sex. Losing too much sperm meant losing that which sperm was believed to manufacture: a man's lifeblood.[19]

Todd and Geddes were not alone in the nineteenth century in using images of business loss and gain to describe physiological processes. Susan Sontag has suggested that nineteenth-century fantasies about disease, especially tuberculosis, "echo the attitudes of early capitalist accumulation. One has a limited amount of energy, which must be properly spent . . . Energy, like savings, can be depleted, can run out or be used up, through reckless expenditure. The body will start 'consuming' itself, the patient will 'waste away.' "[20]

Despite the variety of ways that spending-saving metaphors could be related to gender, the radical difference between these metaphors and the earlier intake-outgo metaphor is key. Whereas in the earlier model, male and female ways of secreting were not only analogous but desirable, now the way became open to denigrate, as Geddes overtly did, functions that for the first time were seen as uniquely female, without analogue in males. For our purposes, what happened to accounts of menstruation is most interesting: by the nineteenth century, the process itself was seen as soundly pathological. In Geddes's terms,

it yet evidently lies on the borders of pathological change, as is evidenced not only by the pain which so frequently accompanies it, and the local and constitutional disorders which so frequently arise in this connection, but by the general systemic disturbance and local histological changes of which the discharge is merely the outward expression and result.[21]

Whereas in earlier accounts the blood itself may have been considered impure, now the process itself is seen as a disorder.

Nineteenth-century writers were extremely prone to stress the debilitating nature of menstruation and its adverse impact on the lives and activities of women.[22] Medical images of menstruation as pathological were remarkably vivid by the end of the century. For Walter Heape, the militant antisuffragist and Cambridge zoologist, in menstruation the entire epithelium was torn away,

leaving behind a ragged wreck of tissue, torn glands, ruptured vessels, jagged edges of stroma, and masses of blood corpuscles, which it would seem hardly possible to heal satisfactorily without the aid of surgical treatment.[23]

A few years later, Havelock Ellis could see women as being "periodically wounded" in their most sensitive spot and "emphasize the fact that even in the healthiest woman, a worm however harmless and unperceived, gnaws periodically at the roots of life."[24]

If menstruation was consistently seen as pathological, menopause, another function which by this time was regarded as without analogue in men, often was too: many nineteenth-century medical accounts of menopause saw it as a crisis likely to bring on an increase of disease.[25] Sometimes the metaphor of the body as a small business that is either winning or losing was applied to menopause too. A late-nineteenth-century account specifically argued against Tilt's earlier adjustment model: "When the period of fruitfulness is ended the activity of the tissues has reached its culmination, the secreting power of the glandular organs begins to diminish, the epithelium becomes less sensitive and less susceptible to infectious influences, and atrophy and degeneration take the place of the active up-building processes."[26] But there were other sides to the picture. Most practitioners felt the "climacteric disease," a more general disease of old age, was far worse for men than for women.[27] And some regarded the period after menopause far more positively than it is being seen medically in our century, as the " 'Indian summer' of a woman's life—a period of increased vigor, optimism, and even of physical beauty.' "[28]

Perhaps the nineteenth century's concern with conserving energy and limiting expenditure can help account for the seeming anomaly of at least some positive medical views of menopause and the climacteric. As an early-twentieth-century popular health account put it,

[Menopause] is merely a conservative process of nature to provide for a higher and more stable phase of existence, an economic lopping off of a function no longer needed, preparing the individual for different forms of activity, but is in no sense pathologic. It is not sexual or physical decrepitude, but belongs to the age of invigoration, marking the fullness of the bodily and mental powers.[29]

Those few writers who saw menopause as an "economic" physiological function might have drawn very positive conclusions from Geddes's description of females as anabolic, stressing their "thriftiness" instead of their passivity, their "growing bank accounts" instead of their sluggishness.

If the shift from the body as an intake-outgo system to the body as a small business trying to spend, save, or balance its accounts is a radical one, with deep importance for medical models of female bodies, so too in another shift that began in the twentieth century with the development of scientific medicine. One of the early-twentieth-century engineers of our system of scientific medicine, Frederick

T. Gates, who advised John D. Rockefeller on how to use his philan-
thropies to aid scientific medicine, developed a series of interrelated
metaphors to explain the scientific view of how the body works:

> It is interesting to note the striking comparisons between the
> human body and the safety and hygienic appliances of a great
> city. Just as in the streets of a great city we have "white angels"
> posted everywhere to gather up poisonous materials from the
> streets, so in the great streets and avenues of the body, namely
> the arteries and the blood vessels, there are brigades of corpus-
> cles, white in color like the "white angels," whose function it
> is to gather up into sacks, formed by their own bodies, and
> disinfect or eliminate all poisonous substances found in the
> blood. The body has a network of insulated nerves, like tele-
> phone wires, which transmit instantaneous alarms at every point
> of danger. The body is furnished with the most elaborate police
> system, with hundreds of police stations to which the criminal
> elements are carried by the police and jailed. I refer to the great
> numbers of sanitary glands, skillfully placed at points where
> vicious germs find entrance, especially about the mouth and
> throat. The body has a most complete and elaborate sewer sys-
> tem. There are wonderful laboratories placed at convenient
> points for a subtle brewing of skillful medicines ... The fact is
> that the human body is made up of an infinite number of micro-
> scopic cells. Each one of these cells is a small chemical labora-
> tory, into which its own appropriate raw material is constantly
> being introduced, the processes of chemical separation and com-
> bination are constantly taking place automatically, and its own
> appropriate finished product being necessary for the life and
> health of the body. Not only is this so, but the great organs of
> the body like the liver, stomach, pancreas, kidneys, gall bladder
> are great local manufacturing centers, formed of groups of cells
> in infinite numbers, manufacturing the same sorts of products,
> just as industries of the same kind are often grouped in spe-
> cific districts.[30]

Although such a full-blown description of the body as a model of
an industrial society is not often found in contemporary accounts
of physiology, elements of the images that occurred to Gates are
commonplace. In recent years, the "imagery of the biochemistry of

the cell [has] been that of the factory, where functions [are] specialized for the conversion of energy into particular products and which [has] its own part to play in the economy of the organism as a whole."[31] There is no doubt that the basic image of cells as factories is carried into popular imagination, and not only through college textbooks: the illustration from *Time* magazine shown in Figure 6 depicts cells explicitly as factories (and AIDS virus cells as manufacturing armored tanks!).

Still more recently, economic functions of greater complexity have been added: ATP is seen as the body's "energy currency": "Produced in particular cellular regions, it [is] placed in an 'energy bank' in which it [is] maintained in two forms, those of 'current account' and 'deposit account.' Ultimately, the cell's and the body's energy books must balance by an appropriate mix of monetary and fiscal policies."[32] Here we have not just the simpler nineteenth-century saving and spending, but two distinct forms of money in the bank, presumably invested at different levels of profit.

Development of the new molecular biology brought additional metaphors based on information science, management, and control. In this model, flow of information between DNA and RNA leads to the production of protein.[33] Molecular biologists conceive of the cell as "an assembly line factory in which the DNA blueprints are interpreted and raw materials fabricated to produce the protein end products in response to a series of regulated requirements."[34] The cell is still seen as a factory, but, compared to Gates's description, there is enormous elaboration of the flow of information from one "department" of the body to another and exaggeration of the amount of control exerted by the center. For example, from a college physiology text:

> All the systems of the body, if they are to function effectively, must be subjected to some form of control ... The precise control of body function is brought about by means of the operation of the nervous system and of the hormonal or endocrine system ... The most important thing to note about any control system is that before it can control anything it must be supplied with information ... Therefore the first essential in any control system is an adequate system of collecting information about the state of the body ... Once the CNS [central nervous system] knows what is happening, it must then have a means for rectify-

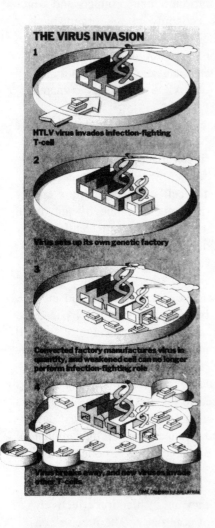

THE VIRUS INVASION

1

HTLV virus invades infection-fighting T-cell

2

Virus sets up its own genetic factory

3

Converted factory manufactures virus in quantity, and weakened cell can no longer perform infection-fighting role

4

Virus breaks away, and new viruses invade other T-cells.

TIME Diagram by Joe Lertola

Fig. 6 A contemporary image of cells as factories. (*Time* magazine, 30 April 1984:67. Copyright 1984 by Time, Inc. All rights reserved. Reprinted by permission from TIME.)

ing the situation if something is going wrong. There are two available methods for doing this, by using nerve fibres and by using hormones. The motor nerve fibres ... carry instructions from the CNS to the muscles and glands throughout the body ... As far as hormones are concerned the brain acts via the pituitary gland ... the pituitary secretes a large number of hormones ... the rate of secretion of each one of these is under the direct control of the brain.[35]

The illustration in Figure 7 reiterates this account vividly: there is a "co-ordinating centre" which transmits messages to and receives messages from peripheral parts, for the purpose of integration and control. Although there is increasing attention to describing physiological processes as positive and negative feedback loops so that like a thermostat system no single element has preeminent control over any other, most descriptions of specific processes give preeminent control to the brain, as we will see [on the following page].

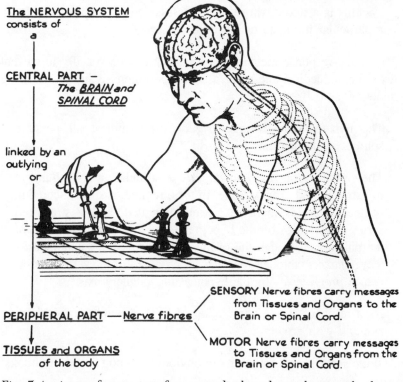

NERVOUS SYSTEM

The Nervous System is concerned with the INTEGRATION and CONTROL of all bodily functions.
It has specialized in IRRITABILITY – *the ability to receive and respond to messages from the external and internal environments*
and also in CONDUCTION – *the ability to transmit messages to and from CO-ORDINATING CENTRES*.

The NERVOUS SYSTEM consists of a

↓

CENTRAL PART –
        The *BRAIN* and
        SPINAL CORD

linked by an outlying or

PERIPHERAL PART — Nerve fibres

↓

TISSUES and ORGANS
        of the body

SENSORY Nerve fibres carry messages from Tissues and Organs to the Brain or Spinal Cord.

MOTOR Nerve fibres carry messages to Tissues and Organs from the Brain or Spinal Cord.

Fig. 7 An image from a text for premedical students showing the brain as a coordinating center transmitting messages to and receiving them from outlying parts. (McNaught and Callander 1983:204. Reprinted by permission of Churchill Livingstone.)

METAPHORS IN DESCRIPTIONS
OF FEMALE REPRODUCTION

In overall descriptions of female reproduction, the dominant image is that of a signaling system. Lein, in a textbook designed for junior colleges, spells it out in detail:

> Hormones are chemical signals to which distant tissues or organs are able to respond. Whereas the nervous system has characteristics in common with a telephone network, the endocrine glands perform in a manner somewhat analogous to radio transmission. A radio transmitter may blanket an entire region with its signal, but a response occurs only if a radio receiver is turned on and tuned to the proper frequency . . . the radio receiver in biological systems is a tissue whose cells possess active receptor sites for a particular hormone or hormones.[36]

The signal-response metaphor is found almost universally in current texts for premedical and medical students (emphasis in the following quotes is added):

> The hypothalamus *receives signals* from almost all possible sources in the nervous system.[37]

> The endometrium *responds directly* to stimulation or withdrawal of estrogen and progesterone. In turn, regulation of the secretion of these steroids involves a well-integrated, highly structured series of activities by the hypothalamus and the anterior lobe of the pituitary. Although the ovaries do not function autonomously, they *influence,* through *feedback* mechanisms, the level of performance *programmed* by the hypothalamic-pituitary axis.[38]

> As a result of strong stimulation of FSH, a number of follicles *respond* with growth.[39]

And the same idea is found, more obviously, in popular health books:

> Each month from menarch on, [the hypothalamus] acts as elegant interpreter of the body's rhythms, *transmitting messages* to the pituitary gland that set the menstrual cycle in motion.[40]

Each month, *in response to a message* from the pituitary gland, one of the unripe egg cells develops inside a tiny microscopic ring of cells, which gradually increases to form a little balloon or cyst called the Graafian follicle.[41]

Although most accounts stress signals or stimuli traveling in a "loop" from hypothalamus to pituitary to ovary and back again, carrying positive or negative feedback, one element in the loop, the hypothalamus, a part of the brain, is often seen as predominant. Just as in the general model of the central nervous system shown in Figure 7, the female brain-hormone-ovary system is usually described not as a feedback loop like a thermostat system, but as a hierarchy, in which the "directions" or "orders" of one element dominate (emphasis in the following quotes from medical texts is added):

Both positive and negative feedback control must be invoked, together with *superimposition* of control by the CNS through neurotransmitters released into the hypophyseal portal circulation.[42]

Almost all secretion by the pituitary is *controlled* by either hormonal or nervous signals from the hypothalamas.[43]

The hypothalamus is a collecting center for information concerned with the internal well-being of the body, and in turn much of this information is used *to control* secretions of the many globally important pituitary hormones.[44]

As Lein puts it into ordinary language, "The cerebrum, that part of the brain that provides awareness and mood, can play a significant role in the control of the menstrual cycle. As explained before, it seems evident that these higher regions of the brain exert their influence by modifying the actions of the hypothalamus. So even though the hypothalamus is a kind of master gland dominating the anterior pituitary, and through it the ovaries also, it does not act with complete independence or without influence from outside itself . . . there are also pathways of control from the higher centers of the brain."[45]

So this is a communication system organized hierarchically, not a committee reaching decisions by mutual influence.[46] The hierarchical nature of the organization is reflected in some popular literature meant to explain the nature of menstruation simply: "From first menstrual cycle to menopause, the hypothalamus acts as the conductor of a highly trained orchestra. Once its baton signals the downbeat to the pituitary, the hypothalamus-pituitary-ovarian axis is united in purpose and begins to play its symphonic message, preparing a woman's body for conception and child-bearing.'' Carrying the metaphor further, the follicles vie with each other for the role of producing the egg like violinists trying for the position of concertmaster; a burst of estrogen is emitted from the follicle like a ''clap of tympani.''[47]

The basic images chosen here—an information-transmitting system with a hierarchical structure—have an obvious relation to the dominant form of organization in our society.[48] What I want to show is how this set of metaphors, once chosen as the basis for the description of physiological events, has profound implications for the way in which a change in the basic organization of the system will be perceived. In terms of female reproduction, this basic change is of course menopause. Many criticisms have been made of the medical propensity to see menopause as a pathological state.[49] I would like to suggest that the tenacity of this view comes not only from the negative stereotypes associated with aging women in our society, but as a logical outgrowth of seeing the body as a hierarchical information-processing system in the first place. (Another part of the reason menopause is seen so negatively is related to metaphors of production, which we discuss later in this chapter.)

What is the language in which menopause is described? In menopause, according to a college text, the ovaries become ''unresponsive'' to stimulation from the gonadotropins, to which they used to respond. As a result the ovaries ''regress.'' On the other end of the cycle, the hypothalamus has gotten estrogen ''addiction'' from all those years of menstruating. As a result of the ''withdrawal'' of estrogen at menopause, the hypothalamus begins to give ''inappropriate orders.''[50] In a more popular account, ''the pituitary gland during the change of life becomes disturbed when the ovaries fail to respond to its secretions, which tends to affect its control over other glands. This results in a temporary imbalance existing among all the endocrine glands of the body, which could very well lead to disturbances that may involve a person's nervous system.''[51]

In both medical texts and popular books, what is being described is the breakdown of a system of authority. The cause of ovarian ''decline'' is the ''decreasing ability of the aging ovaries to respond to pituitary gonadotropins.''[52] At every point in this system, functions

MENOPAUSE

Between the ages of 42 and 50years OVARIAN tissue gradually ceases to respond to stimulation by ANTERIOR PITUITARY GONADO-TROPHIC HORMONES.

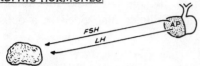

OVARIAN CYCLE becomes irregular and finally ceases ⟶ Ovary becomes small and fibrosed and no longer produces ripe Ova.
OESTROGEN and PROGESTERONE levels in Blood stream fall.

TISSUES of the body — begin to show changes which mark the end of REPRODUCTIVE LIFE.

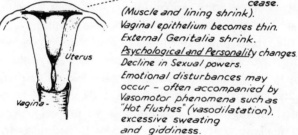

Sometimes final redistribution of fat → less typically feminine distribution.
Regression of *Secondary Sex Characteristics*
........Breasts shrink.
Ducts) Acini) Atrophy   Hair becomes sparse in axillae and on pubis.
Secondary Sex Organs atrophy.
Fallopian tubes shrink.
Uterine Cycle and Menstruation cease.
(Muscle and lining shrink).
Vaginal epithelium becomes thin.
External Genitalia shrink.
Psychological and Personality changes
Decline in Sexual powers.
Emotional disturbances may occur - often accompanied by Vasomotor phenomena such as "Hot Flushes" (vasodilatation), excessive sweating and giddiness.

Uterus

Vagina -

After the MENOPAUSE a woman is usually unable to bear children.

Fig. 8 A summary diagram from a text for premedical students that emphasizes menopause as a process of breakdown, failure, and decline. (McNaught and Callander 1983:200. Reprinted by permission of Churchill Livingstone.)

"fail" and falter. Follicles "fail to muster the strength" to reach ovulation.[53] As functions fail, so do the members of the system decline: "breasts and genital organs gradually atrophy,"[54] "wither,"[55] and become "senile."[56] Diminished, atrophied relics of their former vigorous, functioning selves, the "senile ovaries" are an example of the vivid imagery brought to this process. A text whose detailed illustrations make it a primary resource for medical students despite its early date describes the ovaries this way:

> The *senile ovary* is a shrunken and puckered organ, containing few if any follicles, and made up for the most part of old corpora albincantia and corpora atretica, the bleached and functionless remainders of corpora lutia and follicles embedded in a dense connective tissue stroma.[57]

The illustration in Figure 8 summarizes the whole picture: ovaries cease to respond and fail to produce. Everywhere else there is regression, decline, atrophy, shrinkage, and disturbance.

The key to the problem connoted by these descriptions is functionlessness. Susan Sontag has written of our obsessive fear of cancer, a disease that we see as entailing a nightmare of excessive growth and rampant production. These images frighten us in part because in our stage of advanced capitalism, they are close to a reality we find difficult to see clearly: broken-down hierarchy and organization members who no longer play their designated parts represent nightmare images for us. . . . [O]ne woman I talked to said her doctor gave her two choices for treatment of her menopause: she could take estrogen and get cancer or she could not take it and have her bones dissolve. Like this woman, our imagery of the body as a hierarchical organization gives us no good choice when the basis of the organization seems to us to have changed drastically. We are left with breakdown, decay, and atrophy. Bad as they are, these might be preferable to continued activity, which because it is not properly hierarchically controlled, leads to chaos, unmanaged growth, and disaster.

But let us return to the metaphor of the factory producing substances, which dominates the imagery used to describe cells. At the cellular level DNA communicates with RNA, all for the purpose of the cell's production of proteins. In a similar way, the system of communication involving female reproduction is thought to be geared toward production of various things. . . . It is clear that the system is thought to produce many good things: the ovaries produce estrogen, the pituitary produces FSH and LH, and so on. Follicles also produce eggs in a sense, although this is usually described as "maturing" them since the entire set of eggs a woman has for her lifetime is known to be present at birth. Beyond all this the system is seen as organized for a single preeminent purpose: "transport" of the egg along its journey from the ovary to the uterus[58] and preparation of an appropriate place for the egg to grow if it is fertilized. In a chapter titled "Prepregnancy Reproductive Functions of the Female, and the Female Hormones," Guyton puts it all together: "Female reproductive functions can be divided into two major phases: first, preparation of the female body for conception and gestation, and second, the period of gestation itself."[59] This view may seem commonsensical and entirely justified by the evolutionary development of the species, with its need for reproduction to ensure survival.

Yet I suggest that assuming this view of the purpose for the process slants our description and understanding of the female cycle unnecessarily. Let us look at how medical textbooks describe menstruation. They see the action of progesterone and estrogen on the lining of the uterus as "ideally suited to provide a hospitable environment for implantation and survival of the embryo"[60] or as intended to lead to "the monthly renewal of the tissue that will cradle [the ovum]."[61] As Guyton summarizes, "The whole purpose of all these endometrial changes is to produce a highly secretory endometrium containing large amounts of stored nutrients that can provide appropriate conditions for implantation of a fertilized ovum during the latter half of the monthly cycle."[62] Given this teleological interpretation of the purpose of the increased amount of endometrial tissue, it should be no surprise that when a fertilized egg does not implant, these texts describe the next event in very negative terms. The fall in blood progesterone and estrogen "deprives" the "highly developed endometrial lining of its hormonal support," "constriction" of blood vessels leads to a "diminished" supply of oxygen and nutrients, and finally "disintegration starts, the entire lining begins to slough, and the menstrual flow begins." Blood vessels in the endometrium "hemorrhage" and the menstrual flow "consists of this blood mixed with endometrial debris."[63] The "loss" of hormonal stimulation causes "necrosis" (death of tissue.)[64]

The construction of these events in terms of a purpose that has failed is beautifully captured in a standard text for medical students (a text otherwise noteworthy for its extremely objective, factual descriptions) in which a discussion of the events covered in the last paragraph (sloughing, hemorrhaging) ends with the statement "When fertilization fails to occur, the endometrium is shed, and a new cycle starts. This is why it used to be taught that 'menstruation is the uterus crying for lack of a baby.' "[65]

I am arguing that just as seeing menopause as a kind of failure of the authority structure in the body contributes to our negative view of it, so does seeing menstruation as failed production contribute to our negative view of it. We have seen how Sontag describes our horror of production gone out of control. But another kind of horror for us is *lack* of production: the disused factory, the failed business, the idle machine. In his analysis of industrial civilization, Winner terms the stopping and breakdown of technological systems in modern society "apraxia" and describes it as "the ultimate horror, a condition to be avoided at all costs."[66] This horror of idle workers or machines seems to have been present even at earlier stages of industrialization. A nineteenth-century inventor, Thomas Ewbank, elaborated his view that the whole world "was designed for a Factory."[67] "It is only as a Factory, a *General Factory,* that the whole materials and influences of the earth are to be brought into play."[68] In this great workshop, humans' role is to produce: "God employs no idlers—creates none."[69]

> Like artificial motors, we are created for the work we can do—for the useful and productive ideas we can stamp upon matter. Engines running daily without doing any work resemble men who live without labor; both are spendthrifts dissipating means that would be productive if given to others.[70]

Menstruation not only carries with it the connotation of a productive system that has failed to produce, it also carries the idea of production gone awry, making products of no use, not to specification, unsalable, wasted, scrap. However disgusting it may be, menstrual blood will come out. Production gone awry is also an image that fills us with dismay and horror. Amid the glorification of machinery common in the nineteenth century were also fears of what machines could do if they went out of control. Capturing this fear, one satirist wrote of a steam-operated shaving machine that "sliced the noses off too many customers."[71] This image is close to the one Melville created in "The Bell-Tower," in which an inventor, who can be seen as an allegory of America, is killed by his mechanical slave,[72] as well as to Mumford's sorcerer's apprentice applied to modern machinery:[73]

> Our civilization has cleverly found a magic formula for setting both industrial and academic brooms and pails of water to work by themselves, in ever-increasing quantities at an ever-increasing

speed. But we have lost the Master Magician's spell for altering the tempo of this process, or halting it when it ceases to serve human functions and purposes.[74]

Of course, how much one is gripped by the need to produce goods efficiently and properly depends on one's relationship to those goods. While packing pickles on an assembly line, I remember the foreman often holding up improperly packed bottles to us workers and trying to elicit shame at the bad job we were doing. But his job depended on efficient production, which meant many bottles filled right the first time. This factory did not yet have any effective method of quality control, and as soon as our supervisor was out of sight, our efforts went toward filling as few bottles as we could while still concealing who had filled which bottle. In other factories, workers seem to express a certain grim pleasure when they can register objections to company policy by enacting imagery of machinery out of control. Noble reports an incident in which workers resented a supervisor's order to "shut down their machines, pick up brooms, and get to work cleaning the area. But he forgot to tell them to stop. So, like the sorcerer's apprentice, diligently and obediently working to rule, they continued sweeping up all day long."[75]

Perhaps one reason the negative image of failed production is attached to menstruation is precisely that women are in some sinister sense out of control when they menstruate. They are not reproducing, not continuing the species, not preparing to stay at home with the baby, not providing a safe, warm womb to nurture a man's sperm. I think it is plain that the negative power behind the image of failure to produce can be considerable when applied metaphorically to women's bodies. Vern Bullough comments optimistically that "no reputable scientist today would regard menstruation as pathological,"[76] but this paragraph from a recent college text belies his hope:

If fertilization and pregnancy do not occur, the corpus luteum degenerates and the levels of estrogens and progesterone decline. As the levels of these hormones decrease and their stimulatory effects are withdrawn, blood vessels of the endometrium undergo prolonged spasms (contractions) that reduce the bloodflow to the area of the endometrium supplied by the vessels. The resulting lack of blood causes the tissues of the affected region to degenerate. After some time, the vessels relax, which allows

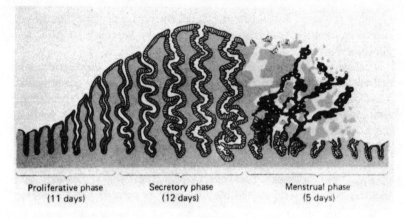

Proliferative phase   Secretory phase   Menstrual phase
(11 days)   (12 days)   (5 days)

Fig. 9 An illustration from a current physiology text showing changes in the endometrium during the monthly cycle. The menstrual phase is represented visually as disintegration of the uterine lining. (Guyton 1984:624. Copyright © 1984 by CBS College Publishing. Reprinted by permission of CBS College Publishing.)

blood to flow through them again. However, capillaries in the area have become so weakened that blood leaks through them. This blood and the deteriorating endometrial tissue are discharged from the uterus as the menstrual flow. As a new ovarian cycle begins and the level of estrogens rises, the functional layer of the endometrium undergoes repair and once again begins to proliferate.[77]

In rapid succession the reader is confronted with "degenerate," "decline," "withdrawn," "spasms," "lack," "degenerate," "weakened," "leak," "deteriorate," "discharge," and, after all that, "repair."

In another standard text, we read:

The sudden lack of these two hormones [estrogen and progesterone] causes the blood vessels of the endometrium to become spastic so that blood flow to the surface layers of the endometrium almost ceases. As a result, much of the endometrial tissue dies and sloughs into the uterine cavity. Then, small amounts of blood ooze from the denuded endometrial wall, causing a blood loss of about 50 ml during the next few days. The sloughed endometrial tissue plus the blood and much serous exudate from the denuded uterine surface, all together called the *menstrum,* is gradually expelled by intermittent contractions of the uterine muscle for about 3 to 5 days. This process is called *menstruation.*[78]

The illustration that accompanies this text (see Figure 9) captures very well the imagery of catastrophic disintegration: "ceasing," "dying," "losing," "denuding," and "expelling."

These are not neutral terms; rather, they convey failure and dissolution. Of course, not all texts contain such a plethora of negative terms in their descriptions of menstruation. But unacknowledged cultural attitudes can seep into scientific writing through evaluative words. Coming at this point from a slightly different angle, consider this extract from a text that describes male reproductive physiology. "The mechanisms which guide the *remarkable* cellular transformation from spermatid to mature sperm remain uncertain . . . Perhaps the most *amazing* characteristic of spermatogenesis is its *sheer magnitude:* the normal human male may manufacture several hundred million sperm per day (emphasis added)."[79] As we will see, this text has no parallel appreciation of female processes such as menstruation or ovulation, and it is surely no accident that this "remarkable" process involves precisely what menstruation does not in the medical view: production of something deemed valuable. Although this text sees such massive sperm production as unabashedly positive, in fact, only about one out of every 100 billion sperm ever makes it to fertilize an egg: from the very same point of view that sees menstruation as a waste product, surely here is something really worth crying about!

When this text turns to female reproduction, it describes menstruation in the same terms of failed production we saw earlier.

The fall in blood progesterone and estrogen, which results from *regression* of the corpus luteum, *deprives* the highly developed endometrial lining of its hormonal support; the immediate result is *profound constriction* of the uterine blood vessels due to production of vasoconstrictor prostaglandins, which leads to *diminished* supply of oxygen and nutrients. *Disintegration* starts, and the entire lining (except for a thin, deep layer which will regenerate the endometrium in the next cycle) begins to slough . . .

The endometrial arterioles dilate, resulting in *hemorrhage* through the weakened capillary walls; the menstrual flow consists of this blood mixed with endometrial *debris* ... The menstrual flow ceases as the endometrium *repairs* itself and then grows under the influence of rising blood estrogen concentration. (Emphasis added.)[80]

And ovulation fares no better. In fact part of the reason ovulation does not merit the enthusiasm that spermatogenesis does may be that all the ovarian follicles containing ova are already present at birth. Far from being *produced* as sperm is, they seem to merely sit on the shelf, as it were, slowly degenerating and aging like overstocked inventory.

At birth, normal human ovaries contain an estimated one million follicles, and no new ones appear after birth. Thus, in marked contrast to the male, the newborn female already has all the germ cells she will ever have. Only a few, perhaps 400, are destined to reach full maturity during her active productive life. All the others degenerate at some point in their development so that few, if any, remain by the time she reaches menopause at approximately 50 years of age. One result of this is that the ova which are released (ovulated) near menopause are 30 to 35 years older than those ovulated just after puberty; it has been suggested that certain congenital defects, much commoner among children of older women, are the result of aging changes in the ovum.[81]

How different it would sound if texts like this one stressed the vast excess of follicles produced in a female fetus, compared to the number she will actually need. In addition, males are also born with a complement of germ cells (spermatogonia) that divide from time to time, and most of which will eventually differentiate into sperm. This text could easily discuss the fact that these male germ cells and their progeny are also subject to aging, much as female germ cells are. Although we would still be operating within the terms of the production metaphor, at least it would be applied in an evenhanded way to both males and females.

One response to my argument would be that menstruation just *is* in some objective sense a process of breakdown and deterioration.

The particular words are chosen to describe it because they best fit the reality of what is happening. My counterargument is to look at other processes in the body that are fundamentally analogous to menstruation in that they involve the shedding of a lining to see whether they also are described in terms of breakdown and deterioration. The lining of the stomach, for example, is shed and replaced regularly, and seminal fluid picks up shedded cellular material as it goes through the various male ducts.

The lining of the stomach must protect itself against being digested by the hydrochloric acid produced in digestion. In the several texts quoted above, emphasis is on the *secretion* of mucus,[82] the *barrier* that mucous cells present to stomach acid,[83] and—in a phrase that gives the story away—the periodic *renewal* of the lining of the stomach.[84] There is no reference to degenerating, weakening, deteriorating, or repair, or even the more neutral shedding, sloughing, or replacement.

> The primary function of the gastric secretions is to begin the digestion of proteins. Unfortunately, though, the wall of the stomach is itself constructed mainly of smooth muscle which itself is mainly protein. Therefore, the surface of the stomach must be exceptionally well protected at all times against its own digestion. This function is performed mainly by mucus that is secreted in great abundance in all parts of the stomach. The entire surface of the stomach is covered by a layer of very small *mucous cells,* which themselves are composed almost entirely of mucus; this mucus prevents gastric secretions from ever touching the deeper layers of the stomach wall.[85]

In this account from an introductory physiology text, the emphasis is on production of mucus and protection of the stomach wall. It is not even mentioned, although it is analogous to menstruation, that the mucous cell layers must be continually sloughed off (and digested). Although all the general physiology texts I consulted describe menstruation as a process of disintegration needing repair, only specialized texts for medical students describe the stomach lining in the more neutral terms of "sloughing" and "renewal."[86] One can choose to look at what happens to the lining of stomachs and uteruses negatively as breakdown and decay needing repair or positively as continual production and replenishment. Of these two sides of the same coin, stomachs, which women *and* men have, fall on the positive side; uteruses, which only women have, fall on the negative.

One other analogous process is not handled negatively in the general physiology texts. Although it is well known to those researchers who work with male ejaculates that a very large proportion of the ejaculate is composed of shedded cellular material, the texts make no mention of a shedding process let alone processes of deterioration and repair in the male reproductive tract.[87]

What applies to menstruation once a month applies to menopause once in every lifetime. As we have seen, part of the current imagery attached to menopause is that of a breakdown of central control. Inextricably connected to this imagery is another aspect of failed production. Recall the metaphors of balanced intake and outgo that were applied to menopause up to the mid-nineteenth century, later to be replaced by metaphors of degeneration. In the early 1960s, new research on the role of estrogens in heart disease led to arguments that failure of female reproductive organs to produce much estrogen after menopause was debilitating to health.

This change is marked unmistakably in successive editions of a major gynecology text. In the 1940s and 1950s, menopause was described as usually not entailing "any very profound alteration in the woman's life current."[88] By the 1965 edition dramatic changes had occurred: "In the past few years there has been a radical change in viewpoint and some would regard the menopause as a possible pathological state rather than a physiological one and discuss therapeutic prevention rather than the amelioration of symptoms."[89]

In many current accounts, menopause is described as a state in which ovaries fail to produce estrogen.[90] The 1981 World Heatlh Organization report defines menopause as an estrogen-deficiency disease.[91] Failure to produce estrogen is the leitmotif of another current text: "This period during which the cycles cease and the female sex hormones diminish rapidly to almost none at all is called the *menopause*. The cause of the menopause is the 'burning out' of the ovaries ... Estrogens are produced in subcritical quantities for a short time after the menopause, but over a few years, as the final remaining primordial follicles become atretic, the production of estrogens by the ovaries falls almost to zero." Loss of ability to produce estrogen is seen as central to a woman's life: "At the time of the menopause a woman must readjust her life from one that has been physiologically stimulated by estrogen and progesterone production to one devoid of those hormones."[92]

Of course, I am not implying that the ovaries do not indeed produce much less estrogen than before. I am pointing to the choice of these textbook authors to emphasize above all else the negative aspects of ovaries failing to produce female hormones. By contrast, one current text shows us a positive view of the decline in estrogen production: "It would seem that although menopausal women do have an estrogen milieu which is lower than that necessary for *reproductive* function, it is not negligible or absent but is perhaps satisfactory for *maintenance of support tissues.* The menopause could then be regarded as a physiologic phenomenon which is protective in nature—protective from undesirable reproduction and the associated growth stimuli."[93]

I have presented the underlying metaphors contained in medical descriptions of menopause and menstruation to show that these ways of describing events are but one method of fitting an interpretation to the facts. Yet seeing that female organs are imagined to function within a hierarchical order whose members signal each other to produce various substances, all for the purpose of transporting eggs to a place where they can be fertilized and then grown, may not provide us with enough of a jolt to begin to see the contingent nature of these descriptions. Even seeing that the metaphors we choose fit very well with traditional roles assigned to women may still not be enough to make us question whether there might be another way to represent the same biological phenomena. . . .[94] And here I suggest some other ways that these physiological events could be described.

First, consider the teleological nature of the system, its assumed goal of implanting a fertilized egg. What if a woman has done everything in her power to avoid having an egg implant in her uterus, such as birth control or abstinence from heterosexual sex. Is it still appropriate to speak of the single purpose of her menstrual cycle as dedicated to implantation? From the woman's vantage point, it might capture the sense of events better to say the purpose of the cycle is the production of menstrual flow. Think for a moment how that might change the description in medical texts: "A drop in the formerly high levels of progesterone and estrogen creates the appropriate environment for reducing the excess layers of endometrial tissue. Constriction of capillary blood vessels causes a lower level of oxygen and nutrients and paves the way for a vigorous production of menstrual fluids. As a part of the renewal of the remaining endometrium, the capillaries begin to reopen, contributing some blood and serous fluid to the volume of endometrial material already beginning to flow." I can see no reason why the menstrual blood itself could not be seen as the desired "product" of the female cycle, except when the woman intends to become pregnant.

Would it be similarly possible to change the nature of the relationships assumed among the members of the organization—the hypothalamus, pituitary, ovaries, and so on? Why not, instead of an organization with a controller, a team playing a game? When a woman wants to get pregnant, it would be appropriate to describe her pituitary, ovaries, and so on as combining together, communicating with each other, to get the ball, so to speak, into the basket. The image of hierarchical control could give way to specialized function, the way a basketball team needs a center as well as a defense. When she did not want to become pregnant, the purpose of this activity could be considered the production of menstrual flow.

Eliminating the hierarchical organization and the idea of a single purpose to the menstrual cycle also greatly enlarges the ways we could think of menopause. A team which in its youth played vigorous soccer might, in advancing years, decide to enjoy a quieter "new game" where players still interact with each other in satisfying ways but where gentle interaction *itself* is the point of the game, not getting the ball into the basket—or the flow into the vagina.

Notes

1. Laqueur 1986:3, 18–19
2. Laqueur 1986:10
3. Rosenberg 1979:5
4. Rosenberg 1979:5–6
5. Tilt 1857:54
6. Tilt 1857:54, 57
7. Crawford 1981:50
8 Crawford 1981:50
9. Rothstein 1972:45–49
10. Crawford 1981:63
11. See Luker 1984:18; Crawford 1981:53–54; Skultans 1985
12. Laqueur 1986:4
13. Laqueur 1986:8
14. Fee 1976:180
15. Bagehot, quoted in Fee 1976:190
16. Geddes 1890:122
17. Geddes 1890:123
18. Geddes 1890:270–71
19. Barker-Benfield 1976:195–96
20. Sontag 1977:61–62
21. Geddes 1890:244; see also Smith-Rosenberg 1974:28–29
22. Smith-Rosenberg 1974:25–27
23. Quoted in Laqueur 1986:32
24. Ellis 1904:284, 293, quoted in Laqueur 1986:32
25. Smith-Rosenberg 1974:30–31; Wilbush 1981:5
26. Currier 1897:25–26
27. Haber 1983:69. See Good 1843:23–25 for an explanation of why the climacteric affects men more severely than women.
28. Smith-Rosenberg 1974:30
29. Taylor 1904:413
30. Quoted in Berliner 1982:170–71
31. Lewontin et al. 1984:58
32. Lewontin et al. 1984:59; see also Guyton 1986:23–24
33. In an extremely important series of papers, Donna Haraway 1978, 1979 has traced the replacement of organic functional views of biology by cybernetic systems views and shown the permeation of genetics and population biology by metaphors of investment, quality control, and maximization of profit.

34. Lewontin et al. 1984:59
35. Horrobin 1973:7–8. See also Guyton 1984:7. In general, more sophisticated advanced texts such as Guyton 1986:879 give more attention to feedback loops.
36. Lein 1979:14
37. Guyton 1986:885
38. Benson 1982:129
39. Netter 1965:115
40. Norris 1984:6
41. Dalton and Greene 1983:6
42. Mountcastle 1980:1615
43. Guyton 1986:885
44. Guyton 1986:885
45. Lein 1979:84
46. Evelyn Fox Keller 1985:154–56 documents the pervasiveness of hierarchical models at the cellular level.
47. Norris 1984:6
48. Giddens 1975:185
49. McCrea 1983
50. Lein 1979:79, 97
51. O'Neill 1982:11
52. Vander et al. 1985:597
53. Norris 1983:181
54. Vander et al. 1985:598
55. Norris 1983:181
56. Netter 1965:121
57. Netter 1965:116
58. Vander et al. 1985:580
59. Guyton 1986:968
60. Vander et al. 1985:576
61. Lein 1979:43
62. Guyton 1986:976
63. Vander et al. 1985:577
64. Guyton 1986:976; see very similar accounts in Lein 1979:69, Mountcastle 1980: 1612, Mason 1983:518, Benson 1982:128–29.
65. Ganong 1985:63
66. Winner 1977:185, 187
67. Ewbank 1855:21–22
68. Ewbank 1855:23
69. Ewbank 1855:27
70. Ewbank 1855:141; on Ewbank, see Kasson 1976:148–51.
71. Fisher 1967:153
72. Fisher 1967:153; 1966
73. Mumford 1967:282
74. Mumford 1970:180
75. Noble 1984:312
76. Bullough 1975:298
77. Mason 1983:525
78. Guyton 1984:624
79. Vander et al. 1980:483–84. The latest edition of this text has removed the first of these sentences, but kept the second (Vander et al. 1985:557).
80. Vander et al. 1985:577
81. Vander et al. 1985:567, 568
82. Mason 1983:419; Vander et al. 1985:483
83. Ganong 1986:776
84. Mason 1983:423
85. Guyton 1984:498–99
86. Sernka and Jacobson 1983:7

87. Vander et al. 1985:557–58; Ganong 1985:356
88. Novak 1944:536; Novak and Novak 1952:600
89. Novak et al. 1965:642
90. See McCrea and Markle 1984 for the very different clinical treatment for this lack in the United States and the United Kingdom.
91. Kaufert and Gilbert 1986:8–9; World Health Organization Scientific Group 1981
92. Guyton 1986:979
93. Jones and Jones 1981:799
94. Sadly enough, even the women's health movement literature contains the same negative view of menstruation—failed production—as does scientific medicine. See Boston Women's Health Book Collective 1984:217 and Federation of Feminist Women's Health Centers 1981:74. As in the case of prepared childbirth literature, this is evidence of the invisible power of the ideology of the dominant culture.

Works Cited

Barker-Benfield, G. J. 1976 *The Horrors of the Half-Known Life: Male Attitudes Toward Women and Sexuality in Nineteenth-Century America.* New York: Harper and Row.

Benson, Ralph C. 1982 *Current Obstetric and Gynecologic Diagnosis and Treatment.* Los Altos, CA: Lange Medical Publishers.

————. 1982 "Medical Modes of Production," pp. 162–71 in *The Problem of Medical Knowledge: Examining the Social Construction of Medicine,* Peter Wright and Andrew Treacher, eds. Edinburgh: Edinburgh University Press.

Boston Women's Health Book Collective 1984 *The New Our Bodies, Our Selves.* New York: Simon and Schuster.

Bullough, Vern L. 1975 "Sex and the Medical Model." *The Journal of Sex Research* 11(4):291–303.

Crawford, Patricia 1981 "Attitudes of Menstruation in Seventeenth-Century England." *Past and Present* 91:47–73.

Currier, Andrew F. 1897 *The Menopause.* New York: Appleton.

Dalton, Katharina and Raymond Greene 1983 "The Premenstrual Syndrome." *British Medical Journal,* May: 1016–17.

Ellis, Havelock 1904 *Man and Woman.* London: Walter Scott.

Ewbank, Thomas 1855 *The World a Workshop: or the Physical Relationship of Man to the Earth.* New York: Appleton.

Fanon, Frantz 1963 *The Wretched of the Earth.* New York: Grove Press.

Federation of Feminist Women's Health Centers 1981 *The New View of a Woman's Body.* New York: Simon and Schuster.

Fee, Elizabeth 1976 "Science and the Woman Problem: Historical

Perspectives," pp. 175–223 in *Sex Difference: Social and Biological Perspectives,* Michael S. Teitelbaum, ed. New York: Doubleday.

———. 1981 "Is Feminism a Threat to Scientific Objectivity?" *International Journal of Women's Studies* 4:378–92.

Fisher, Marvin 1967 *Workshops in the Wilderness: The European Response to American Industrialization, 1830–1860.* New York: Oxford University Press.

Ganong, William F. 1983 *Review of Medical Physiology.* 11th Edition. Los Altos, CA: Lange.

———. 1985 *Review of Medical Physiology.* 12th Edition. Los Altos, CA: Lange.

Geddes, Patrick and J. Arthur Thompson 1890 *The Evolution of Sex.* New York: Scribner and Welford.

Giddens, Anthony 1975 *The Class Structure of the Advanced Societies.* New York: Harper and Row.

Good, John Mason 1843 *The Study of Medicine,* V. 2. New York: Harper and Bros.

Guyton, Arthur C. 1981 *Textbook of Medical Physiology.* Philadelphia: W. B. Saunders.

———. 1984 *Physiology of the Human Body.* 6th Edition. Philadelphia: Saunders College Publishing.

———. 1986 *Textbook of Medical Physiology.* 7th Edition. Philadelphia: W. B. Saunders.

Haber, Carole 1983 *Beyond Sixty-Five: The Dilemma of Old Age in America's Past.* Cambridge: Cambridge University Press.

Haraway, Donna 1978 "Animal Sociology and a Natural Economy of the Body Politic." *Signs* 4:21–36.

———. 1979 "The Biological Enterprise: Sex, Mind, and Profit from Human Engineering to Sociobiology." *Radical History Review* 20:206–37.

Horrobin, David F. 1973 *Introduction to Human Physiology.* Philadelphia: F. A. Davis.

Jones, Howard W. and Georgeanna Seegar Jones 1981 *Novak's Textbook of Gynecology.* 10th Edition. Baltimore, MD: Williams and Wilkins.

Kaufert, Patricia A. and Penny Gilbert 1986 "Women, Menopause and Medicalization." *Culture, Medicine and Psychiatry* 10(1):7–21.

Keller, Evelyn Fox 1985 *Reflections on Gender and Science.* New Haven, CT: Yale University Press.

Laqueur, Thomas 1986 "Female Orgasm, Generation, and the Politics of Reproductive Biology." *Representations* 14 (Spring): 1–82.

Lein, Allen 1979 *The Cycling Female: Her Menstrual Rhythm.* San Francisco: W. H. Freeman.

Lewontin, R. C., Steven Rose, and Leon J. Kamin 1984 *Not in Our Genes: Biology, Ideology, and Human Nature.* New York: Pantheon.

Luker, Kristin 1984 *Abortion and the Politics of Motherhood.* Berkeley: University of California Press.

Mason, Elliott B. 1983 *Human Physiology.* Menlo Park, CA: Benjamin Cummings Publishing Co.

McCrea, Frances B. 1983 "The Politics of Menopause: The 'Discovery' of a Deficiency Disease." *Social Problems* 31(1):111–23.

McCrea, Frances B. and Gerald E. Markle 1984 "The Estrogen Replacement Controversy in the USA and UK: Different Answers to the Same Question?" *Social Studies of Science* 14:1–26.

Mountcastle, Vernon B. 1980 *Medical Physiology.* 14th Edition, V. II. St. Louis, MO: C. V. Mosby Co.

Mumford, Lewis 1967 *The Myth of the Machine: Technics and Human Development.* V. I. New York: Harcourt, Brace and World.

———. 1970 *The Myth of the Machine: The Pentagon of Power.* V. 2. New York: Harcourt, Brace and World.

Netter, Frank H. 1965 *A Compilation of Paintings on the Normal and Pathologic Anatomy of the Reproductive System.* The CIBA Collection of Medical Illustrations, V. II. Summit, NJ: CIBA.

Norris, Ronald V. 1984 *PMS: Premenstrual Syndrome.* New York: Berkley Books.

Novak, Emil 1941 "Gynecologic Problems of Adolescence." *Journal of the American Medical Association* 117:1950–53.

———. 1944 *Textbook of Gynecology.* 2nd Edition. Baltimore, MD: Williams and Wilkins Co.

Novak, Emil and Edmund Novak 1952 *Textbook of Gynecology.* Baltimore, MD: Williams and Wilkins Co.

Novak, Edmund, Georgeanna Seegar Jones, and Howard W. Jones 1965 *Novak's Textbook of Gynecology.* 7th Edition. Baltimore, MD: Williams and Wilkins Co.

O'Neill, Daniel J. 1982 *Menopause and Its Effect on the Family.* Washington, DC: University Press of America.

Rosenberg, Charles E. 1979 "The Therapeutic Revolution: Medicine, Meaning, and Social Change in Nineteenth-Century America," pp.

3–25 in *The Therapeutic Revolution: Essays in the Social History of American Medicine,* Morris J. Vogel and Charles E. Rosenberg, eds. Philadelphia: University of Pennsylvania Press.

Rothstein, William G. 1972 *American Physicians in the Nineteenth Century: From Sects to Science.* Baltimore: Johns Hopkins University Press.

Sernka, Thomas and Eugene Jacobson 1983 *Gastrointestinal Physiology: The Essentials.* Baltimore: Williams and Wilkins.

Skultans, Vieda 1970 "The Symbolic Significance of Menstruation and the Menopause." *Man* 5(4):639–51.

———. 1985 "Vicarious Menstruation." *Social Science and Medicine* 21(6): 713–14.

Smith-Rosenberg, Carroll 1974 "Puberty to Menopause: The Cycle of Femininity in Nineteenth-century America," pp. 23–37 in *Clio's Consciousness Raised,* Mary Hartman and Lois W. Banner, eds. New York: Harper and Row.

Sontag, Susan 1979 *Illness as Metaphor.* New York: Vintage.

Taylor, J. Madison 1904 "The Conservation of Energy in Those of Advancing Years." *Popular Science Monthly,* 64:343–414, 541–49.

Tilt, Edward John 1857 *The Change of Life in Health and Disease.* London: John Churchill.

Vander, Arthur J., James H. Sherman, and Dorothy S. Luciano 1980 *Human Physiology: The Mechanisms of Body Function.* 3rd Edition. New York: McGraw-Hill.

———. 1985 *Human Physiology: The Mechanisms of Body Function.* 4th Edition, New York: McGraw-Hill.

Wilbush, Joel 1981 "What's in a Name? Some Linguistic Aspects of the Climacteric." *Maturitas* 3:1–9.

Winner, Langdon 1977 *Autonomous Technology: Technics-out-of-Control as a Theme in Political Thought.* Cambridge: MIT Press.

World Health Organization Scientific Group 1981 *Research on the Menopause.* World Health Organization Technical Report Series 670. Geneva: World Health Organization.

Kristin Luker

---

from *Abortion: Understanding Differences*
"Abortion and the Meaning of Life"

Kristin Luker, Professor of Sociology at the University of California at Berkeley, examines the debate between prolife and prochoice activists as a clash between two fundamentally different viewpoints of the world in which we live, die and are born. Luker has also written *Taking Chances: Abortion and the Decision Not to Contracept* and *Abortion and the Politics of Motherhood.*

The following autobiographical note introduces Ms. Luker's essay.

As a social scientist who has spent the last seven years probing the whys and wherefores of how people come to feel the way they do about abortions, I am embarrassed to say that I am not entirely sure where my own interest in the topic comes from. I myself have never had an abortion, and my mother underwent lengthy and painful fertility treatments in order to have her three children.

Of course, as I am in my late thirties and have lived for many years in California, abortion is very much a part of my life: Almost all my friends have had abortions, a predictable number of my students have abortions every year, and many of those closest to me have faced the abortion dilemma. In addition, because most of my professional life has focused on abortion, people who know of my research interest often feel compelled to tell me about their experiences with abortion, partly because they feel that I will take a professional interest and partly because they have never been able to discuss this intimate event with anyone else. (Although it may be hard for people in their twenties to imagine, until the latter part of the 1960s, abortion was simply not discussed in polite company. I lived through the period when women suddenly felt the opportunity for the first time to speak freely about abortion.) My elderly Berkeley landlady once told me shyly of an abortion she had had in 1926; my best friend's mother told me of going to Mexico during World War II. Thus I, more than most, have come to see what abortion means to women, and to the men who care about them.

If I had to choose a single event that triggered my interest in abortion, it would probably be my college roommate's illegal abortion in the early 1960s. As a loyal friend, I accompanied her for her pregnancy test (she, demurely attired with a borrowed wedding ring on her finger, which she twisted nervously throughout). Once the pregnancy was confirmed, her choices seemed stark: Her boyfriend had left her, the shame and stigma of a home for unwed mothers seemed out of the question, and an illegal abortion seemed the only remaining option. Like the activists I studied, my roommate and I *were drawing on tacit beliefs about the nature of the embryo, women's roles, and the role of human control over unforeseen events. The abortion was a nightmare, as were so many in that era. She was met on a street corner in Mexico by a taxicab driver, aborted without anesthesia, and unceremoniously dumped, shivering and retching, on still another street corner. This was my introduction to abortion and—when I realized how totally a woman's life can be changed by one microscopic, wayward sperm—my introduction to feminism, although it took me years to make the connection.*

My personal and professional experiences have convinced me of several inescapable conclusions. First, there is no reason to assume that the answer to the abortion problem is contraception. Americans smoke, drive when they've been drinking, and steadfastly refuse to fasten their seat belts. Why should we expect contraceptive behavior to be of a higher standard, when everyone agrees that correct behavior in these other areas can literally save lives? Unintended pregnancies, like lung cancer and automobile deaths, are a fact of life. The only real policy choice that confronts Americans is whether a significant portion of those pregnancies will be ended legally or illegally. (My conversations with elderly women make it clear that many unintended pregnancies will be ended, no matter what law or social policy says.) Finally, I am convinced that this policy choice cannot be made rationally. Feelings about abortion draw too much on deeply held, tacit values about the meaning of life for people to admit of any compromise.

Abortion polarizes. Much like abolition, civil rights, and the prohibition of alcohol, abortion is an issue whose advocates see little in the way of nuances. People who care about the issue of abortion care intensely, and the abortion debate is marked by passionate heat and very little light.

This paper argues that the opportunities for a rational resolution of this issue appear to be dim. Drawing on a five-year study of prolife and prochoice activists,[1] I argue that prolife and prochoice people come from very different parts of the social world, have very different sets of resources with which to confront that world, and have visions of the world that both ratify and shape their own places in it. For these activists to examine closely their own beliefs about abortion, much less to change those beliefs, would mean calling into question everything in which they believe.

In the course of this research, 212 activists were interviewed on both sides of the issue[2] and were routinely asked about a number of "background variables," sociodemographic characteristics such as where they were born, their education, their income, the number of their children, and their occupation. When these activists were compared with one another (and with their opposite numbers on the other side of the debate), certain broad characteristics of status, style, and values unified those on a given side of the issue and simultaneously differentiated them from their opponents.

As one crude measure, the prolife and the prochoice activists lived in very different financial worlds. Whereas one third of all prolife people made less than $20,000 a year, only one prochoice person in five made that little, and some considerable portion of them were accounted for by young, single women just starting out on a career. Conversely, whereas a little over a third (35 percent of prolife people made more than $30,000 a year, over half of the prochoice people made that much. Prochoice income was, in fact, clustered in the upper end of the income scale: Almost one prochoice person in four in this study made $50,000 a year or more.[3]

This discrepancy was in large part due to the different educational and occupational levels attained by the two sides. More than half of the prochoice people had gone on to further education after finishing college: 37 percent had undertaken some graduate work beyond the B.A., and another 18 percent had an M.D., a law degree, a Ph.D., or a similar postgraduate degree. Prolife people were by comparison less well educated: 8 percent of the prolife people in this study had only a high-school degree or less education, and another 22 percent had not finished college. In comparison, only 2 percent of the prochoice people were high-school graduates, and only 8 percent had not finished college. Also 22 percent of the prolife activists had a college degree, whereas 27 percent of the prochoice people did. These differences were in large part a product of differences among women activists, and they became even more dramatic when women activists alone were examined (see Table 1).

These educational differences were reflected in occupational differences as well. Because of the past history of the two movements, in which elite professionals predominated, both sides had a roughly equal number of people engaged in the major professions: 14 percent of the prochoice people were doctors, lawyers, and the like, whereas 13 percent of the prolife people were. However, even here, the differ-

TABLE 1. Education

	All prolife (%)	All prochoice (%)	Female prolife (%)	Female prochoice (%)
Less than high school	2.2	0.0	1.7	0.0
High-school graduate	6.6	2.0	8.6	2.9
Some college	22.0	8.2	29.3	8.6
College graduate	28.6	26.5	31.0	31.4
Graduate/professional	16.5	36.7	13.8	37.1
M.D., Ph.D., J.D.	18.7	18.4	6.0	17.1
Technical training	5.5	2.0	8.6	2.9

ences among *women* were striking. Most of the pro*choice* doctors, lawyers, and Ph.D.'s were women, whereas most of the pro*life* professionals were men. The occupations of the remaining prolife and prochoice people were also quite different. Of the prochoice people, 20 percent were executives in large businesses, or managers, as compared to 12 percent of the prolife people, and 51 percent were small-business people, or administrators, in contrast to only 34 percent of the prolife people. Perhaps most dramatically, 31 percent of the prolife people described themselves as primarily homemakers, in contrast to none of the prochoice people.

These economic and social differences had their counterparts in the choices that the two sides had made with respect to marriage and family life. Although both prolife and prochoice people were almost equally likely to have never been married (19 percent and 22 percent, respectively), only 3 percent of the prolife people had ever been divorced, compared to 10 percent of the prochoice people. Similarly, 5 percent of prochoice people described their marital status as "living together," whereas none of the prolife people did so. The prochoice families were also on the whole smaller than the prolife families: The average prochoice family had between one and two children (and was more likely to have one); the prolife families had between two and three and were more likely to have three. (One prolife woman in five had six or more children.) The prolife people had also married at a slightly younger age than did their prochoice counterparts and were likely to have had their first child earlier.

In terms of religious affiliation, almost eight of every ten people active in the prolife movement in this study were Catholics, but two of these eight were converts. The remainder were Protestants (11 percent), a scattering were Jewish (1 percent), and a few said that they had no religion (5 percent). Prochoice people, in contrast, did not consider themselves religiously affiliated. Over half (55 percent) said that they had no religion, 22 percent thought of themselves as vaguely Protestant, 6 percent were Jewish, and 8 percent had what they called a "personal" religion. There were in this group of pro-choice activists none who currently described themselves as being Catholic, although 20 percent of the prochoice activists in this study were raised in that religion. These differences in orientation were buttressed by differences in behavior. Prolife people found their religion vital to their daily lives: half of them attended church once a week, and 13 percent attended more often. Only 2 percent of all the prolife activists never attended church. Conversely, only 20 percent of the prochoice people *ever* attended church, and the overwhelming majority said that organized religion was not an important part of their lives.

If we keep in mind the inherent difficulties in the statistical use of averages, who were the "average" prochoice and prolife advocates? When the background data of the two sides are considered carefully, two very different "average" activists emerge. The average prochoice activist is a forty-four-year-old married woman who grew up in a large, metropolitan area. She was married at twenty-two, has one or two children, and has had some graduate or professional training after the B.A. Education was a tradition in her family: Her father graduated from college. This average prochoice activist is married to a professional man and is herself employed in the paid labor force, and her family income is more than $50,000 a year. She is not religiously active, feels that religion is not important to her, and attends church very rarely, if at all.

The average prolife activist is also a forty-four-year-old married woman who grew up in a large, metropolitan area. Unlike her pro-choice counterpart, she married at seventeen and has three children (and a substantial minority have six or more children). Her father was a high-school graduate, and she herself either did not finish college or has only the B.A. She is not employed in the paid labor force, she is married to a small-business man or a lower white-collar worker, and her family income is $30,000 a year. She is Catholic (and may have converted to Catholicism), and her religion is one of the most important aspects of her life: She attends church at least once a week, and occasionally more often.

INTERESTS AND PASSIONS

To the social scientist (and perhaps to most of us), these social background characteristics connote lifestyles and values as well. We intuitively clothe these bare statistics with assumptions about these activists' beliefs and values. The prochoice women, for example, emerge as educated, affluent, liberal professionals, whose lack of religious affiliation suggests secular, "modern"—or, as prolife people would put it, "utilitarian"—outlooks on life. Similarly, prolife people's income, education, marital patterns, and religious devotion mark them as traditional, hard-working people who hold conservative views on life, "polyester-types" to their opponents.

These assumptions, as I shall show, are in large part true. But their relationship to the abortion issue, and to the world of resources in which these activists find themselves, is more complicated than one might think at first glance. Because prochoice activists live with certain kinds of resources (education, occupation, income, and "status"), it is true that they tend as a group to hold beliefs and values that are consonant with these resources. Highly educated prochoice women, for example, feel that it is important to "get ahead," and their feelings about abortion are intermingled with beliefs that parents should have children only when they can give those children the best educational, emotional, and financial opportunities. Similarly, prolife women, whose economic fate rests not in their own hands but in those of their husbands, and who are, in turn, relatively less well equipped to get ahead, reject in principle the idea that individuals are in control of their own fates. Moreover, this is a dynamic and on-going process. Individuals are constantly reshaping both the world in which they live and their beliefs about that world, and their beliefs about the way the world is organized shape how much of it they see as open to change, as well as determining how active they choose to be in molding it.

Thus, individual attitudes about abortion do not exist in a vacuum. On the contrary, beliefs and attitudes about motherhood; about sexuality; about men and women; about the role of children; and, more broadly, about such global things as morality and the role of rational planning in human affairs—all are intricately related, and all shape an individual's attitudes toward abortion. At issue is an attitude not only about a single issue—abortion—but about an entire view of the world. On almost every relevant dimension of life, prolife and pro-choice values are internally coherent, vigorously defended, and mutually antagonistic.

Prolife Views of the World

Regarding the proper roles in life for men and women, for example, prolife activists as a group believe that men and women are intrinsically different, and that this difference is both a cause and a product of the fact that they have different roles in life:

> Mrs. Osprey: [Men and women] were created differently and we are meant to complement each other, and when you get away, speaking on a purely natural plane, when you get away from our roles as such, you start obscuring them. That's another part of the confusion that's going on now, people don't know where they stand, they don't know how to act, they don't know where they're coming from, so your psychiatrists' couches are filled with lost souls, with lost people that for a long time now have been gradually led into confusion and don't even know it.

Consequently, prolife activists concur that men and women, as a result of these intrinsic differences, have different roles to play: Men are best suited to the public world of work, whereas women are best suited to rearing children, managing homes, and loving and caring for husbands. Because of this view of the nature of men and women, most prolife activists believe that motherhood—children and families—is the most fulfilling role that women can have. To be sure, they, like the rest of us, live in a world where over half of all women work, and they do acknowledge that some women are employed. But although almost all of them say they believe that women who do work should have equal pay for equal work, this belief does not necessarily translate into a belief that women *should* work. On the contrary, they subscribe quite strongly to the traditional belief that women should be wives and mothers *first,* and that if women *must* work, they should do so only as an adjunct to their primary role.

Mothering, in their view, is itself a full-time job, and any woman who cannot commit herself fully to mothering should eschew it entirely. In short, working and mothering are either-or choices; one can do one or the other, but not both.

> MRS. KESSEN: Well, if that's what you've decided in life, I mean I don't feel that there's anything wrong with not being a wife or mother. If someone wants a career, that's fine. But if you are a mother, I think you have an important job to do. I think you're responsible for your home, and I think you're responsible for the children you bring into the world, and you're responsible for, as far as you possibly can, to educate and teach them; obviously, you have to teach them what you believe is right. Moral values and responsibilities and rights and I think ... it's a huge job and you never know how well you're doing until it's too late.

As Mrs. Kessen suggested, because prolife activists see having a family as a demanding (and in particular an *emotionally* demanding), labor-intensive job, they find it hard to imagine that a woman could put forty hours a week into her job and still have time for her husband and children. Equally important, they feel that different kinds of emotional ''sets'' are called for in the workplace and in the home place.

Because prolife people see the world as inherently divided both emotionally and socially into two separate spheres, a male sphere and a female sphere, they see the loss of one of those spheres as a very deep loss indeed. If tenderness, morality, caring, emotionality, and self-sacrifice are the exclusive province of women, when women cease to be traditional women, who will provide the caring and the tenderness? Dr. Ulrich made the point that although women may have suffered from the softening influence they provide for men and for the society as a whole, they have much to gain as well:

> I think women's lib is on the wrong track. I think they've got every gripe and they've always been that way. The women have been the superior people, they're more civilized, they're more unselfish by nature, but now they want to compete with men at being selfish. And so there's nobody to give an example, and what happens is that men become *more* selfish. See, the women

used to be an example, and they had to take it on the chin for that then, but civilization was due to them, but they also benefited from it because we don't want to go back to the cavemen where you drag the woman around and treat her like nothing. Women were to be protected, respected, and treated like something important.

In this view, everyone loses something when traditional roles are lost. Men lose the nurturing that women offer, and this nurturing is what gently encourages men to give up their potentially destructive and aggressive urges. Women, by extension, lose the protection and the cherishing that men offer. And children lose full-time loving by at least one parent, as well as clear models for their own future. Thus, abortion is offensive to these people not only *per se,* but because it implicitly challenges their visions of maleness and femaleness.

By the same token, these different views about the intrinsic nature of men and women also shape prolife views about sex. The nineteenth century introduced new terms to describe the two faces of sexual activity, distinguishing between *procreative love* and *amative love.* As the names imply, *procreative love* was used to describe sexual activity whose main goal was reproductive, and *amative love* was used to describe sexual activity whose goal was sensual pleasure and mutual enjoyment. Borrowing these two terms permits us to encapsulate the differences between the prochoice and the prolife points of view on sex.

For the prolife people in this study, most of whom were ideologically committed to the idea that women should be wives and mothers first, the relative worth of procreative and amative sex was clear, in part because many of them, being Catholic, accepted some version of a natural law theory of sex that holds that a body part is destined to be used for its physiological function:

> MR. ESTER: You perceive a certain purpose to sexuality. It must be there for some reason. You're not just given arms and legs for no purpose; it's not just an appendage that just floats around. So there must be some cause [for sex] and you begin to think, well, it must be for procreation ultimately, and certainly procreation in addition to fostering a loving relationship with your spouse.

But more important, these views are intimately related to the fact that prolife people have chosen a lifestyle based on traditional roles, and a commitment to amative sex is at odds with a primary commitment to mothering.

Because many prolife people see sex as literally sacred, *and because, for women, procreative sex is a fundamental part of their "career,"* they are disturbed by values that seem to them both to secularize to and profane sex. That whole constellation of values that supports amative sex (sometimes, in modern times, called *recreational sex*) is seen by them as doing just that. Values that define sexuality as a wholesome physical activity, as healthy as volleyball but somewhat more fun, call into question everything that prolife people believe in. Sex is sacred because in their world view it has the capacity to be transcendent—to bring into existence another human life. To routinely eradicate that capacity with premarital sex (where very few people seek the opportunity to bring a new life into existence), contraception, or abortion is, from their point of view, to turn the world upside down.

As might be imagined, given the discussion so far, prolife attitudes about contraception are rooted in these views about the inherent differences between men and women and about the nature and purpose of sexuality. Although the prolife activists in this study often pointed out that the movement is officially neutral on the topic of contraception, their interviews suggested that this statement does not fully capture the complexity of their views and feelings. Virtually all of the activists in this study felt very strongly that the pill and the IUD were abortifacients (that is, that they cause the death of a very young embryo, at least sometimes) and were entirely confident that both the pill and the IUD would be banned by any law that banned abortion. Most of them, furthermore, did not themselves use contraception, basing their nonuse on moral grounds:

DR. IVY: I think it's quite clear that the IUD is an abortifacient 100 percent of the time, and the pill is sometimes an abortifacient and it's hard to know just when, so I think we need to treat it as an abortifacient. It's not really that much of an issue with me, even if it weren't. I think there's a respect for germinal life that is in my mind equivalent to a respect for individual life, and if one doesn't respect one's generative capacity, I think one will not respect one's own life or the progency that one has. So I think there's a spectrum there that begins with oneself and one's generative capacity.

The stance of prolife activists toward other people's use of contraception is therefore ambivalent. They are confident that should a human life law pass, pills and IUDs would no longer be available, so that when they discuss "artificial" contraception, they in fact mean the condom, the diaphragm, and vaginal spermicides. But many of them feel that the answer to the problems of contraception—not only for people with their moral views, but for others as well—is natural family planning (NFP), the modern version of the rhythm method.

When profile people use natural family planning as a form of fertility control, not only is the underlying moral rationale different from the prochoice side's use of contraception, so is the goal. Although prolife people support "natural" methods that do not "frustrate" the procreative function, they are using these methods to *time* the arrival of children, *not to foreclose entirely the possibility of having them.* Thus, the risk of pregnancy with natural family planning is not only *not* a drawback, but prolife people see it as a positive force that can enhance the marriage:

MR. APPLE: I'll tell you, when you're using a so-called natural method, if you try to be perceptive you can be incredibly perceptive as to when the fertile period is. But you're not going to be so perceptive that you're going to shut off every pregnancy. You know, there are a lot of things that people are just—in my opinion, add this note—simply do not understand because they've had no experience with it. It's like somebody who eats in restaurants all the time, and they've never been on the farm and had a natural meal—you know, where the food comes from the freshly killed animals the same day, from the fields. They don't have any concept of what a natural meal is like, and I think the same thing is true in the sexual area. I think that when you begin, when you take a step of cutting off all possibility of conception indefinitely, that it puts emotional and physical restraints on a relationship which divest or remove from it some of its most beautiful values, and it's hard—How do you share that kind of information? The frame of mind in which you know there might be a conception, in the midst of a sex act, is quite different from that in which you know there could not be a conception, and it's the difference between eating this processed prepared food in a restaurant and eating a natural meal on the farm. Now, I don't know how meaningful that comment is, but I don't think that people who are constantly using physical, chemical means of contraception really ever experience the sex act in all of its beauty. That's my opinion.

Ironically, therefore, the one thing it is commonly assumed that everyone wants from a contraceptive—that it be 100 percent reliable and effective—is precisely what prolife people do *not* want from their method of fertility control.

Prolife values on the issue of abortion—and, by extension, on motherhood—are intimately tied to these preceding values. But they also draw more directly on notions of motherhood (and fatherhood) that are not shared by their prochoice opponents. In part, this might seem obvious; after all, prolife people account for their own activism by referring to the notion that babies are being murdered in their mothers' wombs. But prolife feelings about the nature of parenthood draw on other, more subtle dimensions as well.

Prolife people feel that one becomes a parent by being a parent. Parenthood is for them a "natural" rather than a social role. One is a parent by virtue of having a child, and the kinds of values implied by the in-vogue term *parenting* (as in "parenting classes") are alien to them. By extension, the preparations one makes for parenting are decidedly secondary. The kind of material and educational preparations that prochoice people see as necessary achievements before one can even consider the idea of becoming a parent are seen as a serious distortion of values by prolife people. When life focuses on job achievement, home owning, and money in the bank *before* one has children, then prolife people fear that children will be seen as a barrier. Interestingly, in this context, a number of prolife people made the point that few people actually *enjoy* the state of being pregnant:

Mrs. Nehr: You know, which reminds me, I never wanted to have a baby, I never planned to have five children, I never felt the total joy that comes from being pregnant. Oh I was sick, I mean *sick,* for nine months. I mean my general attitude was "Hell, I'm pregnant again." But I thought pregnancy was a natural part of marriage, and I believed so much in the word *natural,* and so I loved the babies when they were born and I realized that a lot of women have abortions in that first trimester out of the fear and sense . . . it's a physical as well as a psychological fear that they experience, the depression, whatever, the changes that are happening to your body that I mean a lot of them will regret having that abortion later on. They work too fast, the doctors advise them too fast. They can outgrow that feeling of fear and reaction if they give themselves a chance.

Prolife activists are concerned, therefore, that women will seek abortions before they have had a chance to accommodate themselves to what they see as the admittedly unpleasant reality of being pregnant.

Prolife values on children, therefore, represent an intersection of a number of values already discussed. Because they feel that the point of sexuality is to have children, they cannot plan the exact number and timing of children with total confidence. As they cannot plan the exact number and timing of children, they feel that it is wrong (and foolish) to make entirely detailed life plans predicated on exact control of fertility. Given that children will influence one's life plans more than life plans will influence one's life plans more than life plans will influence the number of one's children, it is also wrong to value those things—primarily money and what it will buy— over the intangibles that children can bring. Thus, reasoning backward, prolife people object to every step of prochoice logic: If one values material things overly much, one will be tempted to try to plan stringently in order to achieve those material things. If one tries to plan overly stringently, one will be tempted to use highly effective contraception, which removes all potential of childbearing from a marriage. Once all potential for children is eliminated, the sexual act is distorted (and for religious people, morally wrong), and husbands and wives lose an important mutual bond. Finally, should contraception fail, a husband and wife who have accepted the logic of all of these previous steps are ready and willing to resort to abortion in order to achieve their goals.

This is not to say that prolife people do not approve of planning. They do. But because of their world view, their religious faith, and the concrete circumstances of their lives, they see human planning as having concrete limits. To them, it is a matter of priorities: If individuals want fame, money, and worldly success, they have every right to achieve them. But if they are willing to take a chance on the roulette wheel of the sexually active, they have an obligation to subordinate all other parts of life to the responsibilities that such activity entails.

Prolife values with respect to sex and contraception are also located in still deeper feelings—strongly felt, but rarely articulated beliefs about the nature of morality. Prolife people as a group subscribe to explicit and well-articulated moral codes. (After all, many of them are veterans of childhood ethics and religion classes.) Morality for them, therefore, is a straightforward and unambiguous set of rules that specifies what moral behavior is.

Because prolife people believe that these rules originate in a divine plan, they believe that these rules are in principle true and valid across time, across cultural settings, and across individual values. "Thou shalt not kill," they argue, is as true now as it was 2,000 years ago, and the cases to which it applies are still the same. Thus, they tend to locate their morality in traditional, ancient codes (the Ten Commandments, the "Judeo-Christian" law) that have stood the test of time and that exist as external standards against which behavior is measured.

Moreover, a clear-cut moral code leaves little room for nuances in the reasoning of prolife people. Either the embryo is a human life or it is not, but the idea of an intermediate category—a *potential* human life—is one that is incomprehensible to prolife people. Also, the prochoice concept that individuals should personally decide on the moral status of this intermediate category is strange to the average prolife person, given their view of morality. Moral codes dictate, humans obey. The concept of an individually negotiated moral code is simply not a part of their moral repertoire.

This lack of nuances in a strict moral code also has its repercussions in private life: Prolife people, their rhetoric notwithstanding, do have abortions. In the present study, prolife people active in "life centers" volunteered information about the fact that other prolife people had been known to seek abortions. Life centers are organizations staffed and funded by the prolife movement, located in hostipals or other medical settings. They offer free pregnancy tests and pregnancy counseling, should the pregnancy test prove positive, although counselors in life centers, of course, actively encourage women to continue their pregnancies. Because most places that offer free tests and counseling are also abortion referral centers, many women come to life centers in the mistaken belief that they can get a referral for an abortion, and life center counselors estimate that as many as a third of the women they see go on to have an abortion, even after prolife counseling. Because life centers are, by definition, prolife, when employees reveal that prolife people (and in particular, the children of prolife people) have come to these centers seeking abortions, this is persuasive. Prolife people, after all, have something to lose in admitting that their own members (and their own children), like the rest of us, have trouble in always living up to their ideals.

PROCHOICE VIEWS OF THE WORLD

On almost all of the dimensions just considered, the values and beliefs of prochoice people are very different from those of prolife people. Prochoice men and women live in very different social worlds from those of prolife men and women, and their values reflect that fact. For example, in contrast to the prolife view that men and women are inherently different and therefore have different "natural" roles not in life, prochoice people believe that men and women are substantially equal. As a result, they see women's reproductive and family roles not as a "natural" niche, but as a two-sided category: on the one hand, a satisfying option when freely chosen; on the other, a barrier to full equality when coerced. The organization of society, they argue, means that motherhood, as long as it is involuntary, is always potentially a low-status, unrewarding role to which women can be banished at any time. Thus, from their point of view, *control* over reproduction is an essential part of women's being able to live up to their full human potential:

> Ms. ELAN: I just feel that one of the main reasons that culturally women have been in a secondary situation is because of the natural way things happen, that women would bear children; they had no way to prevent this, except for, you know, nonsexual involvement. And that was not a practical thing down through the years, so without knowing what to do to prevent it, women would continually have children. And, then, if they were the ones bearing the child, nursing the child, it just made sense that they were the one to rear the child where they would be in that situation. I think that was the natural order. When we advanced and found

KRISTIN LUKER • *113*

that we could control our reproduction, we could then choose the size of our families, or if we wanted families. But that changed the whole role of women in our society. Or it opened it up to change the role. To allow us to be more than just the bearer of children and the homemaker. It's not to say that we shouldn't continue in that role, but that it's a good role, but not the *only* role for women.

Although prochoice people agree that women (and men) do find children and families a satisfying part of life, they also believe that it is foolhardy for women to believe that this is the only life role that they will ever have. They argue, in essence, that prolife women who do not work outside of the home, who do not wish to, and who try to limit other women from doing so are just one man away from disaster. A death, a divorce, desertion, or disability can plunge a woman with no career skills or experience perilously close to the edge. Pointing to the ever-increasing numbers of "displaced home-makers"—women who have spent a life in a marriage and find themselves suddenly divorced or widowed, in penury with virtually no financial or employment resources—the prochoice activists argue that the prolife women, who in both their values and their lives put work in the paid labor force secondary, live in a precarious world of wishful thinking.

At the same time, prochoice people value what I have earlier called *amative sex.* Prolife values that hold that sex is important—and indeed sacred—because of its inherent reproductive capacity strike many prochoice people as absurd. From their point of view, if the purpose of sex were reproduction, no rational Creator would have arranged things so that people have literally hundreds of acts of intercourse over their lifetimes and literally thousands (and in the case of men, millions) of sex cells—egg and sperm—at the ready. More to the point, if sex is basically procreational in nature, then it *must be highly socially regulated,* lest a baby be created when none is intended. In particular, *women* must be protected—and, in their viewpoint, repressed—because an otherwise free and uninhibited expression of sexual wishes might land individual women "in trouble" and overpopulate the species. In prochoice values, both the "double standard" and "purdah"—the ancient custom of veiling women and keeping them entirely out of the public eye, lest they be too sexually arousing to men—are the logical outcomes of focusing too intensely on the protection of women's reproductive capacities.

Significantly in this context, many of the prochoice people describe themselves as having grown up in families with very traditional sexual values that they now see as "sex-negative" because they focus on the dangers of sexual feelings let out of control. They see themselves as adults now seeking a set of "sex-positive" values for themselves and for the society as a whole, values that emphasize the pleasure, beauty, and joy of sex rather than its dangers. When prochoice people speak of sex-negative values, they mean that in their families sex was not openly talked about, that it was not portrayed as something to be enjoyed for its own sake, and that budding childish sexuality—masturbaton, adolescent flirting—was often treated harshly. Premarital sexuality, especially when pregnancy ensued, was a "fate worse than death."

Such harsh treatment of sex makes sense if there is a presumption that sexuality can lead to genital expression and that pregnancy can (and indeed *should*) result from such genital expression. But for people who plan anyway to have small families, who have no moral opposition to contraceptives, who value rational planning in all realms including pregnancy, and whose other values focus them on the here and now and on other people rather than on the future and God, treating sex as a taboo seems irrelevant at best and potentially damaging at worst.

Prochoice people, therefore, believe that sexual activity is good as an end in itself, and they therefore see sex as primarily amative. The main role of sexuality for them is not the possibility of children—at least, for much of a lifetime—but pleasure, human contact, and, most important perhaps, intimacy.

Despite Mr. Ester's claims earlier, prochoice people *do* believe that sex can be sacred, but it is a different kind of sacredness that they have in mind. For them, sex is sacred when it is mystical, when it dissolves the boundaries between the self and the other, when it brings one closer to one's partner, and when it conveys a sense of the infinite. Transcendent sex for them is rooted in present feeling, rather than in something that may happen in the future.

An important corollary is that, whereas sex for prochoice people has the *capacity* to touch on the sacred, sacredness is a goal to be attained, not an intrinsic part of the situation. That kind of sex can be achieved only when people feel security, trust, and a love for themselves and for their partner. As the spiritual aspect of sex is something to be attained rather than a given (although sometimes, like a state of grace, it just occurs), it follows that prochoice people do not denigrate sexuality that does not achieve this goal. After all, sex is something that needs practice if it calls on such delicate social and emotional resources as trust, caring, and intimacy. As a result, premarital sex, contraception, and infidelity are evaluated by prochoice people according to their ability to enhance or detract from these conditions of trust and caring. In their value scheme, something that enables people to be closer to one another—to create opportunities for intimacy—simply cannot be wrong.

These attitudes about the nature and the meaning of sex also shape prochoice views on contraception. To be sure, contraception *per se* is not a salient issue for most prochoice people. Like vaccines and dental hygiene, it is a necessary, straightforward, and not very controversial part of life. (Indeed, they find prolife objections to contraception mysterious and dismiss them by assuming that such objections are merely medieval—or "religious"—in nature.) Although prochoice people have some pragmatic concerns about contraception—how unpleasant some methods are, how safe other methods may be—they make no moral associations with contraception *per se*. Because their primary moral value in sexuality is amative, focusing on attaining intimacy with the self and the other, then a good (and hence, moral, if one can stretch the term) contraceptive is one that is safe, undistracting, and pleasant to use. Because their moral concerns do focus on intimacy and caring, and because they furthermore *do* use contraception to postpone childbearing for long periods of time, their ideal contraception is easy to use, *highly effective,* and not a risk to their health.

The one moral concern that prochoice people do have about contraception (or, more precisely, birth control) is that many of them feel uncomfortable with the use of abortion as a routine way of controlling fertility, when abortion is used in place of, rather than as a backup for, traditional methods of contraception. In part, such opposition is pragmatic: Repeated abortions have their own set of health risks.

INTERVIEWER: Who are the "extremists"?
REV. OWENS: Those people who are happy to use abortion as a means of birth control, who are advocates of using no form of contraception and relying upon abortion. I cannot agree with that position for physical reasons; I believe it's unhealthy.

But physical risks are not the whole story. The interviewer pursued the question with this respondent:

> INTERVIEWER: Do you have some moral concerns about that, too?
>
> REV. OWENS: Yes, and they're vaguer. Last time at my class in human sexuality, a young woman brought this up, and I was grateful to her because I seldom bring it up myself because it's a spiritual issue. There's a spiritual force within a woman when she's pregnant and people of great spiritual sensitivity have to deal with the reality of that potential life, and a lot of people don't think there's this kind of subtlety, and when they do, I'm very supportive of them. Yes, there's a spiritual issue involved. I take the idea of ending the life of the fetus very, very gravely. I'm troubled by that, but this doesn't in any way diminish my conviction that a woman has the right to do that, but I become distressed when people regard pregnancy lightly and ignore the spiritual significance of a pregnancy.

As the Reverend Owens's response suggests, opposition to abortion as a routine form of birth control is based on a very complex and subtle moral reasoning. For most prochoice people, the personhood of the embryo does not exist at conception but develops at some later point. (Some activists choose viability as the point when personhood begins; others choose birth itself.) Unlike the prolife stand, however, which sees personhood conferred at the moment of conception, the prochoice view of personhood is a *gradualist one.* Thus, although an embryo may not be a full person until viability, it has the rights of a potential person at all times, and those rights become more morally compelling over the length of the pregnancy. (Therefore, wearing an IUD is morally acceptable to all prochoice people, as in their view very early embryos are little more than fertilized eggs.) Prochoice people accept that sometimes the potential rights of the embryo have to be sacrificed to the actual rights of the mother. But a woman who arbitrarily or capriciously brings an embryo into existence, *when she had an alternative,* is seen as usurping even the potential rights of the embryo by trivializing them, and this attitude offends the moral sense of the prochoice activists.

Because they see at least three categories during pregnancy—a fertilized egg without much moral significance (whose life can be ended by wearing an IUD, for example); an embryo, which is a transitional state; and a baby, who makes full moral claim on the human community—prochoice people make sense of the embryo by referring both backward and forward in time. A "menstrual extraction," which is a very early abortion performed within the first three weeks of pregnancy, is less morally troubling than a later, second-trimester abortion, and the moral justification for the later abortion must therefore be correspondingly stronger.

It is in this context that prochoice values about parenting—about the kind of life that the baby-to-be might reasonably expect to have—play such an important role. Prochoice people, for example, have very clear standards about what parenting entails: It means giving a child the very best set of emotional, psychological, social, and financial resources that one possibly can as preparation for future life. Prochoice people feel that it is the duty of a parent to prepare the child for the future, and good parents are seen as arranging life (and childbearing) so that they can do this most effectively:

> Ms. MORRIS: Well, I think that there's a difference between saying that a family should have *all* the children that whoever, the Lord or someone, sends them. And to me, caring about your family means not to have more children than you can give— than you have enough to give them . . . nurturing and . . . not just financially, but in all ways. And I really believe that more families are broken up by unwanted pregnancies and unplanned pregnancies than are ever held together by them.

These values about what a good parent is support and shape prochoice attitudes toward children and the timing of their arrival. Because children demand financial sacrifices, for example, couples should not have them until they are in a financial position to give their children the best. Otherwise, under pressure, parents will come to resent a child, and the lack of emotional and financial resources available to the parents will limit their ability to be caring, attentive, and nurturing to their children. As a corollary, prochoice people want children who feel loved, who have self-esteem, and who "feel good about themselves," and they feel that parents should postpone childbearing until they have the proper *emotional* resources to do the intense one-to-one psychological caring that good parenting takes. (The combination of financial and emotional considerations is what they have in mind when they make the statement that prolife people find unfathomable, that they are not "ready" for childbearing.)

Because prochoice people see the optional raising of children as requiring financial resources, large amounts of "human capital" skills, and emotional maturity, they often worry about how easy it is to have children. In their view, people stumble into parenthood without appreciating what it takes:

> Ms. NEWSOME: I would say that the tip of the iceberg is purposeful parenthood, yes, I am interested. I think life is too cheap. I think we're too easy-going. The automaticness that everybody shall be a mother, that's Garrett Hardin's "compulsory motherhood" concept. Hell, it's a privilege, it's not special enough. The contraceptive agent affords us the opportunity to make motherhood real, real special, and I think again, we have a moral obligation, in the sense of Emerson: New occasions teach new duties. In that sense, with new technology, when you can go to the moon, you can no longer be casual about going to the moon because now it's an act of commission rather than omission. And the same is true—motherhood used to be an act of omission, I mean, you just didn't have any choices, philosophically speaking. You did it because there wasn't anything else to do. And now we have to change the question. We used to say, Why not have a baby? And now we say, Why? So that things have changed just plain philosophically about parenthood, and that's just one part of it.

Because prochoice activists feel that abortion in the long run will enhance the quality of parenting by making it optional, in this respect they see themselves as being on the side of children when they advocate abortion. Consequently, in contrast to prolife people, who feel that parenthood will be enhanced by making it *inclusive* and that all married people should be open to the arrival of children, prochoice people feel that the way to upgrade the quality of parenthood is to make it more *exclusive*:

> REV. OSTER: It stems out of, I think, the same basic concern about the right to share the good life and all these things; that children, once born, have rights which we consistently deny them. I remember giving a talk, that I thought that one of my

roles was to be an advocate for the fetus, and for the fetus's right not to be born. I think the right-to-lifers thought I was great until that point. . . . In this sense, that I think if I had my druthers I would probably pursue a course which would, as I do advocate verbally, the need for licensing pregnancies, which seems to contradict what I've just said, but I don't think it really does.

In part, this view is connected to prochoice views about planning. A planned child is a wanted child, and a child who is wanted starts out on a much better footing than one who is not. Not that the prochoice activists necessarily accept a narrow view of "wantedness":

Ms. HOLMES: Yes, I think that raising a child is a contract of twenty years at least, and I've still found it going on after thirty some, so I think that if you're not in a life situation where you can possibly undertake the commitment to raising a child, you should have the choice of not doing so at the present time. Maybe I'm not being logical, and I don't mean to say that every child is initially unwanted, would remain unwanted, and becomes a social problem. Of course, many people don't want the child when they find out that they're pregnant but they re-solve negative feelings, and by the time the child is born, they do want it, and that's probably far more common. But if they don't want it enough to seek an abortion, then probably they shouldn't have [that child]. And I'm as much concerned with the child as the rights of the woman, but I am also concerned with the rights of the woman.

Not surprisingly, the values that prochoice people hold about sex, contraception, and abortion have their roots in deep values about the nature of morality, as was exactly the case for their opponents. Either implicitly or explicitly, prochoice people believe in "situation ethics." Partly because they are pluralists, they seriously doubt whether any one moral code can serve everyone. Partly because they are secularists, they see the traditional Judeo-Christian codes not as abso-lute moral rules, but as ethical guidelines that emerged in a specific historical time and that may or may not be relevant now. Perhaps most centrally, morality for prochoice people is not a blind "take it or leave it" set of rules, like the Ten Commandments, but the application of a few general ethical principles to a vast array of cases. All of these factors, combined with their staunch belief in the rights of the individual, lead to a belief that only individuals, not governments or churches, can ultimately make ethical decisions. It is tempting to describe their moral positions as quintessentially "Protestant," if one takes this term as being descriptive of a style rather than a religious history. In other words, prochoice people tend to see ethical isssues as matters of individual conscience, guided by moral principles, rather than as moral codes *per se.* Hence, the emphasis that prochoice people put on abortion as an *individual, private* choice:

> Ms. HOLMES: Well, of course you can't deny that [abortion] is ending something that's alive, but we took the position that the decision to bear a child, to raise a child, is a private decision between—it's a private decision, an ethical private decision, and the state has no interest in regulating it. Now if this is a matter of conscience, and if your beliefs would be contrary to abortion, then of course you can decide not to have an abortion, even if it meant some other sacrifice.

This quote illustrates three key features of prochoice moral logic. First, there is the implied distinction between an embryo and a child, which all prochoice people take for granted. Second, and perhaps more interesting, is the idea already noted that the embryo, although not a child, is nonetheless "alive" and thus has some implicit moral rights. Finally, there is a pluralist view: If a person has a different moral view of abortion, she should follow her conscience, "even if it meant some other sacrifice." These three features summarize the core of prochoice morality: Morality consists of weighing a number of competing situations and rights and trying to reconcile them under general moral principles, rather than explicit moral rules.

To use a religious metaphor again, the prochoice activists seem to have a New Testament approach to morality. Although relatively few mention either the New Testament or Joseph Fletcher's situation ethics by name, they do call on the moral principles associated with these two sources. That is, when trying to decide what is the moral thing to do, prochoice people ask what is the *loving* thing to do. The choice of the word *loving* emphasizes the fact that moral judgments rely on a subjectively reasoned application of moral principles, rather than on an externally existing moral code.

THE FORESEEABLE FUTURE

This study suggests that the abortion debate will continue to be a bitter one for the foreseeable future. At stake are not only two different definitions of the embryo, but also two different definitions of the world: Motherhood, the appropriate roles of men and women, and the nature of morality. Because individual values about these related issues run so deep and literally so close to home, reasoned discussion, calm dialogue, and compromise are all equally unlikely. Individuals are unwilling to discuss, much less compromise, their views on abortion. For all of the activists in the study, abortion was merely the tip of the iceberg.

Notes

1. The full report of this research is contained in Kristin Luker, *Abortion and the Politics of Motherhood* (Berkeley: University of California Press, 1984).
2. These activists were those who met the strict criteria of the term *activist,* and who were located in the state of California. Comparative interviews were undertaken in six other states, but those data are not reported here. For details, see "Methodological Appendix" in Luker, *Abortion and the Politics of Motherhood.*
3. Note that this is *family* income in large part. Prochoice people are more well-to-do than prolife people because, if they are women, they are better educated than their prolife counterparts, are far more likely to work, are more likely to work in well-paid jobs than those few prolife women who do work, and are also more likely to be married to elite professionals. Thus, their family income typically represents the conjoined incomes of two elite professionals, whereas prolife family incomes typically represent the income of one upper-blue-collar or lower-white-collar worker.

Nell Irvin Painter

"Who Was Lynched?"

American historian Nell Irvin Painter discusses the 1992 Supreme Court confirmation hearings of Clarence Thomas in terms of lynching (Thomas compared his hearing to a lynching) and the matters of race and gender in the United States. Painter is the author of *Exodusters: Black Migration to Kansas After Reconstruction, The Narrative of Hosea Hudson: His Life as a Negro Communist in the South* and *Standing at Armageddon: The United States 1877–1919.*

In the second part of the Clarence Thomas confirmation hearings, Orrin Hatch and Thomas manipulated what Americans remember of racism and ignored what most Americans have forgotten about women in that same past. The Hatch and Thomas performances did not have black women in view. Any American with a sense of history understood the connotations of Thomas's claim that he was a lynch victim, casting the fourteen white men of the Senate Judiciary Committee as his lynch mob. The lynch victim is an easily recognizable character in our tragic racial past. This character is, like Thomas, black, male and southern, identities that reflect the actual practice of lynching. Here are a few facts on the matter: During Reconstruction lynching functioned as a means of crushing freedmen's political mobilization. After Reconstruction it was used to terrorize southern blacks who transgressed the economic or social mores of white supremacy. Part of a larger phenomenon, the casual slaughter of the poor, lynching in the South has been aimed at the powerless. Lynch victims have not been the protégés of presidents and senators. Since figures began to be kept in 1882, 82 percent of lynchings have occurred in the South, where 84 percent of its victims were black and 95 percent male. From 1882 until the early 1950s, reports show, 4,739 people died at the hands of lynch mobs; the actual number may approach 6,000. The state that ranks first in lynchings—Mississippi, with 581 deaths, of which 539 were black—is also a symbol of everything benighted and impoverished in American life.

Southern historians often speak of a rape-lynch syndrome, since the most popular rhetorical justification for such murders was the rape or attemtped rape of white women. This excuse, however, did not hold up under scrutiny, as a courageous black journalist, Ida B. Wells, discovered in the 1890s. Black lynch victims were accused of rape or attempted rape only about one-third of the time. The most prevalent accusation was murder or attempted murder, followed by a list of infractions that included verbal and physical aggression, spirited business competition and independence of mind. But the association of lynching with rape persists, and even today to mention lynching is to sound the themes of race and sex. Its three emblematic figures are the white woman (the rape victim), the black man (the lynch victim) and the white man (the avenger of the white woman and the black man's murderer). This drama has been playing in American popular culture since the late nineteenth century and is encapsulated most neatly in D.W. Griffith's 1915 film, *The Birth of a Nation.*

Just as the rape-lynch scenario lives on in the minds of Americans (*vide* Willie Horton), so a countertradition of disbelieving that scenario also exists among blacks and well-intentioned whites. Clarence Thomas drew cynically on this countertradition. Casting himself as the black lynch victim was a move that made him the undeserving beneficiary of guilt over our bloody past. But what of the invisible figure in this tableau? It is not by accident that in both the rape-lynch set piece and in Thomas's recitation, one figure in southern society is missing: the black woman.

The black woman's part in the drama (as opposed to the actual history) is usually ignored. Clarence Thomas's little play of a conspiracy of white liberals against his brave, black self caused Anita Hill to vanish completely. Neither prostitute nor welfare mother, Hill, an educated black woman, is hard to fit into clichés of race. As the emblematic woman is white and the emblematic black is male, black women generally are not as easy to cast symbolically. Consider the forgotten figure of Bessie, the first murder victim of Bigger Thomas in Richard Wright's novel *Native Son*, which we recall only as the story of a racial crime with a white woman as victim. Consider the nameless black women Eldridge Cleaver, who wrote *Soul on Ice*, raped for practice before attacking white women and ending up in prison. Just as there is an overlooked drama of victimized black women, there exists an actual, neglected history.

Sexual violence against black women has outlasted slavery and segregation. Since the seventeenth century, black women have been triply vulnerable to rape and other kinds of violence: as members of a stigmatized race, as the subordinate sex and as people who work for others. Even though the testimony is abundant and available in two centuries' worth of black women's autobiographies and novels, black women's condition barely enters the drama of race. Why not? The reasons abound, but I will mention only three: First, as women, black women are discounted within their race, as witnessed by such cultural producitons as men's rap. Second, as blacks, black women are hesitant to speak up loudly, lest they endanger racial unity, for issues of gender are deeply divisive. Third, and most important, race is less salient, as sexual violence against black women indicts black as well as white men.

When a black woman accuses a black man of sexual harassment, there is no racial angle. But the racial angle was absolutely necessary in order to obscure the case and preserve Thomas's nomination. Cognizant of Americans' susceptibility, conservative Republicans once again staged a drama of racial stereotype. This time black as well as white Americans seem to have believed their little show.

Marcia Ann Gillespie

"What's Good for the Race?"

Misogyny among African Americans is often disguised under the banner of a racial consciousness that in fact continually fails to examine the impact of racism upon women, argues Marcia Ann Gillespie. She is the executive editor for *Ms.* magazine.

When Anita Hill publicly confronted Clarence Thomas a lot of folks said she shouldn't have aired "our" dirty linen in public. Wasn't a question of did he do the things she said; for some people race—specifically the need for African Americans to close ranks—was all important. Particularly galling for many was that the charges were being leveled by a black woman, that a sister was dragging a brother down. Even many of the calls I received that fateful weekend from sisters who believed her, were angered by her treatment, and disgusted by his actions, reflected that sense of divided loyalties. We are black, we are women, we are African Americans. We are always aware that in the United States our sexual behavior has long been the stuff of stereotype and destructive myth, used to justify everything from rape to castration, to murder, to court-ordered sterilization, and most recently, forced contraception. And we are equally aware of the fact that for the good of the race, we women have routinely been expected to put our men first, no matter what. But many of us are also painfully conscious of the way that the misogyny in our community is often both heightened and disguised under the banner of racial consciousness.

This fact was brought painfully to mind once again when almost a year after those Senate hearings, an African-American man and woman in New York City were once again at the center of a very public storm raised by charges of sexual harassment. The circumstances were eerily familiar: He, a newly announced deputy mayor, a self-designated key player in the campaign to reelect the city's first African-American mayor. She, a fledgling television reporter, who alleges the harassment took place while they were both working in the office of another highly placed city official five years before. She made the situation known at the time, but did not seek to make a formal complaint. Days before he was named deputy mayor, the rumors surfaced at city hall. Instead of saying something to the effect that "charges of sexual harassment are much too serious to be ignored, we need to investigate this thoroughly," the city's first African-American mayor, a man who had publicly supported Anita Hill the year before, went forward with the appointment. And inevitably, the rumors went public, making front-page news. No sham hearings this time; instead, the equally horrific spectacle of "He said, She said," name-calling, rumors and denials played out in the press, along with charges that he was "set up" and that she was "a dupe" of one of the mayor's archrivals.

Inevitably, the race card got played. Inevitably, some folk in the community chose to paint the woman as "disloyal" to the race. Inevitably, the question of divided loyalties was raised. By the time you read this, the story will be old news. He stepped down. The lawsuit he initiated against her may or may not go forward. We may never know the truth of what did or did not happen between them. But both of their lives have been changed by these events, and within the African-American community the larger issue of the unacknowledged and unaddressed misogyny and sexism continues to simmer.

From the beginning the quest for African-American rights, freedom, and justice has primarily been couched in patriarchal terms. Oft called a "struggle for manhood," it's been a quest for power in which women, with a few notable exceptions, have been and still are expected to play supporting roles. Women's rights and "women's issues" were seen as secondary to the larger goal. In the 1960s many people went so far as to assume that what was best for African-American men was automatically in women's best interest. Yet in the midst of our Freedom Journey, racist stereotyping of black women, instead of being debunked and dismissed, was taken up by black men and used against us. Extremists mockingly declared a woman's position in the movement should be prone, and said that when we weren't on our backs we should be in the kitchen; that we should walk behind our men or serve the cause by having babies for the "revolution." Some vilified our foremothers for having borne children for the slave master, implying they willingly chose sexual enslavement, holding them responsible for the "impurity of our race."

Putting black women down, or in the parlance of the day, "reminding us of our place," was a common practice in many circles. We were castigated for not showing proper respect, i.e., for an unfeminine lack of docility. We were castrating bitches if we complained or questioned men's actions or decisions. We were "Good Sisters" if we dutifully followed orders, or mouthed the party line laid down by the brothers. We were "Strong Black Women" if we spoke out against racism but never about sexism, if we shouldered the burden of raising families on our own and placed all blame for the lack of male responsibility on racism.

Now flash forward two decades to Hill and Thomas, and this more recent incident involving Barbara Wood and Randy Daniels. A frequently repeated remark by many of Daniels's supporters was that Wood was "no Anita Hill." Why? The answers ranged from "she didn't go to Yale Law School" to speculation that "she raised those charges to cover the fact that she wasn't doing her job." Unsaid— perhaps even unconsciously driving that unfavorable comparison— was something else. Many of those who took up the "she's no Anita Hill" line had already expressed their opposition to Thomas way *before* Anita Hill came forward. So no matter how distasteful they may have found the proceedings, Anita Hill could be given the mantle of good sister because she was speaking out against a black man they had already excommunicated from the race for his political views. In short, a version of "the enemy of my enemy is my friend." But in New York City, Daniels was part of the black version of the "good ole boy" network: a black Democrat, a champion of "our" mayor, known and well liked by many in the African-American community. Within the context of that scenario, Woods did not serve the race's agenda (as defined by many of the city's movers and shakers) and therefore she was not a good sister, "no Anita Hill."

That subtlety was lost on many folks in the community who condemn Anita Hill and any African-American woman who dares to place a "woman's issue" above the interests of the race as defined by the patriarchy. And solidarity speak continues to revolve around the impact of racism on men: about how black men are an endangered species. About the need for all male academies to offset what is being done to *them* in the public schools. About how violence impacts on "our" men. About the rising male prison population. As a result, one can call a rally againt the rape of a black woman and be assured a crowd, a full podium of speakers, and the full support of male leadership only if the woman was raped by white men.

But when a women steps forward and dares to bear witness to the misogyny and sexual terrorism that flourishes in our community, all hell breaks loose. She who dares to speak about and hold black men accountable for the everyday acts of incest, battery, rape, domestic violence, and sexual harassment risks becoming a pariah. Black male preachers, who tenaciously cling to male-centered theology and zealously Big Daddy their flocks, will denounce her from their pulpits, calling her misguided (as some did Anita Hill while calling up prayers for Clarence Thomas). Or worse, they will organize petitions on behalf of a Mike Tyson. The "race is all" catechism is deeply ingrained in the collective psyche of our community. But so too is the belief among many women that to get along one must go along with black patriarchy's reasoning. So some African-American women inevitably will be among those calling the sister dupe, pawn, liar, traitor, conniver, jealous, crazy, and cunning, while others deny her by keeping silent.

During the Senate hearings one sister friend asked, "Why must we always be the conscience of this nation?" I had no answer then. Today I would say, "Sister Anita is our conscience as much as she is the nation's. She rebukes our silence as much as theirs. She challenges us to redefine what is good for the race by making women matter."

Catharine A. MacKinnon

---

from *Feminism Unmodified*
Discourses on Life and Law
"Sexual Politics of the First Amendment"

This call for a definition of obscenity that places harm-based restrictions on free speech was originally delivered by University of Michigan law professor Catharine A. MacKinnon in Chicago on March 23, 1986, at the Seventeenth Annual Conference on Women and the Law in a panel on Feminist Ethical Approaches to the First Amendment. MacKinnon is also the author of *Toward a Feminist Theory of State*.

[The Dred Scott case] was a law to be cited, a lesson to be learned, judicial vigor to be emulated, political imprudence to be regretted, but most of all, as time passed, it was an embarrassment—the Court's highly visible skeleton in a transparent closet.

Don E. Ferrenbacher, *The Dred Scott Case: Its Significance in American Law and Politics*

Frankfurter is said to have remarked that Dred Scott was never mentioned by the Supreme Court any more than ropes and scaffolds were mentioned by a family that had lost one of its number to the hangman.

Bruce Catton, in John A. Garraty, ed., *Quarrels That Have Shaped the Constitution*

The Constitution of the United States, contrary to any impression you may have received, is a piece of paper with words written on it. Because it is old, it is considered a document. When it is interpreted by particular people under particular conditions, it becomes a text. Because it is backed up by the power of the state, it is a law.

Feminism, by contrast, springs from the impulse to self-respect in every woman. From this have come some fairly elegant things: a metaphysics of mind, a theory of knowledge, an approach to ethics, and a concept of social action. Aspiring to the point of view of all women on social life as a whole, feminism has expressed itself as a political movement for civil equality.

Looking at the Constitution through the lens of feminism, initially one sees exclusion of women from the Constitution. This is simply to say that we had no voice in the constituting document of this state. From that one can suppose that those who did constitute it may not have had the realities of our situation in mind.

Next one notices that the Constitution as interpreted is structured around what can generically be called the public, or state action. This constituting document pervasively assumes that those guarantees of freedoms that must be secured to citizens begin where law begins, with the public order. This posture is exalted as "negative liberty"[1] and is a cornerstone of the liberal state. You notice this from the feminist standpoint because women are oppressed socially, prior to law, without express state acts, often in intimate contexts. For women this structure means that those domains in which women are distinctively subordinated are assumed by the Constitution to be the domain of freedom.

Finally, combining these first two observations, one sees that women are not given affirmative access to those rights we need most. Equality, for example. Equality, in the words of Andrea Dworkin, was tacked on to the Constitution with spit and a prayer. And, let me also say, late.

If we apply these observations to the First Amendment, our exclusion means that the First Amendment was conceived by white men from the point of view of their social position. Some of them owned slaves; most of them owned women.[2] They wrote it to guarantee their freedom to keep something they felt at risk of losing.[3] Namely—and this gets to my next point—speech which they did not want lost through state action. They wrote the First Amendment so their speech would not be threatened by this powerful instrument they were creating, the federal government. You recall that it reads, "Congress shall make no law abridging . . . the freedom of speech." They were *creating* that body. They were worried that it would abridge something they *did have*. You can tell that they had speech, because what they said was written down: it became a document, it has been interpreted, it is the law of the state.[4]

By contrast with those who wrote the First Amendment so they could keep what they had, those who didn't have it didn't get it. Those whose speech was silenced prior to law, prior to any operation of the state's prohibition of it, were not secured freedom of speech. Their speech was not regarded as something that had to be—and this gets to my next point—affirmatively guaranteed. Looking at the history of the First Amendment from this perspective, reprehensible examples of state attempts to suppress speech exist. But they constitute a history of comparative privilege in contrast with the history of silence of those whose speech has never been able to exist for the state even to contemplate abridging it.

A few affirmative guarantees of access to speech do exist. The *Red Lion* decision is one, although it may be slated for extinction.[5] Because certain avenues of speech are inherently restricted—for instance, there are only so many broadcast frequencies—according to the *Red Lion* doctrine of fairness in access to broadcast media, some people's access has to be restricted in the interest of providing access to all. In other words, the speech of those who could buy up all the speech there is, is restricted. Conceptually, this doctrine works exactly like affirmative action. The speech of those who might be the only ones there, is not there, so that others' can be.

With a few exceptions like that[6] we find no guarantees of access to speech. Take, for example, literacy. Even after it became clear that the Constitution applied to the states, nobody argued that the segregation of schools that created inferior conditions of access to literacy for blacks violated their First Amendment rights. Or the slave codes that made it a crime to teach a slave to read and write or to advocate their freedom.[7] Some of those folks who struggled for civil rights for black people must have thought of this, but I never heard their lawyers argue it. If access to the means of speech is effectively socially precluded on the basis of race or class or gender, freedom from state burdens on speech does not meaningfully guarantee the freedom to speak.

First Amendment absolutism, the view that speech must be absolutely protected, is not the law of the First Amendment. It is the conscience, the superego of the First Amendment, the implicit standard from which all deviations must be justified. It is also an advocacy position typically presented in debate as if it were legal fact. Consider for example that First Amendment bog, the distinction between speech and conduct. Most conduct is expressive as well as active; words are as often tantamount to acts as they are vehicles for removed cerebration. Case law knows this.[8] But the first question, the great divide, the beginning and the end, is still the absolutist question, "Is it speech or isn't it?"

First Amendment absolutism was forged in the crucible of obscenity litigation. Probably its most inspired expositions, its most passionate defenses, are to be found in Justice Douglas's dissents in obscenity cases.[9] This is no coincidence. Believe him when he says that pornography is at the core of the First Amendment. Absolutism has developed through obscenity litigation, I think, because pornography's protection fits perfectly with the power relations embedded in First Amendment structure and jurisprudence from the start. Pornography is exactly that speech of men that silences the speech of women. I take it seriously when Justice Douglas speaking on pornography and others preaching absolutism say that pornography has to be protected speech or else free expression will not mean what it has always meant in this country.

I must also say that the First Amendment has become a sexual fetish through years of absolutist writing in the melodrama mode in *Playboy* in particular. You know those superheated articles where freedom of speech is extolled and its imminent repression is invoked. Behaviorally, *Playboy*'s consumers are reading about the First Amendment, masturbating to the women, reading about the First Amendment, masturbating to the women, reading about the First Amendment, masturbating to the women. It makes subliminal seduction look subtle. What is conveyed is not only that using women is as legitimate as thinking about the Constitution, but also that if you don't support these views about the Constitution, you won't be able to use these women.

This general approach affects even religious groups. I love to go speaking against pornography when the sponsors dig up some religious types, thinking they will make me look bad because they will agree with me. Then the ministers come on and say, "This is the first time we've ever agreed with the ACLU about anything . . . why, what she's advocating would *violate the First Amendment.*" This isn't their view universally, I guess, but it has been my experience repeatedly, and I have personally never had a minister support me on the air. One of them finally explained it. The First Amendment, he said, also guarantees the freedom of religion. So this is not only what we already know: regardless of one's politics and one's moral views, one is into using women largely. It is also that, consistent with this, First Amendment absolutism resonates historically in the context of the long-term collaboration in misogyny between church and state. Don't let them tell you they're "separate" in that.

In pursuit of absolute freedom of speech, the ACLU has been a major institution in defending, and now I describe their behavior, the Nazis, the Klan, and the pornographers. I am waiting for them to add the antiabortionists, including the expressive conduct of their violence. Think about one of their favorite metaphors, a capitalist metaphor, the marketplace of ideas. Think about whether the speech of the Nazis has historically enhanced the speech of the Jews. Has the speech of the Klan expanded the speech of blacks? Has the so-called speech of the pornographers enlarged the speech of women? In this context, apply to what they call the marketplace of ideas the question we were asked to consider in the keynote speech by Winona LaDuke: Is there a relationship between our poverty in speech and their wealth?

As many of you may know, Andrea Dworkin and I, with a lot of others, have been working to establish a law that recognizes pornography as a violation of the civil rights of women in particular. It recognizes that pornography is a form of sex discrimination. Recently, in a fairly unprecedented display of contempt, the U.S. Supreme Court found that the Indianapolis version of our law violates the First Amendment.[10] On a direct appeal, the Supreme Court invalidated a local ordinance by summary affirmance—no arguments, no briefs on the merits, no victims, no opinion, not so much as a single line of citation to controlling precedent. One is entitled to think that they would have put one there if they had had one.

The Court of Appeals opinion they affirmed[11] expressly concedes that pornography violates women in all the ways Indianapolis found it did. The opinion never questioned that pornography is sex discrimination. Interesting enough, the Seventh Circuit, in an opinion by Judge Frank Easterbrook, conceded the issue of objective causation. The only problem was, the harm didn't matter as much as the materials mattered. They are valuable. So the law that prohibited the harm the materials caused was held to be content-based and impermissible discrimination on the basis of viewpoint.

This is a law that gives victims a civil action when they are coerced into pornography, when pornography is forced on them, when they are assaulted because of specific pornography, and when they are subordinated through the trafficking in pornography. Some of us thought that sex discrimination and sexual abuse were against public policy. We defined pornography as the sexually explicit subordination of women through pictures or words that also includes presentations of women being sexually abused. There is a list of the specific acts of sexual abuse. The law covers men, too. We were so careful that practices whose abusiveness some people publicly question—for example, submission, servility, and display—are not covered by the trafficking provision. So we're talking rape, torture, pain, humiliation: we're talking violence against women turned into sex.

Now we are told that pornography, which, granted, does the harm we say it does, this pornography as we define it is protected speech. It has speech value. You can tell it has value as speech because it is so effective in doing the harm that it does.[12] (The passion of this rendition is mine, but the opinion really does say this.) The more harm, the more protection. This is now apparently the law of the First Amendment, at least where harm to women is the rationale. Judge LaDoris Cordell spoke earlier about the different legal standards for high-value and low-value speech, a doctrine that feminists who oppose pornography have always been averse to. But at least it is now clear that whatever the value of pornography is—and it is universally conceded to be low—the value of women is lower.

It is a matter of real interest to me exactly what the viewpoint element in our law is, according to Easterbrook's opinion. My best guess is that our law takes the point of view that women do not enjoy and deserve rape, and he saw that as just one point of view among many. Where do you suppose he got that idea? Another possible rendering is that our law takes the position that women should not be subordinated to men on the basis of sex, that women are or should be equal, and he regards relief to that end as the enforcement of a prohibited viewpoint.

Just what is and is not valuable, is and is not a viewpoint, is and is not against public policy was made even clearer the day after the summary affirmance. In the *Renton* case the Supreme Court revealed the conditions under which pornography can be restricted: it can be zoned beyond the city limits.[13] It can be regulated this way on the basis of its "secondary effects"—which are, guess what, property values. But it cannot be regulated on the basis of its primary effects on the bodies of the women who had to be ground up to make it.

Do you think it makes any difference to the woman who is coerced into pornography or who has just hit the end of this society's chances for women that the product of her exploitation is sold on the other side of the tracks? Does it matter to the molested child or the rape victim that the offender who used the pornography to get himself up or to plan what he would do or to decide what "type" to do it to had to drive across town to get it? It *does* matter to the women who live or work in the neighborhoods into which the pornography is zoned. They pay in increased street harassment, in an atmosphere of terror and contempt for what other neighborhoods gain in keeping their property values up.

Reading the two decisions together, you see the Court doing what it has always done with pornography: making it available in private while decrying it in public. Pretending to be tough on pornography's effects, the *Renton* case still *gives it a place to exist*. Although obscenity is supposed to have such little value that it is not considered speech at all, *Renton* exposes the real bottom line of the First Amendment: the pornography stays. Anyone who doesn't think absolutism has made any progress, check that.

Why is it that obscenity law can exist and our trafficking provision cannot? Why can the law against child pornography exist and not our law against coercion? Why aren't obscenity[14] and child pornography[15] laws viewpoint laws? Obscenity, as Justice Brennan pointed out in his dissent in *Renton,* expresses a viewpoint: sexual mores should be more relaxed, and if they were, sex would look like pornography.[16] Child pornography also presents a viewpoint: sex between adults and children is liberating, fulfilling, fun, and natural for the child. If one is concerned about the government taking a point of view through law, the laws against these things express the state's opposition to these viewpoints, to the extent of making them crimes to express. Why is a time-place-manner distinction all right in *Renton,* and not our forcing provision, which is kind of time-and-place-like and does not provide for actions against the pornographers at all? Why is it all right to make across-the-board, content-based distinctions like obscenity and child pornography, but not our trafficking provision, not our coercion provision?

When do you see a viewpoint as a viewpoint? When you don't agree with it. When is a viewpoint not a viewpoint? When it's yours.[17] What is and is not a viewpoint, much less a prohibited one, is a matter of individual values and social consensus. The reason Judge Easterbrook saw a viewpoint in our law was because he disagrees with it. (I don't mean to personify it, because it isn't at all personal; I mean, it *is* him, personally, but it isn't him only or only him, as a person.) There is real social disagreement as to whether women are or should be subordinated to men. Especially in sex.

His approach obscured the fact that our law is not content-based at all; it is harm-based. A harm is an act, an activity. It is not just a mental event. Coercion is not an image. Force is not a representation. Assault is not a symbol. Trafficking is not simply advocacy. Subordination is an activity, not just a point of view. The problem is, pornography is both theory and practice, both a metaphor for and a means of the subordination of women. The Seventh Circuit allowed the fact that pornography has a theory to obscure the fact that it is a practice, the fact that it is a metaphor to obscure the fact that it is also a means.

I don't want you to misunderstand what I am about to say. Our law comes nowhere near anybody's speech rights,[18] and the literatures of other inequalities do not relate to those inequalities in the same way pornography relates to sexism. But I risk your misunderstanding on both of these points in order to say that there have been serious movements for liberation in this world. This is by contrast with liberal movements. In serious movements for human freedom, speech is serious, both the attempt to get some for those who do not have any and the recognition that the so-called speech of the other side is a form of the practice of the other side. In union struggles, yellow-dog presses are attacked.[19] Abolitionists attacked slave presses.[20] The monarchist press was not tolerated by the revolutionaries who founded this country.[21] When the White Circle League published a racist pamphlet, it was found to violate a criminal law against libeling groups.[22] After World War II the Nazi press was restricted in Germany by law under the aegis of the Allies.[23] Nicaragua considers it "immoral" and contrary to the progress of education and the cultural development of the people to publish, distribute, circulate, exhibit, transmit, or sell materials that, among other things, "stimulate viciousness," "lower human dignity," or to "use women as sexual or commercial objects."[24]

The analogy Norma Ramos mentioned between the fight against pornography to sex equality and the fight against segregation to race equality makes the analogy between the Indianapolis case and *Brown* vs. *Board of Education*[25] evocative to me also. But I think we may be at an even prior point. The Supreme Court just told us that it is a constitutional right to traffic in our flesh, so long as it is done through pictures and words, and a legislature may not give us access to court to contest it. The Indianapolis case is the *Dred Scott*[26] of the women's movement. The Supreme Court told Dred Scott, to the Constitution, you are property. It told women, to the Constitution, you are speech. The struggle against pornography is an abolitionist struggle to establish that just as buying and selling human beings never was anyone's property right, buying and selling women and children is no one's civil liberty.

Notes

1. Isaiah Berlin distinguishes negative from positive freedom. Negative freedom asks the question, "what is the area within which the subject—a person or group of persons—is or should be left to do or be what [he] is able to do or be, without interference from other persons?" Positive freedom asks the question, "what, or who, is the source of control or interference that can determine someone to do, or be, this rather than that?" "Two Concepts of Liberty," in *Four Essays on Liberty* 121–22 (1970). Is it not obvious that if one group is granted the positive freedom to do whatever they want to another group, to determine that the second group will be and do this rather than that, that no amount of negative freedom guaranteed to the second group will make it the equal of the first? The negative state is thus incapable of effective guarantees of rights in any but a just society, which is the society in which they are needed the least.

2. The analysis here is indebted to Andrea Dworkin, "For Men, Freedom of Speech, For Women, Silence Please" in *Take Back the Night: Women on Pornography* 255–58 (Laura Lederer ed. 1982).

3. *But cf.* the words of framer William Livingston, who said, "Liberty of the press means promoting the common good of society, it does not mean unrestraint in writing." Livingston, "Of the Use, Abuse and Liberty of the Press," *Independent Reflector* (1754), quoted in Richard Buel, *The Press and the American Revolution* 69 (1980). Livingston's press was founded "to oppose superstition, bigotry, priestcraft, tyranny, servitude, public mismanagement and dishonesty in office." Quoted in Leonard W. Levy, *Emergence of a Free Press* 138 (1985). Levy, an absolutist, finds the theory that gave rise to the *Independent Reflector* "in fact reactionary if not vicious . . . That a Framer could ever have held such views surprises" at 138.

4. There is a major controversy about the intent of the framers in relation to existing law and values of the colonial period. The controversy is discussed in T. Terrar, "The New Social History and Colonial America's Press Legacy: Tyranny or Freedom?" (1986) (unpublished manuscript).

5. Red Lion Broadcasting Co. v. F.C.C., 395 U.S. 367 (1969). In F.C.C. v. League of Women Voters, 468 U.S. 364 (1984), the Supreme Court hints that it would be receptive to a challenge to the fairness doctrine on the basis that it impedes rather than furthers the values of the First Amendment, 376 n.11, 378 n.12.

6. Schneider v. State, 308 U.S. 147 (1939) (restricting street circulars because of litter is invalid if it is possible to clean them up).

7. Slave codes prohibited teaching slaves or free blacks to read, write, or spell and giving them reading materials and permitting meetings for schooling. Punishments for blacks included whipping; whites caught in the act could be fined and imprisoned

but never whipped. Alabama: *Clay's Digest* 543, Act of 1832, § 10 (crime to teach black to spell, read, or write); North Carolina: *Revised Statutes* ch. 3, §74 (1836–7) (crime to teach slave to read or write, except figures, to give or sell to slave a book or pamphlet); ch. 3, § 27 (slave who receives instruction receives thirty-nine lashes); Georgia: 2 *Cobb's Digest* 1001 (1829) (crime to teach black to read or write); Virginia: "Every assemblage of Negroes for the purpose of instruction in reading or writing shall be an unlawful assembly." *Virginia Code,* §§ 747–48 (1849); South Carolina: meetings including even one person of color "for the purpose of mental instruction in a confined or secret place are declared to be an unlawful meeeting." Police can "break doors" and may lash participants sufficiently to deter them from future such acts. 7 *Statutes of South Carolina* 440 (1800). *See generally* George M. Stroud, *Sketch of the Laws Relating to Slavery* 58–63 (1856, 1968 ed.). The slaves understood that literacy was as fundamental to effective expression as it was to every other benefit of equality: "It seemed to me that if I could learn to read and write, the learning might—nay I really thought it would, point out to me the way to freedom, influence, and real, secure, happiness." Slave narrative quoted in Thomas L. Webber, *Deep Like the Rivers: Education in the Slave Quarter Community* 144 (1978). The Statutes of Louisiana 208 (1852) state: "Whosoever shall make use of language in any public discourse from the bar, the bench, the stage, the pulpit, or in any place whatsoever, or whoever shall make use of language in private discourses or conversations, or shall make use of signs or actions, having a tendency to produce discontent among the free colored population of this state, or to excite insubordination among the slaves, or whosoever shall knowingly be instrumental in bringing into this state any paper, pamphlet or book having such tendency as aforesaid, shall, on conviction thereof before any court of competent jurisdiction, suffer imprisonment at hard labour not less than three years nor more than twenty-one years, or DEATH, at the discretion of the court" at 208.

8.   The best examples are the laws against treason, bribery, conspiracy, threats, blackmail, and libel. Acts can also be expression, but are not necessarily protected as such. *See, e.g.,* Giboney v. Empire Storage & Ins. Co., 336 U.S. 490 (1946) (labor picketing can be enjoined on the ground the First Amendment does not cover "speech or writing used as an integral part of conduct in violation of a valid criminal statute"). Action "is often a method of expression and within the protection of the First Amendment . . ." but "picketing [is] 'free speech plus' [and] can be regulated when it comes to the 'plus' or 'action' side of the protest." Brandenburg v. Ohio, 395 U.S. 444, 455 (1969) (Douglas, J., concurring). *See also* United States v. O'Brien, 391 U.S. 367 (1968) (burning draft card not protected speech as symbolic protest); Street v. New York, 394 U.S. 576 (1969) (burning flag while speaking not punishable because speech is protected even though burning is crime); Spence v. Washington, 418 U.S. 407 (1974) (altering flag is protected speech despite flag desecration statute); Clark v. Committee for Creative Non-Violence, 468 U.S. 288 (1984) (sleeping in park to protest homelessness not protected as expressive conduct when it violates regulation against camping).

9.   Roth v. U.S., 354 U.S. 476, 508–14 ("The first amendment, in prohibitions in terms absolute" at 514); Memoirs v. Massachusetts, 383 U.S. 413, 424–33 (concurring); Miller v. California, 413 U.S. 15, 37–47; Paris Adult Theatres v. Slaton, 413 U.S. 49, 70–73 (1973).

10.   106 S. Ct. 1172 (1986).

11.   American Booksellers v. Hudnut, 771 F.2d 323 (7th Cir. 1985), *aff'd* 106 S. Ct. 1172 (1986).

12.   771 F.2d at 329.

13.   Renton v. Playtime Theatres, 106 S. Ct. 925 (1986).

14.   *E.g.,* Miller v. California, 413 U.S. 15 (1973).

15.   *E.g.,* New York v. Ferber, 458 U.S. 747 (1982).

16.   106 S. Ct. at 933 n.1 (Brennan, J., dissenting).

17.   Laws against rape also express the view that sexual subordination is impermissible,

and this is not considered repressive of thought, although presumably some thought is involved.

18. An erection is not a thought, either, unless one thinks with one's penis.

19. The most celebrated and equivocal example is the prosecution of unionist McNamara brothers for blowing up the virulently anti-union *Los Angeles Times*. The McNamaras pleaded guilty but doubt remains whether they did it. Although the bombing was criticized as inhumane (many people died), needlessly destructive, and instrategic, I found no argument within the movement that the *Times* should not have been attacked because it was "speech." *See* P. Foner, *History of the Labor Movement in the United States*, vol. 5: *The AFL in the Progressive Era, 1910–1915* ch. 1 (1980).

20. Abraham Lincoln ordered "copperhead" (northern pro-slavery) newspapers closed and editors jailed during the Civil War. The postmaster general barred some "copperhead" newspapers from the mail. Abolitionists "threatened, manhandled, or tarred editors, required changes in editorial policy, [and] burned print shops" of pro-slavery presses. Harold L. Nelson, *Freedom of the Press from Hamilton to the Warren Court* xxvi–xxvii, 236–237 (1967).

21. For example, the Sons of Liberty in 1775 issued the following ultimatum to New York printers: "Sir, if you print, or suffer to be printed in your press anything against the rights and liberties of America, or in favor of our inveterate foes, the King, the Ministry and Parliament of Great Britain, death and destruction, ruin and perdition shall be your portion. Signed by Order of the Committee of Tarring and Feathering." Thomas Jones, *History of New York During the Revolutionary War* (E. F. DeLancey ed. 1879), quoted in Levy, note 3 above, at 175.

22. Beauharnais v. Illinois, 343 U.S. 250 (1952).

23. This was particularly true of the American-occupied zone. German publishers were licensed, and those who published materials inconsistent with the American objectives had their licenses revoked. They were kept under surveillance. Americans also imposed school reform and curriculum changes to reeducate German youth against the Nazi ideology. John Gimbel, *The American Occupation of Germany: Politics and the Military (1945–1949)* 246–47 (1968). Positive steps were also taken. American propaganda efforts included radio and television campaigns against the harm of Nazism and attacks on neo-Nazis. Kurt P. Tauber, *Beyond Eagle and Swastika* 434 (1967). The British and American forces denied that they practiced censorship, but destructive criticism of the occupying powers was forbidden. Clara Menck, *A Struggle for Democracy in Germany* 298–99 (Gabriel L. Almon ed. 1965).

24. *La Gaceta-Diario Oficial* 73–75 (Sept. 13, 1979), Ley General Provisional Sobre los Medios de Comunicacion Arto. 3o prohibits materials "que utilicen a la mujer como objeto sexual o comercial" ("that uses women as sexual or commercial objects") Decree No. 48, Aug. 17, 1979, at 74. I make this reference not to hold up this language or this effort as an ideal to be strictly followed, but rather to remind leftists in particular that some efforts that they otherwise take as admirable do (even under conditions very different from those in the United States) consider that the use of women to sell things, as well as prostitution itself, is the opposite of the liberation of women as intended by their revolutions. It is also instructive to notice that an otherwise hard-headed revolutionary government with a lot to worry about does not regard the issue of sexual sale of women as either too unimportant to address or too moralistic for political concern.

25. Brown v. Board of Education, 347 U.S. 483 (1954).

26. Dred Scott v. Sanford, 60 U.S. (19 How.) 393 (1856).

Adrienne Rich

---

from *Of Woman Born: Motherhood as Experience and Institution*

The "repossession by women of [their own] bodies" would radically redefine—and deinstitutionalize—the nature of motherhood so as to effect changes in human society far more profound than the "the seizing of the means of production by workers," writer and teacher Adrienne Rich compellingly argues in this excerpt. Rich has published fifteen volumes of poetry, among them *The Fact of a Doorframe: Poems Selected and New 1950–1984* and *Time's Power: Poems 1985–1988,* as well as the prose works *On Lies, Secrets and Silence, Blood, Bread, and Poetry* and *What Is Found There: Notebooks on Poetry and Politics.*

... there are ways of thinking that we don't know about. Nothing could be more important or precious than that knowledge, however unborn. The sense of urgency, the spiritual restlessness it engenders, cannot be appeased ...
—Susan Sontag, *Styles of Radical Will*

To seek visions, to dream dreams, is essential, and it is also essential to try new ways of living, to make room for serious experimentation, to respect the effort even where it fails. At the same time, in the light of most women's lives as they are now having to be lived, it can seem naive and self-indulgent to spin forth matriarchal utopias, to "demand" that the technologies of contraception and genetics be "turned over" to women (by whom, and under what kinds of effective pressure?); to talk of impressing "unchilded" women into child-care as a political duty, of boycotting patriarchal institutions, of the commune as a solution for child-rearing. Child-care as enforced servitude, or performed out of guilt, has been all too bitter a strain in our history. If women boycott the laboratories and libraries of scientific institutions (to which we have barely begun to gain access) we will not even know what research and technology is vital to the control of our bodies.[1] Certainly the commune, in and of itself, has no special magic for women, any more than has the extended family or the public day-care center. Above all, such measures fail to recognize the full complexity and political significance of the woman's body, the full spectrum of power and powerlessness it represents, of which motherhood is simply one—though a crucial—part.

Furthermore, it can be dangerously simplistic to fix upon "nurturance" as a special strength of women, which need only be released into the larger society to create a new human order. Whatever our organic or developed gift for nurture, it has often been turned into a boomerang. About women political prisoners under torture, Rose Styron writes:

The imagination, the "emotionalism" a woman is classically assigned—the passion she has developed defending her children, the compassion (or insight into human motive and possibility) she has acquired being alert to the needs and demands of her family or community—can make her into a fierce opponent for her tormentors. *It can also make her exceptionally vulnerable* (Emphasis added).[2]

This has been true for women in general under patriarchy, whether our opponents are individual men, the welfare system, the medical and psychoanalytic establishments, or the organized network of drug traffic, pornography, and prostitution. When an individual woman first opposes the institution of motherhood she often has to oppose it in the person of a man, the father of her child, toward whom she may feel love, compassion, friendship, as well as resentment, anger, fear, or guilt. The "maternal" or "nurturant" spirit we want to oppose to rapism and the warrior mentality can prove a liability so long as it remains a lever by which women can be controlled through what is most generous and sensitive in us. Theories of female power and female ascendancy must reckon fully with the ambiguities of our being, and with the continuum of our consciousness, the potentialities for both creative and destructive energy in each of us.

I am convinced that "there are ways of thinking that we don't yet know about." I take those words to mean that many women are *even now* thinking in ways which traditional intellection denies, decries, or is unable to grasp. Thinking is an active, fluid, expanding process; intellection, "knowing" are recapitulations of past processes. In arguing that we have by no means yet explored or understood our biological grounding, the miracle and paradox of the female body and its spiritual and political meanings, I am really asking whether women cannot begin, at last, to *think through the body,* to connect what has been so cruelly disorganized—our great mental capacities, hardly used; our highly developed tactile sense; our genius for close observation; our complicated, pain-enduring, multipleasured physicality.

I know no woman—virgin, mother, lesbian, married, celebate— whether she earns her keep as a housewife, a cocktail waitress, or a scanner of brain waves—for whom her body is not a fundamental problem: its clouded meaning, its fertility, its desire, it's so-called frigidity, its bloody speech, its silences, its changes and mutilations, its rapes and ripenings. There is for the first time today a possibility of converting our physicality into both knowledge and power. Physical motherhood is merely one dimension of our being. We know that the sight of a certain face, the sound of a voice, can stir waves of tenderness in the uterus. From brain to clitoris through vagina to uterus, from tongue to nipples to clitoris, from fingertips to clitoris to brain, from nipples to brain and into the uterus, we are strung with invisible messages of an urgency and restlessness which indeed cannot be appeased, and of a cognitive potentiality that we are only beginning to guess at. We are neither "inner" nor "outer" constructed; our skin is alive with signals; our lives and our deaths are inseparable from the release or blockage of our thinking bodies.

But the fear and hatred of our bodies has often crippled our brains. Some of the most brilliant women of our time are still trying to think from somewhere outside their female bodies—hence they are still merely reproducing old forms of intellection.[3] There is an inexorable connection between every aspect of a woman's being and every other; the scholar reading denies at her peril the blood on the tampon; the welfare mother accepts at her peril the derogation of her intelligence. These are issues of survival, because the woman scholar and the welfare mother are both engaged in fighting for the mere right to exist. Both are "marginal" people in a system founded on the traditional family and its perpetuation.

The physical organization which has meant, for generations of women, unchosen, indentured motherhood, is still a female resource barely touched upon or understood. We have tended either to *become* our bodies—blindly, slavishly, in obedience to male theories about us—or to try to exist in spite of them. "I don't *want* to be the Venus of Willendorf—or the eternal fucking machine." Many women see any appeal to the physical as a denial of mind. We have been perceived for too many centuries as pure Nature, exploited and raped like the earth and the solar system; small wonder if we now long to become Culture: pure spirit, mind. Yet it is precisely this culture and its political institutions which have split us off from itself. In so doing it has also split itself off from life, becoming the death-culture of quantification, abstraction, and the will to power which has reached its most refined destructiveness in this century. It is this culture and politics of abstraction which women are talking of changing, of bringing to accountablity in human terms.

The repossession by women of our bodies will bring far more

essential change to human society than the seizing of the means of production by workers. The female body has been both territory and machine, virgin wilderness to be exploited and asembly-line turning out life. We need to imagine a world in which every woman is the presiding genius of her own body. In such a world women will truly create new life, bringing forth not only children (if and as we choose) but the visions, and the thinking, necessary to sustain, console, and alter human existence—a new relationship to the universe. Sexuality, politics, intelligence, power, motherhood, work, community, intimacy will develop new meanings; thinking itself will be transformed.

This is where we have to begin.

Notes

1. It is, rather, essential that women become well informed about current developments in genetics, cloning, and extrauterine reproduction. A two-pronged approach is needed: just as more women are receiving medical training, while other women are educating themselves and each other as lay persons in the fields of health-care and childbirth, so we need women scientists within the institutions, *and* lay women who are knowledgeably monitoring the types of decisions and research that go on there, and disseminating the information they gather.

2. "The Hidden Women," in *Women Political Prisoners in the USSR,* Ukrainian National Women's League of America, New York, 1975, pp. 3–4.

3. Even Mary Wollstonecraft, viewing with pain the "passive obedience" and physical weakness she saw in the majority of women around her, remarked that she had been "led to imagine that the few extraordinary women who have rushed in eccentrical directions out of the orbit prescribed to their sex, were *male* spirits, confined by mistake to female frames" (A *Vindication of the Rights of Woman,* 1792 [New York: Norton, 1967], p. 70). I am indebted to Barbara Gelpi for drawing this passage to my attention.

Ursula K. Le Guin

from *Dancing at the Edge of the World*
Thoughts on Words, Women, Places
"Is Gender Necessary?
Redux"

Originally written in 1976 and then "reconsidered" in 1987, this essay continues to prod cultural notions of gender and a gendered society as it examines the significance of the novel *The Left Hand of Darkness,* written by Ursula K. Le Guin in 1967. Best known as a writer of science fiction, Le Guin also writes short stories, children's books, poetry and criticism.

The author's headnote follows.

"Is Gender Necessary?" first appeared in Aurora, *that splendid first anthology of science fiction written by women, edited by Susan Anderson and Vonda N. McIntyre. It was later included in* The Language of the Night. *Even then I was getting uncomfortable with some of the statements I made in it, and the discomfort soon became plain disagreement. But those were just the bits that people kept quoting with cries of joy.*

It doesn't seem right or wise to revise an old text severely, as if trying to obliterate it, hiding the evidence that one had to go there to get here. It is rather in the feminist mode to let one's changes of mind, and the processes of change, stand as evidence—and perhaps to remind people that minds that don't change are like clams that don't open. So I here reprint the original essay entire, with a running commentary in bracketed italics. I request and entreat anyone who wishes to quote from this piece henceforth to use or at least include these reconsiderations. And I do very much hope that I don't have to print reconsiderations in 1997, since I'm a bit tired of chastising myself.

In the mid-1960s, the women's movement was just beginning to move again, after a fifty-year halt. There was a groundswell gathering. I felt it, but I didn't know it was a groundswell; I just thought it was something wrong with me. I considered myself a feminist; I didn't see how you could be a thinking woman and not be a feminist; but I had never taken a step beyond the ground gained for us by Emmeline Pankhurst and Virginia Woolf.

[Feminism has enlarged its ground and strengthened its theory and practice immensely, and enduringly, in these past twenty years; but has anyone actually taken a step "beyond" Virginia Woolf? The image, implying an ideal of "progress," is not one I would use now.]

Along about 1967, I began to feel a certain unease, a need to step on a little farther, perhaps, on my own. I began to want to define and understand the meaning of sexuality and the meaning of gender, in my life and in our society. Much had gathered in the unconscious—both personal and collective—which must either be brought up into consciousness or else turn destructive. It was that same need, I think, that had led Beauvoir to write *The Second Sex,* and Friedan to write *The Feminine Mystique,* and that was, at the same time, leading Kate Millett and others to write their books, and to create the new feminism. But I was not a theoretician, a political thinker or activist, or a sociologist. I was and am a fiction writer. The way I did my thinking was to write a novel. That novel, *The Left Hand of Darkness,* is the record of my consciousness, the process of my thinking.

Perhaps, now that we have all *[well, quite a lot of us, anyhow]* moved on to a plane of heightened consciousness about these matters, it might be of some interest to look back on the book, to see what it did, what it tried to do, and what it might have done, insofar as it is a "feminist" *[strike the quotation marks, please]* book. (Let me repeat that last qualification, once. The fact is that the real subject of the book is not feminism or sex or gender or anything of the sort; as far as I can see, it is a book about betrayal and fidelity. That is why one of its two dominant sets of symbols is an extended metaphor of winter, of ice, snow, cold: the winter journey. The rest of this discussion will concern only half, the lesser half, of the book.)

[This parenthesis is overstated; I was feeling defensive, and resentful that critics of the book insisted upon talking only about its "gender problems," as if it were an essay not a novel. "The fact is that the real subject of the book is . . ." This is bluster. I had opened a can of worms and was trying hard to shut it. "The fact is," however, that there are other aspects to the book, which are involved with its sex/gender aspects quite inextricably.]

It takes place on a planet called Gethen, whose human inhabitants differ from us in their sexual physiology. Instead of our continuous sexuality, the Gethenians have an oestrus period, called *kemmer.* When they are not in kemmer, they are sexually inactive and impotent; they are also androgynous. An observer in the book describes the cycle:

In the first phase of kemmer [the individual] remains completely androgynous. Gender, and potency, are not attained in isolation. . . . Yet the sexual impulse is tremendously strong in this phase, controlling the entire personality. . . . When the individual finds a partner in kemmer, hormonal secretion is further stimulated (most importantly by touch—secretion? scent?) until in one partner either a male or female hormonal dominance is established. The genitals engorge or shrink accordingly, foreplay intensifies, and the partner, triggered by the change, takes on the other sexual role (apparently without exception). . . . Normal individuals have no predisposition to either sexual role in kemmer; they do not know whether they will be the male or the female, and have no choice in the matter. . . . The culminant phase of kemmer lasts from two to five days, during which sexual drive and capacity are at maximum. It ends fairly abruptly, and if conception has not taken place, the individual returns to the latent phase and the cycle begins anew. If the individual was in the female role and was impregnated, hormonal activity of course continues, and for the gestation and lactation periods this individual remains female. . . . With the cessation of lactation the female becomes once more a perfect androgyne. No physiological habit is established, and the mother of several children may be the father of several more.

Why did I invent these peculiar people? Not just so that the book could contain, halfway through it, the sentence "The king was pregnant"—though I admit that I am fond of that sentence. Not, certainly not, to propose Gethen as a model for humanity. I am not in favor of genetic alteration of the human organism—not at our present level of understanding. I was not recommending the Gethenian sexual setup: I was using it. It was a heuristic device, a thought-experiment. Physicists often do thought-experiments. Einstein shoots a light ray through a moving elevator; Schrödinger puts a cat in a box. There is no elevator, no cat, no box. The experiment is performed, the question is asked, in the mind. Einstein's elevator, Schrödinger's cat, my Gethenians, are simply a way of thinking. They are questions, not answers; process, not stasis. One of the essential functions of science fiction, I think, is precisely this kind of question-asking: reversals of a habitual way of thinking, metaphors for what our language has no words for as yet, experiments in imagination.

The subject of my experiment, then, was something like this: Because of our lifelong social conditioning, it is hard for us to see clearly what, besides purely physiological form and function, truly differentiates men and women. Are there real differences in temperament, capacity, talent, psychic processes, etc.? If so, what are they? Only comparative ethnology offers, so far, any solid evidence on the matter, and the evidence is incomplete and often contradictory. The only going social experiments that are truly relevant are the kibbutzim and the Chinese communes, and they too are inconclusive—and hard to get unbiased information about. How to find out? Well, one can always put a cat in a box. One can send an imaginary, but conventional, indeed rather stuffy, young man from Earth into an imaginary culture which is totally free of sex roles because there is no, absolutely no, physiological sex distinction. I eliminated gender, to find out what was left. Whatever was left would be, presumably, simply human. It would define the area that is shared by men and women alike.

I still think that this was a rather neat idea. But as an experiment, it was messy. All results were uncertain; a repetition of the experiment by someone else, or by myself seven years later, would probably give quite different results. *[Strike the word "probably" and replace it with "certainly."]* Scientifically, this is most disreputable. That's all right; I am not a scientist. I play the game where the rules keep changing.

Among these dubious and uncertain results, achieved as I thought, and wrote, and wrote, and thought, about my imaginary people, three appear rather interesting to me.

First: the absence of war. In the thirteen thousand years of recorded history on Gethen, there has not been a war. The people seem to be as quarrelsome, competitive, and aggressive as we are; they have fights, murders, assassinations, feuds, forays, and so on. But there have been no great invasions by peoples on the move, like the Mongols in Asia or the Whites in the New World: partly because Gethenian populations seem to remain stable in size, they do not move in large masses, or rapidly. Their migrations have been slow, no one generation going very far. They have no nomadic peoples, and no societies that live by expansion and aggression against other societies. Nor have they formed large, hierarchically governed nation-states, the mobilizable entity that is the essential factor in modern war. The basic social unit all over the planet is a group of two hundred to eight hundred people, called a *hearth,* a structure founded less on economic convenience than on sexual necessity (there must be others in kemmer at the same time), and therefore more tribal than urban in nature, though overlaid and interwoven with a later urban pattern. The hearth tends to be communal, independent, and somewhat introverted. Rivalries between hearths, as between individuals, are channeled into a socially approved form of aggression called *shifgrethor,* a conflict without physical violence, involving one-upsmanship, the saving and losing of face—conflict ritualized, stylized, controlled. When shifgrethor breaks down there may be physical violence, but it does not become mass violence, remaining limited, personal. The active group remains small. The dispersive trend is as strong as the cohesive. Historically, when hearths gathered into a nation for economic reasons, the cellular pattern still dominated the centralized one. There might be a king and a parliament, but authority was not enforced so much by might as by the use of shifgrethor and intrigue, and was accepted as custom, without appeal to patriarchal ideals of divine right, patriotic duty, etc. Ritual and parade were far more effective agents of order than armies or police. Class structure was flexible and open; the value of the social hierarchy was less economic than aesthetic, and there was no great gap between rich and poor. There was no slavery or servitude. Nobody owned anybody. There were no chattels. Economic organization was rather communistic or syndicalistic than capitalistic, and was seldom highly centralized.

During the time span of the novel, however, all this is changing. One of the two large nations of the planet is becoming a genuine nation-state, complete with patriotism and bureaucracy. It has achieved state capitalism and the centralization of power, authoritarian government, and a secret police; and it is on the verge of achieving the world's first war.

Why did I present the first picture, and show it in the process of changing to a different one? I am not sure. I think it is because I was trying to show a balance—and the delicacy of a balance. To me the "female principle" is, or at least historically has been, basically anarchic. It values order without constraint, rule by custom not by force. It has been the male who enforces order, who constructs power structures, who makes, enforces, and breaks laws. On Gethen, these two principles are in balance: the decentralizing against the centralizing, the flexible against the rigid, the circular against the linear. But balance is a precarious state, and at the moment of the novel the balance, which had leaned toward the "feminine," is tipping the other way.

[*At the very inception of the whole book, I was interested in writ-*

ing a novel about people in a society that had never had a war.
That came first. The androgyny came second. (Cause and effect?
Effect and cause?)

I would now write this paragraph this way: ... *The "female*
principle" has historically been anarchic; that is, anarchy has histor-
ically been identified as female. The domain allotted to women—"the
family," for example—is the area of order without coercion, rule by
custom not by force. Men have reserved the structures of social
power to themselves (and those few women whom they admit to it
on male terms, such as queens, prime ministers); men make the wars
and peaces, men make, enforce, and break the laws. On Gethen, the
two polarities we perceive through our cultural conditioning as male
and female are neither, and are in balance: consensus and authority,
decentralizing with centralizing, flexible with rigid, circular with lin-
ear, hierarchy with network. But it is not a motionless balance, there
being no such thing in life, and at the moment of the novel, it is
wobbling perilously.]

Second: the absence of exploitation. The Gethenians do not rape
their world. They have developed a high technology, heavy industry,
automobiles, radios, explosives, etc., but they have done so very
slowly, absorbing their technology rather than letting it overwhelm
them. They have no myth of Progress at all. Their calendar calls the
current year always the Year One, and they count backward and
forward from that.

In this, it seems that what I was after again was a balance: the
driving linearity of the "male," the pushing forward to the limit, the
logicality that admits no boundary—and the circularity of the "female," the valuing of patience, ripeness, practicality, livableness. A
model for this balance, of course, exists on Earth: Chinese civilization
over the past six millennia. (I did not know when I wrote the book
that the parallel extends even to the calendar; the Chinese historically
never had a linear dating system such as the one that starts with the
birth of Christ.)

[A better model might be some of the pre-Conquest cultures of
the Americas, though not those hierarchical and imperialistic ones
approvingly termed, by our hierarchical and imperialistic standards,
"high." The trouble with the Chinese model is that their civilization
instituted and practiced male domination as thoroughly as the other
"high" civilizations. I was thinking of a Taoist ideal, not of such
practices as bride-selling and foot-binding, which we are trained to

consider unimportant, nor of the deep misogyny of Chinese culture, which we are trained to consider normal.]

Third: the absence of sexuality as a continuous social factor. For four-fifths of the month, a Gethenian's sexuality plays no part at all in his social life (unless he's pregnant); for the other one-fifth, it dominates him absolutely. In kemmer, one must have a partner, it is imperative. (Have you ever lived in a small apartment with a tabby-cat in heat?) Gethenian society fully accepts this imperative. When a Gethenian has to make love, he does make love, and everybody expects him to, and approves of it.

[I would now write this paragraph this way: . . . For four-fifths of the month, sexuality plays no part at all in a Gethenian's social behavior; for the other one-fifth, it controls behavior absolutely. In kemmer, one must have a partner, it is imperative. (Have you ever lived in a small apartment with a tabby-cat in heat?) Gethenian society fully accepts this imperative. When Gethenians have to make love, they do make love, and everybody else expects it and approves of it.]

But still, human beings are human beings, not cats. Despite our continuous sexuality and our intense self-domestication (domesticated animals tend to be promiscuous, wild animals pair-bonding, familial, or tribal in their mating), we are very seldom truly promiscuous. We do have rape, to be sure—no other animal has equaled us there. We have mass rape, when an army (male, of course) invades; we have prostitution, promiscuity controlled by economics; and sometimes ritual abreactive promiscuity controlled by religion; but in general we seem to avoid genuine license. At most we award it as a prize to the Alpha Male, in certain situations; it is scarcely ever permitted to the female without social penalty. It would seem, perhaps, that the mature human being, male or female, is not satisfied by sexual gratification without psychic involvement, and in fact may be *afraid of it,* to judge by the tremendous variety of social, legal, and religious controls and sanctions exerted over it in all human societies. Sex is a great mana, and therefore the immature society, or psyche, sets great taboos about it. The maturer culture, or psyche, can integrate these taboos or laws into an internal ethical code, which, while allowing great freedom, does not permit the treatment of another person as an object. But, however irrational or rational, there is always a code.

Because the Gethenians cannot have sexual intercourse unless both partners are willing, because they cannot rape or be raped, I figured that they would have less fear and guilt about sex than we tend to have; but still it is a problem for them, in some ways more than for us, because of the extreme, explosive, imperative quality of the oestrous phase. Their society would have to control it, though it might move more easily than we from the taboo stage to the ethical stage. So the basic arrangement, I found, in every Gethenian community, is that of the kemmerhouse, which is open to anyone in kemmer, native or stranger, so that he can find a partner *[read: so that they can find sexual partners]*. Then there are various customary (not legal) institutions, such as the kemmering group, a group who choose to come together during kemmer as a regular thing; this is like the primate tribe, or group marriage. Or there is the possibility of vowing kemmering, which is marriage, pair-bonding for life, a personal commitment without legal sanction. Such commitments have intense moral and psychic significance, but they are not controlled by Church or State. Finally, there are two forbidden acts, which might be taboo or illegal or simply considered contemptible, depending on which of the regions of Gethen you are in: first, you don't pair off with a relative of a different generation (one who might be your own parent or child); second, you may mate, but not vow kemmering, with your own sibling. These are the old incest prohibitions. They are so general among us—and with good cause, I think, not so much genetic as psychological—that they seemed likely to be equally valid on Gethen.

These three "results," then, of my experiment, I feel were fairly clearly and successfully worked out, though there is nothing definitive about them.

In other areas where I might have pressed for at least such plausible results, I see now a failure to think things through, or to express them clearly. For example, I think I took the easy way in using such familiar governmental structures as a feudal monarchy and a modern-style bureaucracy for the two Gethenian countries that are the scene of the novel. I doubt that Gethenian governments, rising out of the cellular hearth, would resemble any of our own so closely. They might be better, they might be worse, but they would certainly be different.

I regret even more certain timidities or ineptnesses I showed in following up the psychic implications of Gethenian physiology. Just for example, I wish I had known Jung's work when I wrote the book: so that I could have decided whether a Gethenian had *no* animus or anima, or *both*, or an animum.... *[For another example (and Jung wouldn't have helped with this, more likely hindered) I quite unnecessarily locked the Gethenians into heterosexuality. It is a naively pragmatic view of sex that insists that sexual partners must be of opposite sex! In any kemmer-house homosexual practice would, of course, be possible and acceptable and welcomed—but I never thought to explore this option; and the omission, alas, implies that sexuality is heterosexuality. I regret this very much.]* But the central failure in this area comes up in the frequent criticism I receive, that the Gethenians seem like *men*, instead of menwomen.

This rises in part from the choice of pronoun. I call Gethenians "he" because I utterly refuse to mangle English by inventing a pronoun for "he/she." *[This "utter refusal" of 1968 restated in 1976 collapsed, utterly, within a couple of years more. I still dislike invented pronouns, but I now dislike them less than the so-called generic pronouns he/him/his, which does in fact exclude women from discourse; and which, was an invention of male grammarians, for until the sixteenth century the English generic singular pronoun was they/them/their, as it still is in English and American colloquial speech. It should be restored to the written language, and let the pedants and pundits squeak and gibber in the streets. In a screenplay of* The Left Hand of Darkness *written in 1985, I referred to Gethenians not pregnant or in kemmer by the invented pronouns a/un/a's, modeled on a British dialect. These would drive the reader mad in print, I suppose; but I have read parts of the book aloud using them, and the audience was perfectly happy, except that they pointed out that the subject pronoun, "a" pronounced "uh" [ə], sounds too much like "I" said with a southern accent.]* "He" is the generic pronoun, damn it, in English. (I envy the Japanese, who, I am told, do have a he/she pronoun.) But I do not consider this really very important. *[I now consider it very important.]* The pronouns wouldn't matter at all if I had been cleverer at *showing* the "female" component of the Gethenian characters in *action*. *[If I had realized how the pronouns I used shaped, directed, controlled my own thinking, I might have been "cleverer."]* Unfortunately, the plot and structure that arose as I worked the book out cast the Gethenian protagonist, Estraven, almost exclusively in roles that we are culturally conditioned to perceive as "male"—a prime minister (it takes more than even Golda Meir and Indira Gandhi to break a stereotype), a political schemer, a fugitive, a prison-breaker, a sledge-hauler. . . . I think I did this because I was privately delighted at watching, not a man, but a manwoman, do all these things, and do them with considerable skill and flair. But, for the reader, I left out too much. One does not see Estraven as a mother, with his children *[strike "his"]*, in any role that we automatically perceive as "female": and therefore, we tend to see him as a man *[place "him" in quotation marks, please]*. This is a real flaw in the book, and I can only be very grateful to those readers, men and women, whose willingness to participate in the experiment led them to fill in that omission with the work of their own imagination, and to see Estraven as I saw him *[read: as I did]*, as man and woman, familiar and different, alien and utterly human.

It seems to be men, more often than women, who thus complete my work for me: I think because men are often more willing to identify as they read with poor, confused, defensive Genly, the Earthman, and therefore to participate in his painful and gradual discovery of love.

[I now see it thus: Men were inclined to be satisfied with the book, which allowed them a safe trip into androgyny and back, from a conventionally male viewpoint. But many women wanted it to go further, to dare more, to explore androgyny from a woman's point of view as well as a man's. In fact, it does so, in that it was written by a woman. But this is admitted directly only in the chapter "The Question of Sex," the only voice of a woman in the book. I think women were justified in asking more courage of me and a more rigorous thinking-through of implications.]

Finally, the question arises, Is the book a Utopia? It seems to me that it is quite clearly not; it poses no *practicable* alternative to contemporary society, since it is based on an imaginary, radical change in human anatomy. All it tries to do is open up an alternative viewpoint, to widen the imagination, without making any very definite suggestions as to what might be seen from that new viewpoint. The most it says is, I think, something like this: If we were socially ambisexual, if men and women were completely and genuinely equal in their social roles, equal legally and economically, equal in freedom, in responsibility, and in self-esteem, then society would be a very different thing. What our problems might be, God knows; I only know we would have them. But it seems likely that our central problem would not be the one it is now: the problem of exploitation—exploitation of the woman, of the weak, of the earth. Our curse is alienation, the separation of yang from yin *[and the moralization of yang as good, of yin as bad]*. Instead of a search for balance and integration, there is a struggle for dominance. Divisions are insisted upon, interdependence is denied. The dualism of value that destroys us, the dualism of superior/inferior, ruler/ruled, owner/owned, user/used, might give way to what seems to me, from here, a much healthier, sounder, more promising modality of integration and integrity.

Cynthia Enloe

from *Bananas, Beaches & Bases*
Making Feminist Sense of International Politics
"Gender Makes the World Go Round"

Reinterpretation is a political act, and Cynthia Enloe invites women to share in it by reexamining history and international politics in terms of their particular experience. A professor at Clark University in Massachusetts, Enloe is the author of *Ethnic Soldiers: State Security in Divided Societies, Ethnic Conflict and Political Development, Comparative Politics of Pollution* and *Does Khaki Become You? The Militarization of Women's Lives.*

Ambassadors cabling their home ministries, legislators passing laws to restrict foreign imports, bank executives negotiating overseas loans, soldiers landing on foreign hillsides—these are some of the sites from which one can watch the international political system being made. But if we employ only the conventional, ungendered compass to chart international politics, we are likely to end up mapping a landscape peopled only by men, most élite men. The real landscape of international politics is less exclusively male.

A European woman decides to take her holiday in Jamaica because the weather is warm, it is cheap and safe for tourists. In choosing this form of pleasure, she is playing her part in creating the current international political system. She is helping the Jamaican government earn badly needed foreign currency to repay overseas debts. She is transforming "chambermaid" into a major job category. And, unwittingly, if she travels on holiday with a white man, she may make some Jamaican men, seeing every day the privileges—economic and sexual—garnered by white men, feel humiliated and so nourish nationalist identities rooted in injured masculinity.

A school teacher plans a lesson around the life of Pocahontas, the brave Powhantan "princess" who saved Captain John Smith from execution at Jamestown and so cleared the way for English colonization of America. The students come away from the lesson believing the convenient myth that local women are likely to be charmed by their own people's conquerors.

In the 1930s Hollywood moguls turned Brazilian singer Carmen Miranda into an American movie star. They were trying to aid President Franklin Roosevelt's efforts to promote friendlier relations between the US and Latin America. When United Fruit executives then drew on Carmen Miranda's popular Latinized female image to create a logo for their imported bananas, they were trying to construct a new, intimate relationship between American housewives and a multinational plantation company. With her famous fruited hats and vivacious screen presence, Carmen Miranda was used by American men to reshape international relations. Carmen Miranda alerts us to the fact that it would be a mistake to confine an investigation of regional politics or international agribusiness to male foreign-policy officials, male company executives, and male plantation workers. Omitting sexualized images, women as consumers and women as agribusiness workers, leaves us with a political analysis that is incomplete, even naïve.

When a British soldier on leave from duties in Belize or West Germany decides that he can't tolerate his friends' continuous razzing about being "queer" and so finally joins them in a visit to a local brothel in order to be "one of the boys," he is shaping power relations between the British military and the society it is supposed to be protecting. He is also reinforcing one of the crucial bulwarks—masculinity—which permits the British government to use a military force to carry out its foreign policy among its former colonies and within NATO. Military politics, which occupy such a large part of international politics today, require military bases. Bases are artificial societies created out of unequal relations between men and women of different races and classes.

The woman tourist, the Jamaican chambermaid, Carmen Miranda, the American housewife, the British soldier and Belize prostitute are all dancing an intricate international minuet.

But they aren't all in a position to call the tune. Each has been used by the makers of the international political system, but some are more complicit and better rewarded than others. A poor woman who has been deprived of literacy (especially in the language of the ruling group), bank credit, and arable land is likely to find that the intrusions of foreign governments and companies in her daily life exacerbate, not relieve, those burdens. The woman tourist may not be Henry Kissinger, but she is far removed from the daily realities confronting the Jamaican woman who is changing her sheets. The American housewife who buys United Fruit bananas because the "Chiquita" logo gives her a sense of confidence in the product may not be Margaret Thatcher, but the problems she confronts as a woman are less acute than those facing the Latin American fruit vendor making a living on the streets.

Power infuses all international relationships. Most of us, understandably, would prefer to think that our attraction to a certain food company's marketing logo is a cultural, not a political act. We would like to imagine that going on holiday to Bermuda rather than Grenada is merely a social, even aesthetic matter, not a question of politics. But in these last decades of the twentieth century, that unfortunately isn't so. Company logos are designed to nourish certain presumptions we have about different cultures; usually they reinforce global hierarchies between countries. Similarly, tourism has become a business that is maintaining dozens of governments. Power, not simply taste, is at work here. Ignoring women on the landscape of international politics perpetuates the notion that certain power relations are merely a matter of taste and culture. Paying serious attention to women can expose how *much* power it takes to maintain the international political system in its present form.

American popular culture today demands that any political idea worth its salt should fit on a bumper sticker. A feminist theory bumper sticker might say, "Nothing is natural—well, almost nothing." As one learns to look at this world through feminist eyes, one learns to ask whether anything that passes for inevitable, inherent, "traditional," or biological has in fact been *made*. One begins to ask how all sorts of things have been made—a treeless landscape, a rifle-wielding police force, the "Irishman joke," an all-women typing pool. Asking how something has been made implies that it has been made by someone. Suddenly there are clues to trace; there is also blame, credit, and responsibility to apportion, not just at the start but at each point along the way.

The presumption that something that gives shape to how we live with one another is inevitable, a "given," is hard to dislodge. It seems easier to imagine that something oozes up from an indeterminate past, that it has never been deliberately concocted, does not need to be maintained, that it's just there. But if the treeless landscape or all-women typing pool can be shown to be the result of someone's decision and has to be perpetuated, then it is possible to imagine alternatives. "What if . . . ?" can be a radical question.

Conventionally both masculinity and femininity have been treated as "natural," not created. Today, however, there is mounting evidence that they are packages of expectations that have been created through specific decisions by specific people. We are also coming to realize that the traditional concepts of masculinity and femininity have been surprisingly hard to perpetuate: it has required the daily exercise of power—domestic power, national power, and, as we will see, international power.

So far feminist analysis has had little impact on international politics. Foreign-policy commentators and decision-makers seem particularly confident in dismissing feminist ideas. Rare is the professional commentator on international politics who takes women's experiences seriously. Women's experiences—of war, marriage, trade, travel, factory work—are relegated to the "human interest" column. Women's roles in creating and sustaining international politics have been treated as if they were "natural" and thus not worthy of investigation. Consequently, how the conduct of international politics has *depended* on men's control of women has been left unexamined. This has meant that those wielding influence over foreign policy have escaped responsibility for how women have been affected by international politics.

Perhaps international politics has been impervious to feminist ideas precisely because for so many centuries in so many cultures it has been thought of as a typically "masculine" sphere of life. Only men, not women or children, have been imagined capable of the sort of public decisiveness international politics is presumed to require. Foreign affairs are written about with a total disregard for feminist revelations about how power depends on sustaining notions about masculinity and femininity. Local housing officials, the assumption goes, may have to take women's experiences into account now and then. Social workers may have to pay some attention to feminist theorizing about poverty. Trade-union leaders and economists have to give at least a nod in the direction of feminist explanations of wage inequalities. Yet officials making international policy and their professional critics are freed from even a token consideration of women's experiences and feminist understandings of those experiences. . . .

By taking women's experiences of international politics seriously, I think we can acquire a more realistic understanding of how international politics actually "works." We may also increase women's confidence in using their own experiences and knowledge as the basis for making sense of the sprawling, abstract structure known as "the international political economy." Women should no longer have to disguise their feminist curiosity when they speak up on issues of international significance.

Even women who have learned how crucial it is to always ask feminist questions—about welfare, science, bus routes, police procedures—have found it hard to ask feminist questions in the midst of a discussion about the international implications of Soviet *perestroika* or Britain's trade policies in the European Economic Community. We are made to feel silly. Many women find it tempting to build up credibility in this still-masculinized area of political discussion by lowering their voices an octave, adjusting their body postures and demonstrating that they can talk "boy's talk" as well as their male colleagues. One result of women not being able to speak out is that we may have an inaccurate understanding of how power relations between countries are created and perpetuated. Silence has made us dumb.

Relations between governments involve the workings of at least two societies—sometimes twenty. Thinking about international politics is most meaningful when it derives from contact with the diverse values, anxieties, and memories of people in those societies. Yet such access is itself gendered. As a British woman explained at the first meeting of the European Forum of Socialist Feminists, "In this world it is men who do the traveling. They are so much more mobile, have so many more forums than women do—military, financial, they even have spy rings! Whereas it's rare for women to have any kind of international forum, organized by and for us."[1]

So when women do manage to get together at their own meetings—not just in caucuses of other people's meetings—they usually become absorbed in making comparisons. In international forums women today are comparing how racism and class barriers divide women in their respective societies. We are comparing different explanations for the persistence of sexism and strategies for ending that sexism, but it is difficult to get the chance to work together to create a feminist description of the larger international frameworks that link women. For instance, when groups of women from several countries in Europe meet, do they try to hammer out a feminist analysis of "Europe," or use their international comparisons as the basis for a fresh explanation of the political workings of NATO and the European Community? Usually they don't have an opportunity to do so. As a result, international politics remains relatively untouched by feminist thought.[2]

It's difficult to imagine just what feminist questioning would sound like in the area of international politics. Some women have come to believe that there is a fundamental difference between men and women. "Virtually everyone at the top of the foreign-policy bureaucracies is male," they argue, "so how could the outcome be other than violent international conflict?" That is, men are men, and men seem almost inherently prone to violence; so violence is bound to come about if men are allowed to dominate international politics. At times this sweeping assertion has the unsettling ring of truth. There's scarcely a woman who on a dark day hasn't had a suspicion this just might be so. Yet most of the women from various cultures who have created the theories and practices which add up to feminism have not found this "essentialist" argument convincing. Digging into the past and present has made them reluctant to accept explanations that rest on an assertion that men and women are inherently different.

Men trying to invalidate any discussion of gender in international politics tend to quote a litany of militaristic women leaders: "Well, if you think it's men who are causing all the international violence, what about Margaret Thatcher, Indira Gandhi, and Jeanne Kirkpatrick?" Most women—or men—who have been treating feminist analyses seriously have little trouble in responding to this now ritualistic jibe. It's quite clear to them that a woman isn't inherently or irreversibly anti-militaristic or anti-authoritarian. It's not a matter of her chromosomes or her menstrual cycle. It's a matter of social processes and structures that have been created and sustained over the generations—sometimes coercively—to keep most women out of any political position with influence over state force. On occasion, élite men *may* let in a woman here or a woman there, but these women aren't randomly selected.

Most of the time we scarcely notice that governments look like men's clubs. We see a photo of members of the Soviet Union's Politburo, or the US Cabinet's sub-committee on national security, of negotiators at a Geneva textile bargaining session, and it's easy to miss the fact that all the people in those photographs are men. One of the most useful functions that Margaret Thatcher has served is to break through our numbness. When Margaret Thatcher stood in Venice with Mitterand, Nakasone, Reagan, and the other heads of state, we suddenly noticed that everyone else was male. One woman in a photo makes it harder to ignore that the men are men.

However, when a woman is let in by the men who control the political élite it usually is precisely because that woman has learned the lessons of masculinized political behavior well enough not to threaten male political privilege. Indeed she may even entrench that privilege, for when a Margaret Thatcher or Jeanne Kirkpatrick uses her state office to foment international conflict, that conflict looks less man-made, more people-made, and thus more legitimate and harder to reverse.

Still, being able to counter the "What about Margaret Thatcher?" taunt isn't by itself a satisfactory basis for a full feminist analysis of international politics. We have to push further, open up new political terrain, listen carefully to new voices.

A fictional James Bond may have an energetic sex life, but neither sexuality nor notions of manhood nor roles of women are taken seriously by most commentators in the "real" world of power relations between societies and their governments. What really matters, conventional international observers imply, are money, guns, and the personalities of leaders—of the men who make up the political élite. The processes holding sway in most societies have been designed so that it is mainly men who have the opportunities to accumulate money, control weaponry, and become public personalities. As a consequence, any investigation that treats money, guns, and personalities as the key ingredients in relations between societies is almost guaranteed to obliterate women from the picture.

WHERE ARE THE WOMEN?
CLUES FROM THE IRAN/CONTRA AFFAIR

In July 1987 I turn on my television to watch the congressional hearings on the Iran/Contra affair. Senior members of the Reagan administration are accused of selling weapons to the Iranian government and funneling the proceeds to the anti-Sandinista rebels in Nicaragua in violation of congressional policy. All of the congressional representatives sitting at their tiers of desks under the media's bright lights are men. All but one of the congressional committees' lawyers asking questions are men. All but two of the scores of witnesses subpoenaed to answer their questions are men. All of their attorneys are men. All of the men have been told that dark blue suits and red ties look best on television. Everyone wears a dark suit and a red tie.

The Iran/Contra hearings are heralded as the event of the decade in international politics. Now we, the ordinary folk, are going to see how foreign policy actually gets made. Some of my friends become hooked on the congressional hearings: watching or listening from morning to evening, arranging their work and social schedules so as not to miss a word. In Britain, Canada, and Australia TV viewers see excerpts every evening. As much as Europe's endless drizzle, the Iran/Contra hearings seem to define the summer of 1987. Information from the hearings is woven into popular culture. There are "instant books," songs, and jokes, "I luv Ollie" T-shirts, even Ollie North and Betsy North haircuts.

Women do appear during the hearings, though their appearances confirm rather than disturb the implied naturalness of the otherwise all-male cast. Maybe it's because all the women captured by the media's eye are so marginalized.

Ellen Garwood is one of the few women called to the witness table. She is a wealthy conservative who has donated over $2 million to the Contras after being appealed to by Colonel North and other American Contra fund raisers. Congressmen and their attorneys ask her about how her donation was solicited. They aren't interested in her views on US foreign policy. She is not a retired general or a former CIA agent. A public opinion survey comes out at about this time showing that American women are signficantly less enthusiastic about US aid to the Contras than are American men, especially American white men.[3] But such revelations do not prompt any of the legislators to ask Ellen Garwood for her foreign policy ideas.

Women appear so infrequently that their very appearance in any authoritative role becomes "news." One day a woman assistant-attorney for the congressional committee appears on TV. She asks a minor witness questions. Feminist viewers sit up and take notice. One viewer counts seven young women sitting on the chairs arranged awkwardly just behind the congressmen. They don't speak in public. They are staff aides, ready to serve their male bosses.

Men comprise the majority of the media people assigned to tell us what each day's revelations "mean." The women reporters covering the hearings for radio and television do take extra care with their gender pronouns, yet shy away from posing any feminist questions. They haven't climbed this high on the news media ladder by questioning how masculinity and femininity might be shaping foreign policy. They must take care to look feminine while still sounding as though gender were irrelevant to their commentary.[4]

The one woman witness who becomes front-page news is Fawn Hall. She is the twenty-seven-year-old who worked in the National Security Council as civil-service secretary to Oliver North and who admits assisting her boss in shredding important government documents. Fawn Hall is routinely described, even by the most low-key media commentators, as "the beautiful Fawn Hall." It's as if Fawn Hall is meant to represent the feminine side of High Politics of the 1980s: worldly, stylish, exciting, sexy. Beauty, secrecy, and state power: they all enhance one another. In the élite politics of the present era, the "beautiful secretary," the "handsome, can-do military officer," and the bureaucratic shredding machine make an almost irresistible combination.[5]

There are at least two sorts of feminized beauty, however: the revealed and the hidden. Fawn Hall is set up as beauty revealed. She stands in stark contrast to the popularly constructed image of beauty hidden: the veiled Muslim woman. Until it began selling weapons to Iran, the Reagan administration liked to emphasize the Iranian regime's wrong-headed regressiveness by pointing to its anti-modern confinement of women. Reagan aides thought their arms sales were giving them access to a moderate "second channel" in the Teheran political élite. Does the Iranian "second channel" insist his secretary wear a veil? I try to imagine what Fawn Hall and the "second channel's" secretary, if they ever had a chance to meet, would find they had in common, as government secretaries to male bosses carrying out secret operations.

Some Republicans deem Fawn Hall worthy of imitation, if not emulation. In Arkansas Republican party activists hold a gathering to celebrate Oliver North with " 'Ollie Dogs' on the grill, tough-talking T-shirts, water melons, and 95° heat," according to the press report. There is also a Fawn Hall look-alike contest. Women entering the contest have to perform dramatic readings of Fawn Hall's congressional testimony and act her feeding documents into a paper shredder. The winner is sixteen-year-old Renee Kumpee, who, when asked about her attitude to Oliver North, replies, "I like him OK."[6]

Women supply most of the clerical labor force that has made the complex communications, money transfers, and arms shipments possible. They handle the procedures and technology, and more importantly, they provide many male officials with on-the-job encouragement. In today's international political system, large bureaucracies are vehicles for making, implementing, and remembering decisions. Since the deliberate feminization of clerical work in the early twentieth century, every government has required women to acquire certain skills and attitudes towards their work, their superiors, and themselves. Even in small states without the huge bureaucratic machines the public agencies rely on women for their smooth running. If secretaries went out on strike, foreign affairs might grind to a standstill. Without women's willingness to fill these positions in acceptably feminine ways, many men in posts of international influence might be less able to convince themselves of their own rationality, courage, and seriousness.

Other Washington secretaries felt ambivalent toward Fawn Hall. They resented the media for treating Fawn Hall as the quintessential government secretary. "I guess the media wouldn't be making such a big deal out of it if she had been fifty years old and not blond." Still, they also saw Fawn Hall's dilemma as their own. "You develop personal relationships when you work in a high-pressure operation like that . . . She was more than a receptionist or a typist, and she was expected to keep things confidential." Patricia Holmes, a black woman working as a secretary in the Department of the Interior, summed up many Washington secretaries' feelings: Fawn Hall was caught "between a rock and a hard place."[7]

Each woman who appears in person during the Iran/Contra proceedings is considered peripheral to the "real" political story. None of their stories is interpreted in a way that could transform the masculinized meaning of complex international political relationships. Most of us see them as marginal characters who simply add "color" to the all-male, blue-suited, red-tied political proceedings.

Several of the male witnesses assure their congressional interrogators that they took their state jobs so seriously that they didn't tell "even their wives" about the secrets they were guarding. On the other hand, they expected to receive from their wives an automatic stamp of moral approval. This is the kind of marriage on which the national-security state depends.

Thousands of women today tailor their marriages to fit the peculiar demands of states operating in a trust-starved international system. Some of those women are married to men who work as national-security advisors; others have husbands who are civilian weapons-engineers working on classified contracts; still others are married to foreign-service careerists. Most of these men would not be deemed trustworthy if they were not in "stable" marriages. Being a reliable husband and a man the state can trust with its secrets appear to be connected.

And yet it is precisely that elevation to a position of state confidence which can shake the foundations of a marriage. Patriotic marriages may serve the husbands, giving them a greater sense of public importance and less of a sense of guilt for damaging the lives of people in other countries. And they serve the national-security state. But they don't necessarily provide the women in those marriages with satisfaction or self-esteem. Typically, it is left up to the wife to cope with the tensions and disappointments. She may respond by trying to cultivate interests of her own outside her marriage, investing her relationship with her distracted husband with less importance than she once did. Or she may continue to see her relationship with her husband as her most important friendship, but adjust her notion of it so that it becomes a marriage of unequals: she will continue to confide in him all her hopes and worries, while resigning herself to hearing from him only what is "unclassified." In such cases some women express admiration for their husbands' patriotism, a patriotism they believe, as wives, they cannot match. This is the stance taken by Betsy North. She is praised. Her haircut becomes the new fashion.

Marriages between élite men and patriotic wives are a building block holding up the international political system. It can continue to work the way it now does, dependent on secrecy, risk-taking, and state loyalty, only if men can convince women to accept the sorts of marriages that not only sustain, but also legitimize, that system. And it isn't just marriages at the pinnacles of power that must be made to fit. As we will see, marriages up and down the international pyramid can jeopardize power relations between governments if the women refuse to play their parts. They must be willing to see their husbands leave home for long periods of time—as multinational plantation workers, as migrant workers on Middle East construction projects, as soldiers posted to foreign bases. Women working as domestic servants must be willing to leave their husband and children to service other families and, in the process, their country's foreign debt. But no one asked either Betsy North or the wife of a Honduran banana-plantation worker what her analysis was of the international political system that produced the Iran/Contra affair.

One of the beliefs that informs this [argument] is this: if we listened to women more carefully—to those trying to break out of the strait-jacket of conventional femininity *and* to those who find security and satisfaction in those very conventions—and if we made concepts such as "wife," "mother," "sexy broad" central to our investigations, we might find that the Iran/Contra affair and international politics generally looked different. It's not that we would abandon our curiosity about arms dealers, presidents' men, and concepts such as "covert operations." Rather, we would no longer find them sufficient to understand how the international political system works.

MASCULINITY AND INTERNATIONAL POLITICS

Making women invisible hides the workings of both femininity and masculinity in international politics. Some women watching the Iran/Contra hearings found it useful to speculate about how the politics of masculinity shape foreign-policy debates. They considered the verbal rituals that public men use to blunt the edges of their mutual antagonism. A congressman would, for instance, preface a devastating attack on Admiral Poindexter's rationale for destroying a document by reassuring the admiral—and his male colleagues—that he believed the admiral was "honorable" and "a gentleman." Another congressman would insist that, despite his differences with Reagan officials Robert McFarlane and Oliver North, he considered them to be "patriots." Would these same male members of Congress, selected for this special committee partly because they had experience of dealing with military officers and foreign-policy administrators, have used the word "honorable" if the witness had been a woman? Would "patriot" have been the term of respect if these men had been commending a woman? There appeared to be a platform of trust holding up these investigations of US foreign policy. It was a platform that was supported by pillars of masculinity, pillars that were never subjected to political scrutiny, but which had to be maintained by daily personal exchanges, memos, and formal policy.

A theme that surfaced repeatedly during the weeks of the Iran/Contra hearings was "We live in a dangerous world." Critics as well as supporters of selling arms to Iran and using the profits to fund the Contras were in agreement on this view of the world in 1987. No one chimed in with, "Well, I don't know; it doesn't feel so dangerous to me." No one questioned this portrayal of the world as permeated by risk and violence. No one even attempted to redefine "danger" by suggesting that the world may indeed be dangerous, but especially so for those people who are losing access to land or being subjected to unsafe contraceptives. Instead, the vision that informed these male officials' foreign-policy choices was of a world in which two superpowers were eyeball-to-eyeball, where small risks were justified in the name of staving off bigger risks—the risk of Soviet expansion, the risk of nuclear war. It was a world in which taking risks was proof of one's manliness and therefore of one's qualification to govern. Listening to these officials, I was struck by the similarity to the "manliness" now said to be necessary for success in the international financial markets. With Britain's "Big Bang," which deregulated its financial industry, and with the French and Japanese deregulators following close behind, financial observers began to warn that the era of gentlemanliness in banking was over. British, European, and Japanese bankers and stockbrokers would now have to adopt the more robust, competitive form of manliness associated with American bankers. It wouldn't necessarily be easy. There might even be some resistance. Thus international finance and international diplomacy seem to be converging in their notions of the world and the kind of masculinity required to wield power in that world in the 1990s.[8]

At first glance, this portrayal of danger and risk is a familiar one, rooted in capitalist and Cold War ideology. But when it's a patriarchal world that is "dangerous," masculine men and feminine women are expected to react in opposite but complementary ways. A "real man" will become the protector in such a world. He will suppress his own fears, brace himself and step forward to defend the weak, women, and children. In the same "dangerous world" women will turn gratefully and expectantly to their fathers and husbands, real or surrogate. If a woman is a mother, then she will think first of her children, protecting them not in a manly way, but as a self-sacrificing mother. In this fashion, the "dangerous world" evoked repeatedly in the Iran/Contra hearings is upheld by unspoken notions about masculinity. Ideas of masculinity have to be perpetuated to justify foreign-policy risk-taking. To accept the Cold War interpretation of living in a "dangerous" world also confirms the segregation of politics into national and international. The national political arena is dominated by men but allows women some select access; the international political arena is a sphere for men only, or for those rare women who can successfully play at being men, or at least not shake masculine presumptions.

Notions of masculinity aren't necessarily identical across generations or across cultural boundaries. An Oliver North may be a peculiarly American phenomenon. He doesn't have a carbon copy in current British or Japanese politics. Even the Hollywood character "Rambo," to whom so many likened Oliver North, may take on rather different meanings in America, Britain, and Japan.[9] A Lebanese Shiite militiaman may be fulfilling an explicitly masculinist mandate, but it would be a mistake to collapse the values he represents into those of a British SAS officer or an American "Rambo." Introducing masculinity into a discussion of international politics, and thereby making men visible as men, should prompt us to explore differences in the politics of masculinity between countries—and between ethnic groups in the same country.

These differences have ignited nationalist movements which have challenged the existing international order, dismantling empires, ousting foreign bases, expropriating foreign mines and factories. But there have been nationalist movements which have engaged in such world challenges without upsetting patriarchal relationships within that nation. It is important, I think, to understand which kinds of nationalist movement rely on the perpetuation of patriarchal ideas of masculinity for their international political campaigns and which kinds see redefining masculinity as integral to reestablishing national sovereignty. Women do not benefit automatically every time the international system is reordered by a successful nationalist movement. It has taken awareness, questioning, and organizing by women inside those nationalist movements to turn nationalism into something good for women.

In conventional commentaries men who wield influence in international politics are analyzed in terms of their national identities, their class origins, and their paid work. Rarely are they analyzed as men who have been taught how to be manly, how to size up the trustworthiness or competence of other men in terms of their manliness. If international commentators do find masculinity interesting, it is typically when they try to make sense of "great men"—Teddy Roosevelt, Winston Churchill, Mao Tse-t'ung—not when they seek to understand humdrum plantation workers or foreign tourists. Such men's presumptions about how to be masculine in doing their jobs, exercising influence, or seeking relief from stress are made invisible. Here are some examples:

• In 1806 executives of the Northwest Company decided it was no longer good international company politics for their trappers to take Native Canadian women as their wives; they calculated that it was more advantageous to encourage their Canadian white male employees to import European women. That was a self-conscious use of power to reshape the relationships between women and men for the sake of achieving specific international goals. The decisions of managers in London altered the way in which Canada was integrated into the British empire. It was an imperial strategy that relied on the currencies of gender and race.[10]

• When US Defense Department officials insisted that the Philippines government take responsibility for conducting physical examinations of all women working in the bars around the American military bases in the Philippines, it affected the lives of thousands of young Filipinas and sent a clear message to thousands of American sailors and Air Force pilots. The message symbolized the unequal alliance between the US and Philippines governments. Its implementation rooted that government-to-government inequality in the everyday lives of American military men and Filipino working women.[11]

[We will] explore some accepted arenas of international politics: nationalist movements, diplomacy, military expansion, international debt. However, we will examine these familiar realms from unconventional vantage points. We will listen to male nationalist leaders worrying about their women abandoning traditional feminine roles. Those masculine worries and nationalist women's responses to them will be taken as seriously as male nationalists' strategies for ousting colonial rulers. We will look at diplomacy by listening to wives of foreign-service careerists. To understand how military alliances actually work, we will consider the experiences of women who live and work around military bases and women who have camped outside those bases in protest. We will explore bankers' international operations by paying attention to women who have to live on austerity budgets or work in factories, hotels, and other people's kitchens in order for government debts to be serviced.

Later [we'll] explore areas assumed to fall outside "international politics." Looking at fashions in clothing and food sheds light on the relationships between affluent and developing countries. The often difficult relationships between domestic servants and the middle-class women who hire them will be examined to make sense of new trends in international politics. We will take a close look at the foreign travel of Victorian women explorers and present-day businessmen to understand how power between countries is made and challenged. We will listen to women married to diplomats in order to see to what extent governments' foreign-policy machinery depends on notions of wifely duty.

BEYOND THE GLOBAL VICTIM

Some men and women active in campaigns to influence their country's foreign policy—on the right as well as the left—have called on women to become more involved in international issues, to learn more about "what's going on in the world:" "You have to take more interest in international affairs because it affects how you live." The gist of the argument is that women need to devote precious time and energy to learning about events outside their own country because as women they are the objects of those events. For instance, a woman working in a garment factory in Ireland should learn more about the European Economic Community because what the EEC commissioners do in Brussels is going to help determine her wages and maybe even the hazards she faces on the job. An American woman will be encouraged to learn the difference between a cruise and Pershing missile because international nuclear strategies are shaping her and her children's chances of a safe future.

Two things are striking about this line of argument. First, the activists who are trying to persuade women to "get involved" are not inviting women to reinterpret international politics by drawing on their own experiences as women. If the explanations of how the EEC or nuclear rivalry works don't already include any concepts of femininity, masculinity, or patriarchy, they are unlikely to after the women join the movement. Because organizers aren't curious about what women's experiences could lend to an understanding of international politics, many women, especially those whose energies are already stretched to the limit, are wary of becoming involved in an international campaign. It can seem like one more attempt by privileged outsiders—women and men—to dilute their political efforts. If women are asked to join an international campaign—for peace, against communism, for refugees, against apartheid, for religious evangelism, against hunger—but are not allowed to define the problem, it looks to many locally engaged women like abstract do-good-ing with minimal connection to the battles for a decent life in their households and in their communities.

Second, the typical "women-need-to-learn-more-about-foreign-affairs" approach usually portrays women as victims of the international political system. Women should learn about the EEC, the United Nations, the CIA, the IMF, NATO, the Warsaw Pact, the "greenhouse effect" because each has an impact on them. In this world view, women are forever being acted upon; rarely are they seen to be actors.

It's true that in international politics women historically have not had access to the resources enabling them to wield influence. Today women are at the bottom of most international hierarchies: women are routinely paid less than even the lowest-paid men in multinational companies; women are two thirds of all refugees. Women activists have a harder time influencing struggling ethnic nationalist movements than do men; women get less of the ideological and job rewards from fighting in foreign wars than do men. Though a pretty dismal picture, it can tell us a lot about how the international political system has been designed and how it is maintained every day: some men at the top, most women at the bottom.

But in many arenas of power feminists have been uncovering a reality that is less simple. First, they have discovered that some women's class aspirations and their racist fears lured them into the role of controlling other women for the sake of imperial rule. British, American, Dutch, French, Spanish, Portuguese women may not have been the architects of their countries' colonial policies, but many of them took on the roles of colonial administrators' wives, missionaries, travel writers, and anthropologists in ways that tightened the noose of colonial rule around the necks of African, Latin American, and Asian women. To describe colonization as a process that has been carried on solely by men overlooks the ways in which male colonizers' success depended on some women's complicity. Without the willingness of "respectable" women to see that colonization offered them an opportunity for adventure, or a new chance of financial security or moral commitment, colonization would have been even more problematic.[12]

Second, feminists who listen to women working for multinational corporations have heard these women articulate their own strategies for coping with their husbands' resentment, their foremen's sexual harassment, and the paternalism of male union leaders. To depict these women merely as passive victims in the international politics of the banana or garment industries doesn't do them justice. It also produces an inaccurate picture of how these global systems operate. Corporate executives and development technocrats need some women to depend on cash wages; they need some women to see a factory or plantation job as a means of delaying marriage or fulfilling daughterly obligations. Without women's own needs, values, and worries, the global assembly line would grind to a halt. But many of those needs, values, and worries are defined by patriarchal structures and strictures. If fathers, brothers, husbands didn't gain some privilege, however small in global terms, from women's acquiescence to those confining notions of femininity, it might be much harder for the foreign executives and their local élite allies to recruit the cheap labor they desire. Consequently, women's capacity to challenge the men in their families, their communities, or their political movements, will be a key to remaking the world.

"So what?" one may ask. A book about international politics ought to leave one with a sense that "I can do something." A lot of books about international politics don't. They leave one with the sense that "it's all so complex, decided by people who don't know or care that I exist." The spread of capitalist economics, even in countries whose officials call themselves socialists, can feel as inevitable as the tides. Governments' capacity to wound people, to destroy environments and dreams, is constantly expanding through their use of science and bureaucracy. International relationships fostered by these governments and their allies use our labor and our imaginations, but it seems beyond our reach to alter them. They have added up to a world that can dilute the liveliest of cultures, a world that can turn tacos and sushi into bland fast foods, globalize video pornography, and socialize men from dozens of cultures into a common new culture of technocratic management. One closes most books on "international political economy" with a sigh. They explain how it works, but that knowledge only makes one feel as though it is more rewarding to concentrate on problems closer to home.

Hopefully, [my book] will provoke quite a different feeling. They suggest that the world is something that has been made; therefore, it can be remade. The world has been made with blunt power, but also with sleights of hand. Perhaps international policy-makers find it more "manly" to think of themselves as dealing in guns and money rather than in notions of femininity. So they—and most of their critics as well—have tried to hide and deny their reliance on women as feminized workers, as respectable and loyal wives, as "civilizing influences," as sex objects, as obedient daughters, as unpaid farmers, as coffee-serving campaigners, as consumers and tourists. If we can expose their dependence on feminizing women, we can show that this world system is also dependent on artificial notions of masculinity: this seemingly overwhelming world system may be more fragile and open to radical change than we have been led to imagine.

Some women have already begun the difficult process of trying to create a new international political system. Many point to the conference in Nairobi, Kenya, in 1985 to mark the end of the United Nations Decade of Women as a watershed. For eighty years Nairobi women had been trying to build new international alliances, especially to end men's exclusive right to vote in national elections and to end the exploitation of women as mothers and as prostitutes by national and imperial armies. Some of those efforts made international élites nervous. Occasionally, they wittingly or unwittingly entrenched gendered hierarchies of international power. They elevated motherhood to a political status; they made feminine respectability a criterion for political legitimacy; they proposed that white women should be the political mentors of women of color. An international feminist alliance, as we will see, doesn't automatically weaken male-run imperialist ventures. In the late 1980s there are fresh understandings, therefore, of the ways in which international feminist theorizing and organizing has to be rooted in clear explanations of how women from different, often unequal societies, are used to sustain the world patterns that feminists seek to change. Women organizing to challenge UN agencies, the International Monetary Fund, or multinational corporations are developing theory and strategies simultaneously. A feminist international campaign lacking a feminist analysis of international politics is likely to subvert its own ultimate goals. Among the sectors—"subsystems"—of the world political system that are being most affected by internationalized feminist organizing today are prostitution; population politics; development assistance; military alliances; textile and electronics production.

It takes a lot of information-gathering, a lot of thinking, a lot of trial and error, and a lot of emotionally draining work to understand how notions about femininity and masculinity create and sustain global inequalities and oppressions in just one of these sectors. Yet a truly effective international feminism requires us to make sense of how patriarchal ideas and practices link all of these sectors to each other—and to other relationships whose gendered dynamics we have scarcely begun to fathom. . . .

Notes

1. Cynthia Cockburn, quoted by Melissa Benn, "In and Against the European Left: Socialist Feminists Get Organized," *Feminist Review,* No. 26, July, 1987, p. 89.
2. Some notable exceptions are: Swasti Mitter, *Common Fate, Common Bond,* London, Pluto Press, 1987; Gita Sen and Caren Grown, *Development, Crises and Alternative Visions: Third World Women's Perspectives,* New York, Monthly Review Press, 1987; Eva Isaksson, editor, *Women and the Military System,* Brighton, Wheatsheaf Books, and New York, St. Martin's Press, 1988; Wendy Chapkis and Cynthia Enloe, editors, *Of Common Cloth: Women in the Global Textile Industry,* Amsterdam and Washington, Transnational Institute and Institute for Policy Studies, 1983; Wendy Chapkis, editor, *Loaded Questions: Women in the Military,* Amsterdam and Washington, Transnational Institute and Institute for Policy Studies, 1981; Kathleen Barry, Charlotte Bunch and Shirley Castley, editors, *International Feminism: Networking Against Female Sexual Slavery,* New York, International Tribune Center, 1984; *Millennium: Journal of International Studies* special issue on "Women and International Relations," London School of Economics, vol. 17, no. 3, Winter, 1988.
3. *New York Times*/CBS poll, reported in the *New York Times,* July 18, 1987. Only 25 percent of the American women sampled said that they approved of the US government giving aid to the anti-Sandinista Contra forces; 37 percent of the American men polled approved of US aid to the Contras, though proportionately fewer black men approved than did white men.
4. For an interesting exploration of the contradictions behind women as television-news reporters, see Patricia Holland, "When a Woman Reads the News," in Helen Baehr and Gillian Dyers, editors, *Boxed In: Women and Television,* London and Winchester, MA, Pandora Press, 1988, pp. 133–50.
5. For more of the politics of beauty, see Wendy Chapkis, *Beauty Secrets,* Boston, South End Press, 1986, London, Women's Press, 1987.
6. *Boston Globe,* August 10, 1987.
7. Barbara Gamarekian, "Consequences of Fawn Hall," *New York Times,* February 28, 1987. For Fawn Hall's own views on a secretary's professional relationships, see Mary Sit, "Hall Tells Secretaries: 'Stand by Your Boss,' " *Boston Globe,* September 30, 1988. See also Beatrix Campbell's analysis of the Sara Keayes–Cecil Parkinson scandal in Britain in her *Iron Ladies,* London, Virago Press, 1987, pp. 274–5.
8. For a suggestive report on the changing images of male bankers in the era of internationalized and deregularized banking, see "City of London, Survey," *The Economist,* July 25, 1988, pp. 25–9; Sebastian Kinsman, "Confessions of a Commodity Broker," *New Statesman,* 19 February 1988, pp. 10–11; Steve Lohr, "London's Resurgent Markets," *New York Times,* September 22, 1986; "The Risk Game:

A Survey of International Banking," *The Economist,* March 21, 1987; "A Survey of Wall Street," *The Economist,* July 11, 1987; Barbara Rogers, *Men Only,* London and Winchester, MA, Pandora Press, 1988.

9. Cynthia Enloe, "Beyond Rambo," in Eva Isaksson, op. cit.; a somewhat different version appears as "Beyond Rambo and Steve Canyon," in John Gillis, editor, *The Militarization of the World,* New Brunswick, NJ, Rutgers University Press, 1989.

10. Sylvia Van Kirk, *Many Tender Ties: Women in Fur-Trade Society 1670–1870,* Winnipeg, Watson & Dwyer, 1980, Norman, OK, University of Oklahoma Press, 1983; Jennifer H. Brown, *Strangers in Blood: Fur Trade Companies' Families in Indian Countries,* Vancouver, University of British Columbia Press, 1980.

11. Cynthia Enloe, *Does Khaki Become You? The Militarization of Women's Lives,* London and Winchester, MA, Pandora Press, 1988.

12. See, for instance, "Western Women and Imperialism," special issue of *Women's Studies International Forum,* edited by Margaret Strobel and Nupur Chaudhuri, vol. 13, no. 2, 1990.

II

The Call to Action

bell hooks

"Out of the Academy and into the Streets"

In this essay, which originally appeared in a longer version in the *Yale Journal of Law and Feminisim* (Vol. 4, No. 1, pp. 1–12) under the title of "Theory as Liberatory Practice," bell hooks recounts her personal passage from theorist to activist. The author teaches English and women's studies at Oberlin College, and her other titles include *Talking Back, Yearning: Race, Gender, and Cultural Politics* and *Ain't I a Woman: Black Women and Feminism.*

I came to theory because I was hurting. Whenever I tried in childhood to compel folks around me to look at the world differently, I was punished. I remember trying to explain at a very young age to Mama why I thought it was inappropriate for Daddy, this man who hardly spoke to me, to have the right to punish me with whippings: her response was to suggest I was losing my mind and in need of more punishment.

Imagine this young black couple struggling to realize the patriarchal norm (the woman taking care of household and children while the man worked) even though such an arrangement meant that economically they would always be living with less. Try to imagine what it must have been like—each of them working hard all day, struggling to maintain seven children, then having to cope with one bright-eyed child relentlessly questioning, rebelling against the patriarchal norm they were trying so hard to institutionalize. No wonder Mama would say to me, exasperated: "I don't know where I got you from, but I wish I could give you back."

Living in childhood without a sense of home, I found a sanctuary in "theorizing," where I could imagine possible futures. This "lived" experience of critical thinking, of reflection and analysis, became a place where I worked at explaining that theory could be a healing place.

When our lived experience of theorizing is fundamentally linked to processes of self-recovery, of collective liberation, no gap exists between theory and practice. But theory is not inherently healing, liberatory, or revolutionary. It fulfills this function only when we ask that it do so and direct our theorizing toward this end. When I was a child, I certainly did not describe the processes of thought and critique I engaged in as "theorizing." Yet, as I suggested in *Feminist Theory: From Margin to Center* (South End Press, 1984), the possession of a term does not bring a process or practice into being; concurrently one may practice theorizing without ever processing the term, just as we can act in feminist resistance without ever using the word "feminism." The privileged act of naming often affords those in power access to modes of communication that enable them to project a definition of their actions that may obscure what is really taking place. Katie King's essay "Producing Sex, Theory, and Culture: Gay/Straight Remappings in Contemporary Feminism" (*Conflicts in Feminism,* Marianne Hirsch and Evelyn Fox Keller eds., 1990) is a useful discussion of the way in which academic production of feminist theory formulated in hierarchical settings often enables women, particularly white women, with high status and visibility, to draw upon the works of feminist scholars who may have less or no status, less or no visibility, without giving recognition to these sources. Discussing the way work is appropriated and/or the way readers will often attribute ideas to a well-known scholar/feminist thinker—even if that individual has cited in her work that she is building on ideas gleaned from less well-known sources—and focusing particularly on the work of Chicana theorist Chela Sandoval, King states: "Sandoval has been published only sporadically and eccentrically, yet her circulating unpublished manuscripts are much cited and often appropriated, even while the range of her influence is rarely understood." The critical point is that the production of feminist theory is complex, that it is less the individual practice than we often think, and usually emerges from engagement with collective sources.

Critical reflection on contemporary production of feminist theory makes it apparent that the shift from early conceptualizations of feminist theory (that insisted it was most vital when it encouraged and enabled feminist practice) begins to occur or becomes most obvious with the segregation and institutionalization of the feminist theorizing process in the academy, with the privileging of written feminist thought/theory over oral narratives.

Work by women of color and marginalized groups of white women (lesbians, sex radicals), especially if written in a manner accessible to a broad reading public, even if that work enables and promotes feminist practice, is often delegitimized in academic settings. Though such work is often appropriated by the very individuals setting restrictive critical standards, it is this work they most often claim is not really theory. It is evident that one of the uses of theory in academic locations is in the production of an intellectual class hierarchy where the only work deemed theoretical is abstract, jargonistic, difficult to read, and containing obscure references. It is easy to imagine different locations, spaces outside academic exchange, where such theory would not only be seen as useless, but would be seen as politically nonprogressive.

Imagine what a change: when students come to women's studies classes and read what they are told is feminist theory—only to feel that what they are reading cannot be understood, or in no way connects to "lived" realities beyond the classroom. We might ask ourselves of what use is feminist theory that assaults the fragile psyches of women struggling to throw off patriarchy's oppressive yoke? "Feminist theory" that leaves them stumbling bleary-eyed from classroom settings feeling as though they could easily be standing naked with someone who has seduced them or is going to, who subjects them to a process of interaction that humiliates, that strips them of their sense of value? A feminist theory that can do this may legitimize feminist scholarship in the eyes of the ruling patriarchy, but it undermines and subverts feminist movements. It is the purpose of such theory to divide, separate, exclude. And because this theory continues to be used to silence, censor, and devalue various feminist theoretical voices, we cannot simply ignore it. Concurrently, despite its uses as an instrument of domination, it may also contain important ideas that could, if used differently, serve a healing function.

Recently, I went to a gathering of women, predominantly black, where we discussed whether or not black male leaders, like Martin Luther King, Jr., and Malcolm X, should be subjected to feminist critiques that pose hard questions about their stance on gender issues. The entire discussion was less than two hours. As it drew to a close, a black woman who had been silent spoke to say that she was more interested in action, that she was just "tired" of all the talk.

Her response disturbed me. In the world I live in daily, the occasions where black women/women of color thinkers come together to rigorously debate issues of race, gender, class, and sexuality are rare. Hence, from my perspective, we were charting new journeys, claiming for ourselves an intellectual terrain where we could begin the collective construction of feminist theory.

In many black settings, I have witnessed the dismissal of intellectuals, the putting down of theory, and remained silent. I have come to see that silence helps perpetuate the idea that we can engage in revolutionary black liberation and/or feminist struggle without theory. Like many insurgent black intellectuals whose work is often done in predominantly white settings, I am often so pleased to be engaged with a collective group of black folks that I do not want to make myself an outsider by disagreeing with the group. In such settings, I have rarely spoken affirmatively or ecstatically about intellectual process.

I was reminded of this dangerous anti-intellectualism when I agreed to appear on a radio show with a group of black women and men to discuss Shahrazad Ali's *The Blackman's Guide to Under-standing the Blackwoman,* where I listened to speaker after speaker express contempt for the production of theory. Ali's book, though written in a style that makes use of black vernacular, has a theoretical foundation. It is rooted in theories of patriarchy. Many black nationalists will eagerly embrace critical theory as a necessary weapon in the struggle against white supremacy, but suddenly lose the insight when it comes to questions of gender.

We must continually claim theory as necessary practice within a holistic framework of liberatory activism. We must do more than critique the at times reactionary uses some academic women make of feminist theory. We must actively work to call attention to the importance of creating a theory that can advance renewed feminist movements, particularly highlighting that theory that seeks to further feminist opposition to sexist oppression. Doing this, we necessarily celebrate and value theory that can be and is shared in oral as well as written narrative.

Reflecting on my own work in feminist theory, I find writing—theoretical talk—to be most meaningful when it invites readers to engage in critical reflection and in the practice of feminism. To me, this theory emerges from my efforts to make sense of everyday life experiences, efforts to critically intervene in my life and the lives of others. This to me is what makes feminist transformation possible. Personal testimony, personal experience, is such fertile ground for the production of liberatory feminist theory because usually it forms the base of our theory-making. While we work to resolve those issues (our need for literacy, for an end to violence against women and children, for women's health and reproductive rights, for housing, for sexual freedom—to name a few) that are most pressing we engage in a critical process of theorizing that enables and empowers. I continue to be amazed that there is so little feminist theory that strives to speak about ways we might transform our lives via a conversion to feminist politics.

We know that many individuals in the United States have used feminist thinking in ways that allow them to transform their lives. I am often critical of a lifestyle-based feminism, because I fear that any feminist transformational process is easily co-opted if not rooted in a political commitment to a mass-based feminist movement. We have already witnessed the commodification of feminist thinking (just as we experience the commodification of blackness), in ways that make it seem as though one can partake of the "good" these movements produce without any commitment to transformative politics and practice. In this capitalist culture, feminism and feminist theory are fast becoming a commodity only the privileged can afford. This process is disrupted when feminist activists affirm our commitment to a politicized revolutionary feminist movement that has as its central agenda the transformation of society. From such a starting point, we automatically think of creating theory that speaks to the widest audience of people. I have written and talked about my writing style, about not using conventional academic formats, as political decisions motivated by the desire to be inclusive. This decision has had consequences both positive and negative. Students often complain they cannot include my work for degree-oriented qualifying exams because their professors do not see it as scholarly enough. Any of us who create feminist theory in academic settings where we are continually evaluated know that work deemed "not scholarly" can result in not receiving deserved recognition.

These negative responses seem insignificant when compared to the overwhelmingly positive responses to my work both in and outside the academy. I share feminist thinking and practice wherever I am. Recently, I was at a black-owned restaurant in the South and sat for hours with a diverse group of black women and men from various class backgrounds discussing issues of race, gender, and class. Some of us were college-educated, others were not. We had a heated discussion about abortion, discussing whether black women should have the right to choose. Several of the Afrocentric black men were arguing that the male should have as much choice as the female. One of the feminist black women present, a director of a health clinic for women, spoke eloquently about a woman's right to choose.

During this heated discussion, one of the black women present—who had been silent for a long time, who hesitated before she entered the conversation because she was unsure whether she could convey the complexity of her thought in black vernacular speech (in such a way that we would understand and not make fun of her words)—came to voice. As I was leaving, this sister grasped both my hands tightly, and thanked me for the discussion. She prefaced her words of gratitude by sharing that the conversation had not only enabled her to give voice to ideas she had always "kept" to herself, but that it had created a space for her and her partner to change thought and action. She stared at me intently, as we stood facing one another, holding hands, and saying again and again, "There's been so much hurt in me." She gave thanks that our meeting, our theorizing of race, gender, and sexuality, had eased her pain. Standing body to body, eye to eye, she allowed me to share the warmth of that healing.

Our search leads us back to where it all began, to that moment when a woman or child, who may have thought she was all alone, began feminist uprising, began to name her practice, began to formulate theory from experience. I am grateful that I can be a witness, testifying that we can create a feminist theory, a feminist practice, a revolutionary feminist movement, that can speak directly to the pain within folks, and offer them healing words, healing strategies, healing theory. There is no one among us who has not felt the pain of sexist oppression, the anguish male domination can create. If we create theory that addresses this pain, there will be no gap between feminist theory and feminist practice.

Anna Quindlen

---

from *Thinking Out Loud*
On the Personal, the Political, the Public
and the Private
"The Glass Half Empty"

Anger can be creative. It can effect change, and will, for Anna Quindlen as she imagines the ramifications of gender inequality in her daughter's future. A staff member of the *New York Times* since 1977 and winner of the Pulitzer Prize for commentary in 1992, Quindlen currently writes the column "Public & Private" for the newspaper's Op-Ed page. She has also published *Living Out Loud,* a collection of essays from her previous column, "Life in the 30s," as well as the best-selling novel *Object Lessons* and, for children, *The Tree That Came to Stay.*

M y daughter is two years old today. She is something like me, only better. Or at least that is what I like to think. If personalities had colors, hers would be red.

Little by little, in the twenty years between my eighteenth birthday and her second one, I had learned how to live in the world. The fact that women were now making sixty-seven cents for every dollar a man makes—well, it was better than 1970, wasn't it, when we were making only fifty-nine cents? The constant stories about the under-representation of women, on the tenure track in the film industry, in government, everywhere, had become commonplace. The rape cases. The sexual harassment stories. The demeaning comments. Life goes on. Where's your sense of humor?

Learning to live in the world meant seeing the glass half full. Ann Richards was elected governor of Texas instead of a good ol' boy who said that if rape was inevitable, you should relax and enjoy it. The police chief of Houston is a pregnant woman who has a level this-is-my-job look and a maternity uniform with stars on the shoulder. There are so many opportunities unheard of when I was growing up.

And then I had a daughter and suddenly I saw the glass half empty. And all the rage I thought had cooled, all those how-dare-you-treat-us-like-that days, all of it comes back when I look at her, and especially when I hear her say to her brothers, "Me too."

When I look at my sons, it is within reason to imagine all the world's doors open to them. Little by little some will close, as their individual capabilities and limitations emerge. But no one is likely to look at them and mutter: "I'm not sure a man is right for a job at this level. Doesn't he have a lot of family responsibilities?"

Every time a woman looks at her daughter and thinks, She can be anything, she knows in her heart, from experience, that it's a lie. Looking at this little girl, I see it all, the old familiar ways of a world that still loves Barbie. Girls aren't good at math, dear. He needs the money more than you, sweetheart; he's got a family to support. Honey—this diaper's dirty.

It is like looking through a telescope. Over the years I learned to look through the end that showed things small and manageable. This is called a sense of proportion. And then I turned the telescope around, and all the little tableaux rushed at me, vivid as ever. That's called reality.

We soothe ourselves with the gains that have been made. There are many role models. Role models are women who exist—and are photographed often—to make other women feel better about the fact that there aren't really enough of us anywhere, except in the lowest-paying jobs. A newspaper editor said to me not long ago, with no hint of self-consciousness, "I'd love to run your column, but we already run Ellen Goodman." Not only was there a quota; there was a quota of one.

My daughter is ready to leap into the world, as though life were chicken soup and she a delighted noodle. The work of Professor Carol Gilligan of Harvard suggests that sometime after the age of eleven this will change, that even this lively little girl will pull back, shrink, that her constant refrain will become "I don't know." Professor Gilligan says the culture sends a message: "Keep quiet and notice the absence of women and say nothing." A smart thirteen-year-old said to me last week, "Boys don't like it if you answer too much in class."

Maybe someday, years from now, my daughter will come home and say, "Mother, at college my professor acted as if my studies were an amusing hobby and at work the man who runs my department puts his hand on my leg and to compete with the man who's in the running for my promotion who makes more than I do I can't take time to have a relationship but he has a wife and two children and I'm smarter and it doesn't make any difference and some guy tried to jump me after our date last night." And what am I supposed to say to her?

I know?

You'll get used to it?

No. Today is her second birthday and she has made me see fresh this two-tiered world, a world that, despite all our nonsense about post-feminism, continues to offer less respect and less opportunity for women than it does for men. My friends and I have learned to live with it, but my little girl deserves better. She has given me my anger back, and I intend to use it well.

That is her gift to me today. Some birthday I will return it to her, because she is going to need it.

Katha Pollitt

"Marooned on Gilligan's Island
Are Women Morally Superior to Men?"

Reconsidering the concepts of motherhood and woman-hood in America, Katha Pollitt enters the age-old debate as to whether women are morally superior to men, or not. She comes up with some fresh answers. Katha Pollitt is the author of the award-winning *Antarctic Traveller* and a widely published poet.

Some years ago, I was invited by the wife of a well-known writer to sign a women's peace petition. It made the points such documents usually make: that women, as mothers, caregivers, and nurturers, have a special awareness of the precariousness of human life, see through jingoism and cold war rhetoric, and would prefer nations to work out their difficulties peacefully so that the military budget could be diverted to schools and hospitals and housing. It had the literary tone such documents usually have, as well—at once superior and plaintive, as if the authors didn't know whether they were bragging or begging. We are wiser than you poor deluded menfolk, was the subtext, so will you please-please-please listen to your moms?

To sign or not to sign? Of course, I was all for peace. But was I for peace *as a woman*? I wasn't a mother then—I wasn't even an aunt. Did my lack of nurturing credentials make my grasp of the horrors of war and the folly of the arms race only theoretical, like a white person's understanding of racism? Were mothers the natural leaders of the peace movement, to whose judgment nonmothers, male and female, must defer, because after all we couldn't *know,* couldn't *feel* that tenderness toward fragile human life that a woman who had borne and raised children had experienced? On the other hand, I was indeed a woman. Was motherhood with its special wisdom somehow deep inside me, to be called upon when needed, like my uterus?

Complicating matters in a way relevant to this essay was my response to the famous writer's wife herself. Here was a woman in her fifties, her child-raising long behind her. Was motherhood the only banner under which she could gain a foothold on civic life? Perhaps so. Her only other public identity was that of a wife, and wifehood, even to a famous man, isn't much to claim credit for these days. ("To think I spent all those years ironing his underpants!" she once burst out to a mutual friend.) Motherhood was what she had in the work-and-accomplishment department, so it was understandable that she try to maximize its moral status. But I was not in her situation: I was a writer, a single woman, a jobholder. By sending me a petition from which I was excluded even as I was invited to add my name, perhaps she was telling me that, by leading a nondomestic life, I had abandoned the moral high ground, was "acting like a man," but could redeem myself by acknowledging the moral preeminence of the class of women I refused to join.

The ascription of particular virtues—compassion, patience, common sense, nonviolence—to mothers, and the tendency to conflate "mothers" with "women," has a long history in the peace movement but goes way beyond issues of war and peace. At present it permeates discussions of just about every field, from management training to theology. Indeed, although the media like to caricature feminism as denying the existence of sexual differences, for the women's movement and its opponents alike "difference" is where the action is. Thus, business writers wonder if women's nurturing, intuitive qualities will make them better executives. Educators suggest that female students suffer in classrooms that emphasize competition over cooperation. Women politicians tout their playground-honed negotiating skills, their egoless devotion to public service, their gender-based commitment to fairness and caring. A variety of political causes—environmentalism, animal rights, even vegetarianism—are promoted as logical extensions of women's putative peacefulness, closeness to nature, horror of aggression, and concern for others' health. (Indeed, to some extent these causes are arenas in which women fight one another over definitions of femininity, which is why debates over disposable diapers and over the wearing of fur—both rather minor sources of harm, even if their opponents are right—loom so large and are so acrimonious.) In the arts, we hear a lot about what women's "real" subjects, methods, and materials ought to be. Painting is male. Rhyme is male. Plot is male. Perhaps, say the Lacanian feminists, even logic and language are male. What is female? Nature. Blood. Milk. Communal gatherings. The moon. Quilts.

Haven't we been here before? Indeed we have. Woman as sharer and carer, woman as earth mother, woman as guardian of all the small rituals that knit together a family and a community, woman as beneath, above, or beyond such manly concerns as law, reason, abstract ideas—these images are as old as time. Open defenders of male supremacy have always used them to declare women flatly inferior to men; covert ones use them to place women on a pedestal as too good for this naughty world. Thus, in the *Eumenides,* Aeschylus celebrated law as the defeat by males of primitive female principles of bloodguilt and vengeance, while the Ayatollah Khomeini thought women should be barred from judgeships because they were too tenderhearted. Different rationale, same outcome: Women, because of their indifference to an impersonal moral order, cannot be full participants in civic life.

There exists an equally ancient line of thought, however, that uses femininity to posit a subversive challenge to the social order: Think of Sophocles's Antigone, who resists tyranny out of love and piety, or Aristophanes's Lysistrata, the original women's strike-for-peacenik, or Shakespeare's Portia, who champions mercy against the savage letter of the law. For reasons of power, money, and persistent social structures, the vision of the morally superior woman can never overcome the dominant ethos in reality but exists alongside it as a kind of permanent wish or hope: If only powerful and powerless could change places, and the meek inherit the earth! Thus, it is perpetually being rediscovered, dressed in fashionable clothes, and presented, despite its antiquity, as a radical new idea.

"Relational" Women, "Autonomous" Men

In the 1950s, which we think of as the glory days of traditional sex roles, the anthropologist Ashley Montagu argued in "The Natural Superiority of Women" that females had it all over males in every way that counted, including the possession of two X chromosomes that made them stabler, saner, and healthier than men, with their X and Y. Montagu's essay, published in the *Saturday Review* and later expanded to a book, is witty and high-spirited and, interestingly, anticipates the current feminist challenge to male-defined categories. (He notes, for example, that while men are stronger than women in the furniture-moving sense, women are stronger than men when faced with extreme physical hardship and tests of endurance; so when we say that men are stronger than women, we are equating strength with what men have.) But the fundamental thrust of Montagu's essay was to confirm traditional gender roles while revising the way we value them: Having proved to his own satisfaction that women could scale the artistic and intellectual heights, he argued that most would (that is, should) refrain, because women's true genius was "humanness," and their real mission was to "humanize" men before men blew up the world. And that, he left no doubt, was a full-time job.

Contemporary proponents of "difference feminism" advance a variation on the same argument, without Montagu's puckish humor. Instead of his whimsical chromosomal explanation, we get the psychoanalytic one proposed by Nancy Chodorow in *The Reproduction of Mothering:* Daughters define themselves by relating to their mothers, the primary love object of all children, and are therefore empathic, relationship-oriented, nonhierarchical, and interested in forging consensus; sons must separate from their mothers, and are therefore individualistic, competitive, resistant to connection with others, and focused on abstract rules and rights. Chodorow's theory has become a kind of mantra of difference feminism, endlessly cited as if it explained phenomena we all agree are universal, though this is far from the case. The central question Chodorow poses—Why are women the primary caregivers of children?—could not even be asked before the advent of modern birth control, and can be answered without resorting to psychology. Historically, women have taken care of children because high fertility and lack of other options left most of them no choice. Those rich enough to avoid personally raising their children often did, as Rousseau observed to his horror.

Popularizers of Chodorow water down and sentimentalize her thesis. They embrace her proposition that traditional mothering produces "relational" women and "autonomous" men but forget her less congenial argument that it also results in sexual inequality, misogyny, and hostility between mothers and daughters, who, like sons, desire independence but have a much harder time achieving it. Unlike her followers, Chodorow does not romanticize mothering: "Exclusive single parenting is bad for mother and child alike," she concludes; in a tragic paradox, female "caring," "intimacy," and "nurturance" do not soften but *produce* aggressive, competitive, hypermasculine men.

Thus, in her immensely influential book *In a Different Voice,* Carol Gilligan uses Chodorow to argue that the sexes make moral decisions according to separate criteria: women according to an "ethic of care," men according to an "ethic of rights." Deborah Tannen, in the best-selling *You Just Don't Understand,* claims that men and women grow up with "different cultural backgrounds"—the single-sex world of children's play in which girls cooperate and boys compete—"so talk between men and women is cross-cultural communication.'' While these two writers differ in important ways—Tannen, writing at a more popular level, is by far the clearer thinker and the one more interested in analyzing actual human interactions in daily life—they share important liabilities, too. Both largely confine their observations to the white middle class—especially Gilligan, much of whose elaborate theory of gendered ethics rests on interviews with a handful of Harvard-Radcliffe undergraduates—and seem unaware that this limits the applicability of their data. (In her new book, *Meeting at the Crossroads,* Gilligan makes a similar mistake. Her whole theory of ''loss of relationship'' as the central trauma of female adolescence rests on interviews with students at one posh single-sex private school.) Both massage their findings to fit their theories: Gilligan's male and female responses are actually quite similar to each other, as experimenters have subsequently shown by removing the names and asking subjects to try to sort the test answers by gender; Tannen is quick to attribute blatant rudeness or sexism in male speech to anxiety, helplessness, fear of loss of face—anything, indeed, but rudeness and sexism. Both look only at what people say, not what they do. For Tannen this isn't decisive objection because verbal behavior is her subject, although it limits the applicability of her findings to other areas of behavior; for Gilligan, it is a major obstacle, unless you believe, as she apparently does, that the way people say they would resolve farfetched hypothetical dilemmas—Should a poor man steal drugs to save his dying wife?—tells us how they reason in real-life situations or, more important, what they do.

But the biggest problem with Chodorovian accounts of gender difference is that they credit the differences they find to essential, universal features of male and female psychosexual development rather than to the economic and social positions men and women hold, or to the actual power differences between individual men and women. In *The Mismeasure of Woman,* her trenchant and witty attack on contemporary theories of gender differences, Carol Tavris points out that much of what can be said about women applies as well to poor people, who also tend to focus more on family and relationships and less on work and self-advancement; to behave deferentially with those more socially powerful; and to appear to others more emotional and ''intuitive'' than rational and logical in their thinking. Then, too, there is the question of whether the difference theorists are measuring is anything beyond their own willingness to think in stereotypes. If

Chodorow is right, "relational" women and "autonomous" men should be the norm, but are they? Or is it just that women and men use different language, have different social styles, different explanations for similar behavior? Certainly, it is easy to find in one's own acquaintance, as well as in the world at large, men and women who don't fit the models. Difference feminists like to attribute ruthlessness, coldness, and hyperrationality in successful women— Margaret Thatcher is the standard example—to the fact that men control the networks of power and permit only women like themselves to rise. But I've met plenty of loudmouthed, insensitive, aggressive women who are stay-at-home mothers and secretaries and nurses. And I know plenty of sweet, unambitious men whose main satisfactions lie in their social, domestic, and romantic lives, although not all of them would admit this to an inquiring social scientist. We tend to tell strangers what we think will make us sound good. I myself, to my utter amazement, informed a telephone pollster that I exercised regularly, a baldfaced lie. How much more difficult to describe truthfully one's moral and ethical values—even if one knew what they were, which, as Socrates demonstrated at length, almost no one does.

So why are Gilligan and Tannen the toasts of feminist social science, endlessly cited and discussed in academia and out of it too, in gender-sensitivity sessions in the business world and even, following the Anita Hill testimony, in Congress? The success of the difference theorists proves yet again that social science is one part science and nine parts social. They say what people want to hear: Women really are different, in just the ways we always thought. Women embrace Gilligan and Tannen because they offer flattering accounts of traits for which they have historically been castigated. Men like them because, while they urge understanding and respect for "female" values and behaviors, they also let men off the hook: Men have power, wealth, and control of social resources because women don't really want them. The pernicious tendencies of difference feminism are perfectly illustrated by the Sears sex discrimination case, in which Rosalind Rosenberg, a professor of women's history at Barnard College, testified for Sears that female employees held lower-paying salaried jobs while men worked selling big-ticket items on commission because women preferred low-risk, noncompetitive positions that did not interfere with family responsibilities (see Jon Wiener, "Women's History on Trial," September 7, 1985). Sears won its case.

Mother Knows Best

While Chodorow's analysis of psychosexual development is the point of departure for most of the difference feminists, it is possible to construct a theory of gendered ethics on other grounds. The most interesting attempt I've seen is by the pacifist philosopher Sara Ruddick. Although not widely known outside academic circles, her *Maternal Thinking* makes an argument that can be found in such mainstream sources as the columns of Anna Quindlen in the *New York Times*. For Ruddick it is not psychosexual development that produces the Gilliganian virtues but intimate involvement in child-raising, the hands-on work of mothering. Men, too, can be mothers if they do the work that women do. (And women can be Fathers—a word Ruddick uses, complete with arrogant capital letter, for distant, uninvolved, authority-figure parents.) Mothers are patient, peace-loving, attentive to emotional context and so on, because those are the qualities you need to get the job done, the way accountants are precise, lawyers are argumentative, writers self-centered. Thus mothers constitute a logical constituency for pacifist and antiwar politics, and, by extension, a "caring" domestic agenda.

But what is the job of mothering? Ruddick defines "maternal practice" as meeting three demands: preservation, growth, and social acceptability. She acknowledges the enormously varying manifestations of these demands, but she doesn't incorporate into her theory the qualifications, limits, and contradictions she notes—perhaps because to do so would reveal these demands as so flexible as to be practically empty terms.

Almost anything mothers do can be explained under one of these rubrics, however cruel, dangerous, unfair, or authoritarian—the genital mutilation of African and Arab girls, the foot-binding of pre-revolutionary Chinese ones, the sacrifice of some children to increase the resources available for others, as in the killing or malnourishing of female infants in India and China today. I had a Caribbean student whose mother beat all her children whenever one got into trouble, to teach them "responsibility" for one another. In this country, too, many mothers who commit what is legally child abuse *think* they are merely disciplining their kids in the good old-fashioned way. As long as the practices are culturally acceptable (and sometimes even when they're not), the mothers who perform them think of themselves as good parents. But if all these behaviors count as mothering, how can mothering have a necessary connection with any single belief about anything, let alone how to stop war, or any single set of personality traits, let alone nonviolent ones?

We should not be surprised that motherhood does not produce uniform beliefs and behaviors: It is, after all, not a job; it has no standard of admission, and almost nobody gets fired. Motherhood is open to any woman who can have a baby or adopt one. *Not* to be a mother is a decision; becoming one requires merely that a woman accede, perhaps only for as long as it takes to get pregnant, to thousands of years of cumulative social pressure. After that, she's on her own; she can soothe her child's nightmares or let him cry in the dark. Nothing intrinsic to child-raising will tell her what is the better choice for her child (each has been the favored practice at different times). Although Ruddick starts off by looking closely at maternal practice, when the practice contradicts her own ideas about good mothering it is filed away as an exception, a distortion imposed by Fathers or poverty or some other outside force. But if you add up all the exceptions, you are left with a rather small group of people— women like Ruddick herself, enlightened, up-to-date, educated, upper-middle-class liberals.

And not even all of them. Consider the issue of physical punishment. Ruddick argues that experience teaches mothers that violence is useless; it only creates anger, deception, and more violence. Negotiation is the mother's way of resolving disputes and encouraging good behavior. As Ann Crittenden put it in *The Nation* during the Gulf War: "One learns, in theory and in practice, to try to resolve conflict in ways that do not involve the sheer imposition of will or brute force. One learns that violence just doesn't work." Crittenden would have a hard time explaining all those moms in uniform who participated in Desert Storm—but then she'd have a hard time explaining all those mothers screaming at their kids in the supermarket, too.

As it happens, I agree that violence is a bad way to teach, and I made a decision never, no matter what, to spank my daughter. But mothers who do not hit their children, or permit their husbands to do so, are as rare as conscientious objectors in wartime. According to one survey, 78 percent approve of an occasional "good, hard spanking"—because they think violence *is* an effective way of teaching, because they think that hitting children isn't really violence, because they just lose it. Even *Parenting* found that more than a third of its readers hit their kids. And *Parenting*'s audience is not only far more educated, affluent, and liberal than the general population; it consists entirely of people who care what experts think about child development—and contemporary experts revile corporal punishment. Interestingly, the moms who hit tended to be the ones who fretted the most about raising their children well. Mothers who think too much?

Like old-style socialists finding "proletarian virtue" in the working class, Ruddick claims to be describing what mothers do, but all too often she is really prescribing what she thinks they ought to do. "When their children flourish, almost all mothers have a sense of well-being." Hasn't she ever heard of postpartum depression? Of mothers who belittle their children's accomplishments and resent their growing independence? "What mother wouldn't want the power to keep her children healthy ... to create hospitals, schools, jobs, day care, and work schedules that serve her maternal work?" Notice how neatly the modest and common-sensical wish for a healthy child balloons into the hotly contested and by no means universal wish of mothers for day care and flextime. Notice, too, how Ruddick moves from a mother's desire for social institutions that serve *her* children to an assumption that this desire translates into wanting comparable care for *all* children. But mothers feature prominently in local struggles against busing, mergers of rich and poor schools, and the placement of group homes for foster kids, boarder babies, and the retarded in their neighborhoods. Why? The true reason may be property values and racism, but what these mothers often say is that they are simply protecting their kids. Ruddick seems to think Maternal Thinking leads naturally to Sweden; in the United States it is equally likely to lead to Fortress Suburbia.

As Gilligan does with all women, Ruddick scrutinizes mothers for what she expects to find, and sure enough, there it is. But why look to mothers for her peaceful constituency in the first place? Why not health professionals, who spend their lives saving lives? Or historians, who know how rarely war yields a benefit remotely commensurate with its cost in human misery? Or, I don't know, gardeners, blamelessly tending their innocent flowers? You can read almost any kind of work as affirming life and conferring wisdom. Ruddick chooses mothering because she's already decided that women possess the Gilliganian virtues and she wants a non-essentialist peg to hang them on, so that men can acquire them, too. A disinterested observer scouring the world for labor that encourages humane values would never pick child-raising: It's too quirky, too embedded in repellent cultural norms, too hot.

MAN'S WORLD, WOMAN'S PLACE

Despite its intellectual flabbiness, difference feminism is deeply appealing to many women. Why? For one thing, it seems to explain some important phenomena: that women—and this is a cross-cultural truth—commit very little criminal violence compared with men; that women fill the ranks of the so-called caring professions; that women are much less likely than men to abandon their children. Difference feminists want to give women credit for these good behaviors by raising them from the level of instinct and passivity—the Camille Paglia vision of femininity—to the level of moral choice and principled decision. Who can blame women for embracing theories that tell them the sacrifices they make on behalf of domesticity and children are legitimate, moral, even noble? By stressing the mentality of nurturance—the *ethic* of caring, maternal *thinking*—Gilligan and Ruddick challenge the ancient division of humanity into rational males and irrational females. They offer women a way to argue that their views have equal status with those of men and to resist the customary marginalization of their voices in public debate. Doubtless many women have felt emboldened by Gilliganian accounts of moral difference: Speaking in a different voice is, after all, a big step up from silence.

The vision of women as sharers and carers is tempting in another way too. Despite much media blather about the popularity of the victim position, most people want to believe they act out of free will and choice. The uncomfortable truth that women have all too little of either is a difficult hurdle for feminists. Acknowledging the systematic oppression of women seems to deprive them of existential freedom, to turn them into puppets, slaves, and Stepford wives. Deny it, and you can't make change. By arguing that the traditional qualities, tasks, and ways of life of women are as important, valuable, and serious as those of men (if not more so), Gilligan and others let women feel that nothing needs to change except the social valuation accorded to what they are already doing. It's a rationale for the status quo, which is why men like it, and a burst of grateful applause, which is why women like it. Men keep the power, but since power is bad, so much the worse for them.

Another rather curious appeal of difference feminism is that it offers a way for women to define themselves as independent of men. In a culture that sees women almost entirely in relation to men, this is no small achievement. Sex, for example—the enormous amount of female energy, money, and time spent on beauty and fashion and romance, on attracting men and keeping them, on placating male power, strategizing ways around it or making it serve one's own ends—plays a minute role in these theories. You would never guess from Gilligan or Ruddick that men, individually and collectively, are signal beneficiaries of female nurturance, much less that this goes far to explain why society encourages nurturance in women. No, it is always children whom women are described as fostering and sacrificing for, or the community, or even other women—not husbands or lovers. It's as though wives cook dinner only for their kids, leaving the husband to raid the fridge on his own. And no doubt many women, quietly smoldering at their mate's refusal to share domestic labor, persuade themselves that they are serving only their children, or their own preferences, rather than confront the inequality of their marriage.

The peaceful mother and the "relational" woman are a kinder, gentler, leftish version of "family values," and both are modern versions of the separate-spheres ideology of the Victorians. In the nineteenth century, too, some women tried to turn the ideology of sexual difference on its head and expand the moral claims of motherhood to include the public realm. Middle-class women became social reformers, abolitionists, temperance advocates, settlement workers, and even took paying jobs in the "helping professions"—nursing, social work, teaching—which were perceived as extensions of women's domestic role although practiced mostly by single women. These women did not deny that their sex fitted them for the home, but argued that domesticity did not end at the front door of the house, or confine itself to dusting (or telling the housemaid to dust). Even the vote could be cast as an extension of domesticity: Women, being more moral than men, would purify the government of vice and corruption, end war, and make America safe for family life. (The persistence of this metaphor came home to me this summer when I attended a Women's Action Coalition demonstration during the Democratic National Convention. There—along with WAC's funny

and ferocious all-in-black drum corps and contingents of hip downtown artists brandishing Barbara Kruger posters and shouting slogans
like "We're Women! We're Angry! We're Not Going Shopping!"—
was a trio of street performers with housecoats and kerchiefs over
black catsuits and spiky hair, pushing brooms: Women will clean
up government!)

Accepting the separate-spheres ideology had obvious advantages
in an era when women were formally barred from higher education,
political power, and many jobs. But its defects are equally obvious.
It defined all women by a single standard, and one developed by a
sexist society. If offered women no way to enter professions that
could not be defined as extensions of domestic roles—you could be
a math teacher but not a mathematician, a secretary but not a sea
captain—and no way to challenge any but the grossest abuses of
male privilege. Difference feminists are making a similar bid for
power on behalf of women today, and are caught in similar contradictions. Once again, women are defined by their family roles. Child-
raising is seen as women's glory and joy and opportunity for self-
transcendence, while Dad naps on the couch. Women who do not fit
the stereotype are castigated as unfeminine—nurses nurture, doctors
do not—and domestic labor is romanticized and sold to women as a
badge of moral worth.

WHAT'S LOVE GOT TO DO WITH IT?

For all the many current explanations of perceived moral difference
between the sexes, one hears remarkably little about the material
basis of the family. Yet the motherhood and womanhood being valor-
ized cannot be considered apart from questions of power, privilege,
and money. There is a reason a non-earning woman can proudly call
herself a "wife and mother" and a non-earning man is just unem-
ployed: The traditional female role, with its attendant real or imagined character traits, implies a male income. Middle-class women go
to great lengths to separate themselves from this uncomfortable fact.
One often hears women defend their decision to stay at home by
heaping scorn on paid employment—caricatured as making widgets
or pushing papers or dressing for success—and the difference feminists also like to distinguish between altruistic, poorly paid female
jobs and the nasty, profitable ones performed by men. In *Prisoners*

of Men's Dreams, Suzanne Gordon comes close to blaming the modest status of jobs like nursing and flight attending on women's entry into jobs like medicine and piloting, as if before the women's movement those female-dominated occupations were respected and rewarded. (Nurses should be glad the field no longer has a huge captive labor pool of women: The nursing shortage has led to dramatic improvements in pay, benefits, and responsibility. Now nurses earn a man-sized income, and men are applying to nursing school in record numbers—exactly what Gordon wants.) It's all very well for some women to condemn others for "acting like men"—i.e., being ambitious, assertive, interested in money and power. But if their husbands did not "act like men," where would they be? Jean Bethke Elshtain, who strenuously resists the notion of gendered ethics, nevertheless bemoans the loss to their communities when women leave volunteering and informal mutual support networks for paid employment. But money must come from somewhere; if women leave to men the job of earning the family income (an option fewer and fewer families can afford), they will be economically dependent on their husbands, a situation that, besides carrying obvious risks in an age of frequent divorce, weakens their bargaining position in the family and insures that men will largely control major decisions affecting family life.

Difference theorists would like to separate out the aspects of traditional womanhood that they approve of and speak only of those. But the parts they like (caring, nurturing, intimacy) are inseparable from the parts they don't like (economic dependence and the subordination of women within the family). The difference theorists try to get around this by positing a world that contains two cultures—a female world of love and ritual and a male world of getting and spending and killing—which mysteriously share a single planet. That vision is expressed neatly in a recent pop-psychology title, *Men Are From Mars, Women Are From Venus.* It would be truer to say men are from Illinois and women are from Indiana—different, sure, but not in ways that have much ethical consequence.

The truth is, there is only one culture, and it shapes each sex in distinct but mutually dependent ways in order to reproduce itself. To the extent that the stereotypes are true, women have the "relational" domestic qualities *because* men have the "autonomous" qualities required to survive and prosper in modern capitalism. She needs a wage earner (even if she has a job, thanks to job discrimination), and he needs someone to mind his children, hold his hand, and have his emotions for him. This—not, as Gordon imagines, some treason to her sex—explains why women who move into male sectors act very much like men: If they didn't, they'd find themselves back home in a jiffy. The same necessities and pressures affect them, as affect the men who hold those jobs. Because we are in a transition period, in which many women were raised with modest expectations and much emphasis on the need to please others, social scientists who look for it can find traces of empathy, caring, and so on in some women who have risen in the world of work and power, but when they tell us that women doctors will transform American medicine, or women executives will transform the corporate world, they are looking backward, not forward. If women really do enter the work force on equal terms with men—if they become 50 percent of all lawyers, politicians, car dealers, and prison guards—they may be less sexist (although the example of Russian doctors, a majority of them female, is not inspiring to those who know about the brutal gynecological customs prevailing in the former U.S.S.R.). And they may bring with them a distinct set of manners, a separate social style. But they won't be, in some general way, more honest, kind, egalitarian, empathic, or indifferent to profit. To argue otherwise is to believe that the reason factory owners bust unions, doctors refuse Medicaid patients, and New York City school custodians don't mop the floors is because they are men.

The ultimate paradox of difference feminism is that it has come to the fore at a moment when the lives of the sexes are becoming less distinct than they ever have been in the West. Look at the decline of single-sex education (researchers may tout the benefits of all-female schools and colleges, but girls overwhelmingly choose coeducation); the growth of female athletics; the virtual abolition of virginity as a requirement for girls; the equalization of college-attendance rates of males and females; the explosion of employment for married women and mothers even of small children; the crossing of workplace gender lines by both females and males; the cultural pressure on men to be warm and nurturant fathers, to do at least some housework, to choose mates who are their equals in education and income potential.

It's fashionable these days to talk about the backlash against equality feminism—I talk this way myself when I'm feeling blue—but equality feminism has scored amazing successes. It has transformed women's expectations in every area of their lives. However, it has not yet transformed society to meet those expectations. The workplace still discriminates. On the home front few men practice egalitarianism, although many preach it; single mothers—and given the high divorce rate, every mother is potentially a single mother—lead incredibly difficult lives.

In this social context, difference feminism is essentially a way for women both to take advantage of equality feminism's success and to accommodate themselves to its limits. It appeals to particular kinds of women—those in the "helping professions" or the home, for example, rather than those who want to be bomber pilots or neurosurgeons or electricians. At the popular level, it encourages women who feel disadvantaged or demeaned by equality to direct their anger against women who have benefited from it by thinking of them as gender traitors and of themselves as suffering for their virtue—thus the hostility of nurses toward female doctors, and of stay-at-home mothers toward employed mothers.

For its academic proponents, the appeal lies elsewhere: Difference feminism is a way to carve out a safe space in the face of academia's resistance to female advancement. It works much like multiculturalism, making an end-run around a static and discriminatory employment structure by creating an intellectual niche that can be filled only by members of the discriminated-against group. And like other forms of multiculturalism, it looks everywhere for its explanatory force—biology, psychology, sociology, cultural identity—*except* economics. The difference feminists cannot say that the differences between men and women are the result of their relative economic positions because to say that would be to move the whole discussion out of the realm of psychology and feel-good cultural pride and into the realm of a tough political struggle over the distribution of resources and justice and money.

Although it is couched in the language of praise, difference feminism is demeaning to women. It asks that women be admitted into public life and public discourse not because they have a right to be there but because they will improve them. Even if this were true, and not the wishful thinking I believe it to be, why should the task of moral and social transformation be laid on women's doorstep and not on everyone's—or, for that matter, on men's, by the you-broke-it-you-fix-it principle. Peace, the environment, a more humane workplace, economic justice, social support for children—these are issues that affect us all and are everyone's responsibility. By promising to assume that responsibility, difference feminists lay the groundwork for excluding women again, as soon as it becomes clear that the promise cannot be kept.

No one asks that other oppressed groups win their freedom by claiming to be extra-good. And no other oppressed group thinks it must make such a claim in order to be accommodated fully and across the board by society. For blacks and other racial minorities, it is enough to want to earn a living, exercise one's talents, get a fair hearing in the public forum. Only for women is simple justice an insufficient argument. It is as though women don't really believe they are entitled to full citizenship unless they can make a special claim to virtue. Why isn't being human enough?

In the end, I didn't sign that peace petition, although I was sorry to disappoint a woman I liked, and although I am very much for peace. I decided to wait for a petition that welcomed my signature as a person, an American, a citizen implicated, against my will, in war and the war economy. I still think I did the right thing.

Patricia Ireland

"The State of NOW
A Presidential (and Personal) Report"

This reflective essay surveys the distance society has come in addressing women's concerns during Ms. Ireland's lifetime and contemplates where women in all their ethnic, racial and economic diversity need yet to go. Patricia Ireland is the former president of the National Organization for Women.

It seems almost like yesterday. The shrill retort rings clear: "How can they expect me to teach calculus to girls!" All eyes turned to me as I felt myself shrinking in my seat. The outburst of my freshman calculus professor was in response to what I thought was a reasonable question about a math problem. I never asked another question, got a D in the class, and changed my major from math to education.

When I came of age in this society, women were expected to become first and foremost wives and mothers. I grew up hearing that I "could" become a teacher, so I could be there when my kids got home from school, and I would have "something to fall back on" if my husband should die or leave me. I had never even met a woman attorney until 1970. So I became a teacher. One year later, giving up my attempts to teach German in east Tennessee, I could not think of anything else in the world to be except what was then called a "stewardess."

Like so many women, I joined the feminist movement not because of any theoretical conversion, but because of the discrimination I faced. Working for Pan American Airlines for seven years, I learned that "women's work" meant long hours, low pay, and little respect. Airline advertising itself promoted sexual harassment: "We really move our tails for you" and "I'm Cheryl; fly me." The last straw came when I learned that the health benefits I got were worth less than the benefits the men got.

With advice from Dade County, Florida, NOW, I took my complaint about discriminatory benefits to several federal agencies and to my own union. The practice was so blatantly illegal that it was soon changed. So I became an activist. I had discovered I could fight back—and win.

I enrolled in law school to gain tools to fight discrimination. That year, *Ms.* made its first appearance. Today, *Ms.* celebrates its new ad-free incarnation and I serve as NOW's president. In the past two decades, I've seen similar growth in the National Organization for Women. (Pan Am, on the other hand, has gone bankrupt.)

When I became active, only 39 percent of women in the U.S. supported the idea of a women's rights movement. Today, 78 percent of women say they are supporters of the women's movement, including 20 percent who say they are strong supporters. The gains of the past two decades have confirmed the strength of the entire women's movement.

As one organization in that movement, NOW has certainly had—and generated—its share of controversies. Some disputes revolved around strategies or tactics; others around issues. Some remind me of how far we have come; others are still painfully current.

The first words of NOW's statement of purpose are "To take action," a mandate NOW members have always taken seriously. While we lobbied for child care, activists also marched in Mother's Day parades chained to baby carriages. We picketed the Pittsburgh *Press* to end sex-segregated help-wanted ads, and occupied offices of the Equal Employment Opportunity Commission to pressure the agency to enforce Title VII on behalf of women. When I was arrested in 1987 for nonviolently protesting at the Vatican Embassy (against Reagan's recognition of Rome and papal intervention in U.S. policy), some people questioned the target as well as the tactic. In 1967, when NOW activists voted to support the Equal Rights Ammendment, members who felt that women needed protective labor laws left the organization. We lost members again the following year when NOW took a stand in favor of legalizing birth control and abortion. NOW was Red-baited for supporting child care. Richard Nixon vetoed the child care bill in 1971, with a scathing message—written by Pat Buchanan calling child care the "Sovietization of American children."

But I am proud that NOW took these stands and helped turn public opinion around. Such incidents remind us that today's radical issues often become tomorrow's givens. We must be willing to take the heat to move the feminist agenda forward by advocating issues based not on existing politics, but on what women really *need*. As I write this, NOW is building a nonviolent civil disobedience strategy for resistance against all efforts to outlaw abortion, and a nationwide drive to restore full reproductive freedom for all women.

The irony, now that child care is right up there with apple pie, is that we must contend with recycled "NOW-is-anti-family" rhetoric from our opponents, who are uninhibited by reality. In truth, though they continue to call us out-of-touch or irrelevant, NOW has continued to prosper. From a membership of fewer than 20,000 twenty years ago, NOW has grown to more than 280,000. While we usually average 2,000 to 3,000 new members a month, the number more than tripled in the four months following Clarence Thomas's confirmation to the Supreme Court.

As the entire women's movement gains strength and momentum, attacks on all of us increase. Predictably, one of the divide-and-conquer tactics used is lesbian-baiting. But in 1992, the tactic is less effective than it was twenty years ago. The fight for lesbian rights and against heterosexism was, in an earlier period, a source of great controversy in NOW (and in the movement as a whole). All this time later, memories of the attempted purge of the "Lavender Menace" by some NOW leaders and chapters remain painful. But the overwhelming majority of the organization fought back in 1971 with a strong resolution clearly identifying lesbian rights as a feminist issue and a NOW issue. We can take pride that NOW's work since then has been an important part of shaping the movement and changing public opinion on lesbian rights.

Because she is an out lesbian, NOW's Action Vice President Rosemary Dempsey had to fight for custody of her children twenty years ago; last year she also had to battle for the right to provide home care for her mother, who has Alzheimer's disease. Both battles were testimony to the need to fight against oppression, but both were also proof of our ability to win those fights.

When I became president of NOW and my personal life became public, it became clear to me just how far we have come. While I may have vastly underestimated the emotional impact of putting my family and myself in the public spotlight's glare, I also found tremendous support, often where I least expected it. Most people are far more concerned with their own families than with mine. They are also fed up with hypocrisy and are ready for real change, real honesty, and an end to self-serving leadership. There have been many out lesbian and bisexual leaders in NOW—and their leadership has been a boon, not a bane, to the organization.

NOW has also been enhanced by our commitment to fighting racism and by the affirmative action we have taken internally. The Reverend Pauli Murray, an African American and a NOW cofounder, was one of the authors of our statement of purpose. Other women who led NOW in the early years included Addie Wyatt, Shirley Chisholm, Fannie Lou Hamer, and Coretta Scott King. Aileen Hernandez was elected the first African-American president of NOW, in 1971. Still, women of color in NOW's early leadership must have felt isolated. But in 1980, NOW activists voted to require affirmative action on our national board, and since 1987 programs to increase diversity at the chapter and state levels have been mandated.

Ginny Montes, who took office as national secretary last December, brings to our new team of four officers an important perspective as a woman of color and an immigrant from Honduras. She serves an organization with at least 30 percent racial and ethnic diversity represented on the national board and far greater participation by women of color at all levels than NOW had two decades ago. We continue to pursue greater diversity within NOW, including stronger alliances with civil rights groups and organizations of women of color. We have also begun more work on disability rights issues. And as "welfare reform" proposals sweep the country, NOW is determined to fight against those who blame poor women for the nation's economic mess; we have made a major commitment to work with welfare rights, antihunger, and homelessness coalitions.

Change, even strongly desired change, is never easy. Communication between diverse communities and activists can be difficult and confusing. But such a process is crucial if we are to succeed in building the backlash to the backlash. We must empower more women to move into policy-making positions, not just in government but in all institutions—including NOW.

With the capture of the Supreme Court by the Right (and with senators who had pledged to support women's rights voting to confirm each new and more conservative nominee), we learned again and bitterly that no one will fight for us the way we can fight for ourselves. But we've been developing our tactical repertoire for years.

Back in June 1982, Florida's male-dominated senate blocked the Equal Rights Amendment. The vote was not unexpected: backlash had been building for years, and Reagan had taken office eighteen months earlier. We knew the odds when NOW launched the ERA Countdown Campaign in June 1981, but we believed that fighting back would bring real gains.

We did not win the ERA—but it was immediately reintroduced in Congress. Still, although some had seen NOW as singularly focused on the ERA, during the Countdown Campaign we had generated resources for all of the movement: we defeated the so-called Human Life Amendment in Congress. At the end, we had networks of experienced, angry activists, many of whom had enough familiarity with their state legislators to realize, "I could do his job. In fact I could do it better."

The analysis of the legislatures in the fifteen states that failed to pass the ERA showed that 79 percent of the female members, but only 39 percent of the males, favored the amendment. NOW decided to try a new approach: rather than the traditional careful targeting and "husbanding" of our resources, we changed to a tactic of flooding the ticket, recruiting as many women as we could find and persuade to run.

We targeted Florida. Between June and November 1982, we scouted out, supported, and elected enough women to more than double the number in the state senate and to add 50 percent in the house. The following year, Florida NOW drafted an educational equity bill, and the legislators we helped elect made sure it became law. Positive state legislation on violence, health, and economic issues for women followed. Seven years later, NOW's feminization of power campaign was still paying dividends in Florida. After the *Webster* decision, then-Governor Martinez called a special session to pass a major antiabortion package through the legislature. The women legislators were there to stop his antiabortion scheme. The next election, Martinez was voted out of office. We called it "The Revenge of the ERA Nerds."

As the differences in how women and men legislators vote became documented, moving more feminist women into elected office has become a widely accepted strategy. Recruiting large numbers of feminists to run also addresses another long-standing problem: left to their own devices, the two major parties too often present us with a choice of the evil of two lessers.

The Louisiana governor's race in 1991 was a classic case. As important as it was to defeat David Duke, we were hard-pressed to generate much enthusiasm to work for now-Governor Edwin Edwards, or, prior to the primary, any of the other Democrats. But Louisiana ranked dead last in the number of women in the legislature. (Not by coincidence, the legislature in 1990 had passed one of the most restrictive antiabortion laws in the country.) NOW's executive vice president (and a native Louisianan), Kim Gandy headed up a yearlong project that helped generate a record fifty-seven women to run, and elect enough to more than triple the number of women in the state house, elect the first African-American woman to the senate, and replace the antiabortion attorney general with the first woman ever to hold that post. There is no doubt in my mind that every vote we turned out for a feminist woman candidate was also a vote against David Duke—who was soundly defeated.

We know we must defeat Bush in November. Yet, for many women, the Democratic Party's politics-as-usual leaves us cold. When fully half of the eligible voters were not moved even to vote in the last presidential election, we know we are not alone in that perception. Many of us believe that our best hope in the long run is the 21st Century Party, a new feminist party that will hold its first convention in August, the weekend after Women's Equality Day.

Meanwhile, last March, a very surprised U.S. Senator Alan Dixon from Illinois, one of two northern Democrats who voted to confirm Clarence Thomas, was defeated in the Democratic primary by Carol Moseley Braun. The national NOW/PAC endorsed Braun even before she filed as a candidate and, when she did, immediately gave her the maximum legal contribution; Chicago and Illinois NOW activists organized a core of grass-roots support; and Braun inspired both Democratic and Republican women to express their anger over the treatment of Anita Hill and the threats to women's progress.

One month later, more than three quarters of a million people marched on the nation's capital in the largest protest in Washington's history. The organizers of the April 5 March for Women's Lives were the leadership of NOW, with the reinforcements and momentum the Thomas confirmation had produced. We organized the march to demand abortion rights and full reproductive freedom for all women. The front line and the rally speakers represented those literally on the front line of the struggle. Young women. Poor women. Women in the military. Unusually high numbers of women of racial and ethnic diversity (disproportionate to population). Providers whose clinics have been bombed and invaded. Doctors whose children have been harassed at school.

Afterward, NOW activists and staff shifted to NOW/PAC work in Pennsylvania, where we helped another political outsider, Lynn Yeakel, win a come-from-behind primary race against the Democratic party machine's nominee for the U.S. Senate. (Yeakel, of course, is now making a strong run for the seat held by Senator Arlen Specter, the man who so ruthlessly persecuted Hill during the Senate hearings.)

The entire women's movement deserves credit for helping to transform righteous indignation into the concerted political action that expresses itself in Braun and Yeakel. But we all know that our work is not finished. Like the rest of the feminist movement (and despite misperceptions of the extent of our resources), NOW's reach always exceeds our grasp. There are never enough hours in the day, monies in the till, staff in the Action Center, or activists in the field. But we at NOW believe that, working together, women have the strength and determination to change the balance of power in state legislatures, Congress, and even the White House. In this season of discontent, it will be women who can transform the national rage and demoralization into hope. We have been building toward this moment for twenty years.

Elinor Lenz and Barbara Myerhoff

from *The Feminization of America*
"Humanizing the Workplace"

Educational consultant and lecturer Elinor Lenz and anthropology professor Barbara Myerhoff here map the transformation of the workplace environment by women who have entered the work force. Lenz is also the author of *So You Want to Go Back to School* and *Once My Child Now My Friend.* Myerhoff is best known for *Number Our Days,* her award-winning film documentary and book on the Jewish community of Venice, California.

A s women have been moving in ever-increasing numbers into jobs and professions formerly occupied by men, the working environment in which most people spend the major part of their lives has begun to respond to feminine needs and values. As a result, we are seeing a shift to a more humane, more people-centered workplace, a long overdue development that comes in time to counteract a growing discontent with the conditions of work that has been spreading throughout the occupational spectrum.

The discontents that people are voicing about their work are for the most part connected to a feeling of meaninglessness, a sense of being alienated from what one does during the working day, which afflicts people at all salary levels. Some typical comments from interviews with men and women in the $25,000–$50,000 salary range reflect this:

> I spend most of my time writing ad copy for deodorants and after-shave lotion. Eight to ten hours a day, day after day, year after year, agonizing over stuff I don't give a damn about. When I get home at night after an hour's commute, my kids are in bed and I'm so strung out, all I want is a couple of good stiff scotches, and maybe I'll watch a little TV before I turn in. (Mark Nevelson, forty-five-year-old advertising executive, Chicago)
>
> I'm just marking time till I get my pension. Twenty years to go, then if I'm not too old, maybe I can do some of the things I've always wanted to do. My job is just a big fat bore, a waste of time. (Helen Jacoby, forty-two-year-old executive secretary to the financial vice-president of a merchandising conglomerate, Dallas)
>
> I go home on Friday evening, lock the door, and don't leave my apartment until Monday morning. It takes me two days and three nights to calm down so that I can go back on Monday and face five more days of it. I hate my life, I hate myself, I hate

what this is doing to me. (Susan Ellis, thirty-year-old program coordinator in a federally funded community project, Detroit)

Underlying much of this unhappiness is the divorce of work from the rest of life, an inevitable outcome of the work-home schism. Work takes on meaning only in a context that provides wholeness and balance and that gives us a feeling of belonging to a community. The notion that the activity at which we spend the most productive years of our lives can be divided off from the rest of us—from our character, aspirations, and cultural heritage—the assumption that a human being can be split in two with one-half placed on hold for forty hours a week is a recent and dangerous idea that is damaging to the individual's sense of self-worth.

HOW DID WE GET HERE FROM THERE?

In the preindustrial era, men, women, and children worked together, often side by side. The family was the basic economic unit, and families depended upon each other for subsistence. The tasks were, of course, often gender related: men in the family performed the heavy-duty agricultural work; women were in charge of the kitchen garden, poultry yard, and household, which included manufacturing most of the necessities of life. The preindustrial home was actually a hub of industry in which the woman performed not only the customary tasks of cooking, cleaning, and child care but also made soap and candles, spun cloth, wove lace, and sewed and repaired the family's clothes. A similar system existed in the self-contained world of artisans, shopkeepers, and small entrepreneurs who worked in settings that usually combined workplace and home-place, with assistance as needed from family members.

The rise of an industrial economy and the urbanization that accompanied it were the beginning and the end of the integrated home-work system. Farmers and small entrepreneurs flocked to the cities, and goods that had formerly been produced at home were now mass produced in factories. The decrease of productive work in the home brought about the segregation of the sexes during the working day, leading ultimately to the development of two very different, polarized environments.

The home, which was transformed into an exclusively feminine domain, came to represent a refuge from the rigors of work, the place where the heart lay, where the spirit was refreshed and the energies renewed. Home became synonymous with warmth, softness, color. It was the "supreme cultural achievement of women," according to sociologist-philosopher Georg Simmel.

The workplace, which for a rising middle-class white-collar work force was usually an office, came to represent the very antithesis of the homeplace. From the beginning, the office or factory was strictly functional—cold, impersonal, colorless. In the pre-Civil War era, it was strictly a male domain. The clerical work was performed by copyists, or scriveners (Melville's Bartleby was one of these), and it consisted mainly of copying out rough drafts of letters or other documents in a fine hand, using a goose quill pen.

The entry of women into clerical work was brought about by post–Civil War changes in the structure of capitalism, which caused a substantial increase in correspondence and record keeping. Having lost their productive role in the home to the factory system, women who needed to earn a living were attracted to clerical work, which offered them at least a subsistence wage.

But the presence of women in the workplace did not put an end to sexual segregation during working hours. A new form of male-female segregation arose within the workplace itself, facilitated by the growth of hierarchy. A pyramidal structure was designed in response to the growth in size and complexity of commercial enterprises; within this structure, power and responsibility were clearly delineated and ranked from top to bottom. At the bottom of the pyramid were, of course, the clerical workers, who by now were mostly women. Managerial jobs were routinely filled by men, whether or not there were women available with equal or superior qualifications; it was considered a waste of time to train women for managerial positions since it was assumed that they would give up their jobs and return to the home as soon as they were married.

Whereas in 1870 less than 1 percent of women employed outside of agriculture were engaged in clerical work, by 1920 they accounted for nearly 92 percent of the stenographers/typists and nearly 50 percent of the bookkeepers, cashiers, and accountants. Nevertheless, the influx of women into the workplace did not alter the division of labor at home: women continued to be solely responsible for domestic tasks. This meant that, while men's lives had become unidimensional, centering mainly around their work, women were living dual lives: one in the home as the family nurturer and caretaker, the other in the workplace as a performer of routine, repetitive tasks in an impersonal atmosphere. The working environment was alien to the feminine temperament, having been created by and for the men in managerial positions, and it reflected the split between public and private lives that resulted from the separation of work from home, with home life and all that it represented becoming, more than ever before, an exclusive concern of women.

SEPARATE REALITIES

The severing of work from home was like an act of surgery, cutting deeply into the common world of men and women and leaving wounds that only in recent years are beginning to be healed. The idea that "a woman's place is in the home" (except, of course, when she was needed for war work) originated in this separation, as did the man's role as sole breadwinner. The man as producer and the woman as consumer were not, however, two halves neatly fitting together into a whole; women's domestic labor was devalued, while men's labor was viewed as providing the backbone of the nation's economy as well as the family's support. By the 1950s, the flight from the cities added to the work-home schism a geographical separation often involving hours of commuting by car and train.

In the course of this separation, both homeplace and workplace suffered serious losses. The home was deprived of its earlier economic productivity, and work became mainly an endless, repetitive process. With the decline of the extended family and the woman's nearly total preoccupation with child care, the nuclear household, particularly in the suburbs, represented a self-contained nest isolated from the world of action and achievement. (Georg Simmel tempered his effusions by admitting that this "immense cultural achievement" has also proved a prison house.) In this well-appointed dream home, this "haven in a heartless world," the feminine ethnic languished and was assailed by a vague, unfocused discontent, a "problem that had no name," which Betty Friedan labeled "the feminine mystique."

Meanwhile, the workplace, having developed during the nation's rapid industrialization as a masculine construct untempered by feminine influence, was experiencing its own form of deprivation—the lack of nurturing and personalism and the sheltering warmth of home. In the modern large-scale bureaucracy, relations are governed by rational procedures. A masculine ethic of rationality and reason, which can be identified in early bureaucratic models of management, elevates traits that are assumed to belong exclusively to men: a tough-minded approach to problems; analytic ability to abstract and plan; a capacity to set aside personal, emotional considerations in the interests of task accomplishment; and a cognitive superiority in problem solving and decision making. The focus is on goals, output, and efficiency, and managers as well as lower-echelon workers are expected to act in their own self-interest.[1]

Living within their separate realities of work and home left both sexes with a sense of being cheated. The bright, energetic woman could hardly help feeling trapped by the limitations of the full-time domestic role, and the upwardly mobile business executive, the obsessed workaholic, the overstressed professional wore out psychiatrists' couches, wondering, Is that all there is?

For a balanced life, human beings need both love and work, claimed Freud, and when these needs are separated and opposed, men and women are condemned to live half-lives.

Transforming the Workplace

Women bring a positive, humanizing quality to the corporate environment.
—*survey of male CEOs in Fortune 500 companies*

The mass movement of women into the workplace has been hailed by social scientists and historians as a social change of momentous proportions, comparable to the industrial revolution or the waves of immigration in the last century. "It's the single most outstanding phenomenon of this century," says Eli Ginzberg, professor at Columbia University and chairman of the National Commission for Manpower Policy. A *Business Week* article attributes America's rapid economic growth in recent years to one factor: women's entry into the job market as part-time, full-time lifetime workers in virtually all occupations and at all levels of responsibility.

This transfusion of feminine energy and skill from the private to the public world is, the article continues, "boosting economic growth, and helping to reshape the economy dramatically. Women have seized two-thirds of the jobs created in the last decade. And they have been the linchpin in the shift toward services and away from manufacturing. Because a rapidly expanding labor force is a principal element in propelling an economy onto a fast-growth track, the influx of women into the job market may be the major reason that the U.S. has emerged so much healthier than other countries from the economic shocks of the 1970s." Nobel laureate Paul A. Samuelson, professor of economics at M.I.T., adds, "To the degree that women are getting an opportunity that they didn't have in the past, the economy is tapping an important and previously wasted resource."[2]

But the feminization of the workplace is transforming more than just the economy. "Women are neurologically more flexible than men," says Eli Ginzberg, "and they have had cultural permission to be more intuitive, sensitive, feeling. Their natural milieu has been complexity, change, nurturance, affiliation, a more fluid sense of time." As these attributes of feminine culture are brought into the workplace, they are providing a much-needed balance to what has been a predominantly male environment, and slowly but steadily they are eroding some of the obsolete practices and prejudices that have dehumanized work and the work environment.

Much of this change is linked to women's deeply rooted need to integrate love and work. The work-home division grates against the feminine sensibility. "Every woman in America leads a double life," says political scientist Emily Stoper. "She is shaped by a double socialization; she is torn apart by a double pull; often she carries a double burden. One side of her duality turns inward to the world of home, children, 'inner feelings'—femininity, in a word. The other side faces outward to the world of work, achievement, power, money, abstract thought—the 'man's world.' "[3]

Women's efforts to reconcile the two sides of this duality pit them against the structure and rationale of the corporate bureaucracy. As Daniel Boorstin points out in *The End of Ideology,* the contemporary enterprise was set up to obey three "techno-logics": the logic of size, the logic of "metric" time, and the logic of hierarchy. "Each of the three, the product of engineering rationality, has imposed on the worker a set of constraints with which he is forced to wrestle every day." These three technologics, which have defined and delimited work in America for the past century, are giving way—inch by inch, moment by moment, step by step—to the forces of change that are in harmony with feminine culture.

The constraint of "metric time" measurement is loosening as the needs of working mothers challenge rigid work schedules and generate more fluid, flexible time arrangements to include part-time, flexitime, and job sharing. These innovative work patterns, offering more flexibility and the opportunity for choice and self-management on the job, make it possible for women to bring their home and working lives into balance.

But it is not only women who are the beneficiaries of more relaxed work schedules; potential all-around benefits abound: the easing of traffic congestion; the weekday access by employees to shopping, education, recreation; an opportunity for both parents to spend more time with their children. (A 1977 Quality of Employment Survey by the Survey Research Center at the University of Michigan found that 51 percent of wives and 42 percent of husbands with children under eighteen preferred to reduce their work time in order to spend more time with their families.) The time clock may, eventually, be consigned to the ash heap of history as the development of technology converges with new, more leisure-oriented lifestyles to bring about a variety of work schedules that can be adapted to individual needs.

The other two technologics in Boorstin's trio of restrictive practices—size and hierarchy—are being challenged by forces of change that are also in accord with the feminine need to reconcile home and work. A service/information economy does not lend itself to massive bureaucratic organization. As John Naisbitt has noted, this hidebound, elephantine structure, with its rigid ladder of separations, slows down the flow of information "just when greater speed and flexibility is needed." He sees mammoth centralized institutions whose very existence relies upon hierarchies being replaced by smaller, decentralized units, linked informally with each other instead of being clumped together. The eventual replacement for hierarchy, according to current management theory, will be networks, a pattern that is already in evidence and which suits the feminine temperament, with its proclivity for connectedness, far better than the divisive pecking order of the hierarchy. (A recent study of female hierarchies concluded that, though women in general do not like hierarchies, they are able, depending on the task to be performed, to work together, defer to authority, and maintain discipline.)[4]

A New Managerial Agenda

Some of the changes being forged in the crucible of feminization could not have been imagined even a decade ago. Bread-and-butter isssues—comparable pay, for example—are forcing managers as well as economic theorists to rethink the basic American concept of equality. The Equal Pay Act of 1963 required that women be paid equally with men for the same job; and women's pay, though still a long way from parity, has risen from 57 percent of men's wages in 1973 to 64 percent in 1980. But the concept of comparable worth asks: What if the jobs are not the same but are equal in levels of skill, effort, and responsibility? Should a secretary, for example, be paid as much as a truck driver? The controversy has been heating up, with employers and union representatives, particularly those representing public employees, positioning themselves for a protracted battle. A judicial or legislative resolution does not appear to be in the offing, but in the meantime, the underlying question of what equality is, once a preoccupation mainly of academic philosophers, will continue to be argued at corporate seminars and meetings of public officials.

Other strange new issues are appearing on the managerial agenda, issues unrelated to production quotas or profit margins that seem, oddly enough, to be closer to the homeplace than the workplace. In the 1970s, babies were not a concern of such enterprises as the Caltech Jet Propulsion Laboratory. At that time, the laboratory was mostly male. But in 1973, when the federally funded lab initiated an affirmative action program, the number of women employees began growing, until today women constitute a quarter of the five thousand-person work force. And a quarter-mile from the lab is the Child Educational Center of the Caltech/JPL community, which serves 150 preschool children of employees and area residents. Women workers drop in to nurse and play with their children; both mothers and fathers are encouraged to visit.[5]

At present, nearly three thousand corporations nationwide sponsor day-care centers for their employees, or otherwise assist them in finding reliable day care. A recent survey funded by the federal government called employer-supported child care "the fastest growing form of child care today." The survey, conducted for the U.S. Department of Health and Human Services, found that although employer-sponsored programs cover less than 1 percent of children in day care, "the trend is accelerating rapidly."

Obviously, the child-care services currently available are not adequate for the rapidly growing need, but the continuing pressure being placed on officials by working mothers is being felt throughout the economy and is having a significant influence on public policy. The Economic Recovery Tax Act of 1981 offered tax breaks of $2,400 per child to companies that include child care in their benefits package. Several state legislatures are considering similar proposals to encourage local businesses to establish child-care services.

As with any social innovation in its early stages, company-sponsored child care is going through a period of experimentation, during which various child-care systems are being tested. Five Silicon Valley companies make direct contributions to a local service center, which in return ensures employees day care at a discount and priority admission for their children. The Campbell Soup Company operates its own on-site center in Camden, New Jersey. In New York City's Lower East Side, a unique partnership has brought together the International Ladies' Garment Workers Union, a manufacturers' association, and a city agency to establish the Garment Industry Day Care Center of Chinatown. Since most of the parents are recent immigrants from China, the instruction here is bilingual.

So far, the trend seems to favor the Silicon Valley model, in which employers make a corporate contribution to a community-run center in return for which employees receive certain child-care services. In a variation of this model, companies are instituting referral programs or reimbursing employees for child care. The system most advantageous to both parents and children is, of course, the on-site facility that gives parents and children the opportunity for close interaction during the day, but since this is the costliest system, it has not as yet attracted many companies.

We may justifiably question the value system of a society that spends billions on sophisticated weapons yet skimps on care for its children. But as Eric Nelson, codirector of the Caltech/JPL center puts it, "It's going to take people of vision at the top and bottom getting together to solve the day-care problem. In general, management is older and male. Child care is a problem with which they can't easily identify. Child-care experts have to understand that and be able to convince hard-headed businessmen that they should be interested in babies. The fact that women are out of the home is still a shock to some men, and the thought of babies in the workplace is the last straw.''

But the trend is unstoppable, for it reflects a growing public consciousness that day care for the children of working parents is a concern not only of the parents but of the entire society. When children are not adequately cared for, as many studies show, the lack is reflected in rising rates of crime, unemployment, and domestic violence. An argument that is proving more persuasive, however, especially among "hard-headed businessmen," is that day care is good for business, reducing absenteeism, and boosting morale. Most companies would be hard hit by the loss of those female workers who are mothers of small children, and economic analyses indicate that the economy would go into a severe decline without the earnings and purchasing power of working mothers. The facts of economic life make it safe to predict that by the end of this decade, companies without some form of day care will be regarded as dinosaurs, along with those having no employee benefit plans.

The economics of feminine employment has also made parental leave one of the hotter personnel issues of the mid-eighties. With the passage of the federal Pregnancy Discrimination Act, ... pregnancy and childbirth must be treated similarly to any other physical disability, a legislative breakthrough that has forced many companies to change their corporate policies in regard to maternity leave. (It is somewhat ironic that motherhood, to which our public officials regularly pay homage, must be classified as a disability in order for women to be able to have babies and continue working.)

According to a national survey by Catalyst, a New York-based national research organization, companies that had treated maternity differently from other disabilities were required to change their policies after October 1978, with the result that informal, unwritten maternity-leave plans were formalized, and longer-paid leave for maternity was added to company disability plans. Here again, progress has been slow: fewer than half of all working women receive paid maternity leaves of more than six weeks, and the few forward-looking companies that offer paternity leaves find that only a small fraction of eligible fathers apply. But the issue is moving to the top of the corporate agenda as more women return to work after becoming mothers and more fathers are sharing child-care responsibilities from the beginning.

The working mother is also forcing corporations to rethink their policies linking mobility to transferability. Since working wives cannot be moved as easily as the household effects, company personnel divisions are now charged with the responsibility of finding a comparable job for the displaced wife—or for her husband, if she is the one to be transferred. This is not always so simple, and in the case of the professional, a doctor or lawyer with an established practice, it may be virtually impossible. As a result, the mobility-transferability link is no longer a clear-cut either/or choice: either move and climb up the ladder or count yourself out; it has become enmeshed in emotional ties, in friendships and community roots, so that family stability must now be factored into corporate management planning, much to the surprise and, no doubt, chagrin of the more traditional male managers.

This growing interest in the needs of working parents stems less, as we have suggested, from a sudden surge of corporate solicitude for the two-job family than from the new economic realities that business and industry are facing as a result of women entering the work force. The facts and figures are clear and their implications for the workplace are unmistakable: women now constitute one-half of the work force, and of these women, half will become pregnant at some time in their working lives. The majority of these women are no longer leaving their jobs for an extended time to rear their children. According to U.S. census figures for 1982, almost one-third of mothers with infants under six months are working, and a survey of corporations found that the average length of time off work for new mothers is three months. (This coincides with research in infant psychology, which has found that at three months, the infant can be safely separated from the mother for limited time periods.)

These corporate efforts to meet the needs of working mothers, insufficient as they are at present, represent a radical reordering of an institutional mind-set that has been shaped by ''the cult of efficiency.'' Feminization is forcing that mind-set to extend itself to the larger questions of human values and relationships and how these impinge upon people's working lives. For traditional management, confronting such questions has had the effect of shock treatment. To most men in top management, women are ''a foreign country,'' says organizational psychologist Sandra Florstedt. She attributes the slow pace of reform to women's ''different heritage'' of values, behavior, and style, acquired over the centuries and often baffling to men in the workplace, accustomed as they are to working in an all-male environment. Having started her career as a high school language teacher, she identifies as the most difficult problem in organizations today the development of a common language to span the communication gap between men and women in the workplace.

Florstedt, who has fifteen years of experience in organizational development, believes that though tangible reforms have been slow in coming, attitudinal and atmospheric changes have speeded up as the feminine presence has made itself felt throughout the workplace. To encourage better communication among employees and provide a healthier, pleasanter working environment, many large corporations are moving from private offices to open space, installing cheerfully decorated employee lounges and exercise rooms offering recreation and fitness programs, and, as in the case of the new Levi-Strauss corporate headquarters in downtown San Francisco, including in the building complex small parks in which employees can hold meetings or relax during coffee and lunch breaks.

The most important influence of women on the workplace, according to Florstedt, is that "they're keeping men honest. I know a lot of men who like working with women because it's the women who are calling it the way they see it, at least privately—maybe it's because they're new to the situation, they're seeing it differently, more clearly." At the same time, she recognizes that women's creative energies, which are now being diverted from housework and babies to business and the professions, need to be channeled properly if women are to achieve their full potential for productivity. "They need to feel a sense of connection to the workplace and not think of it as a male world in which they are intruders."

It may well be that the growing presence of women in the workplace holds forth the greatest promise for a humanizing transformation in American working lives: the desegregation of the workplace and the restoration in today's egalitarian terms of a working life shared by men and women, which was disrupted by the industrial revolution. "Men and women are rediscovering each other," said a woman who heads a corporate training program. There is still hostility and resentment, she added, by men who see women taking over jobs that were formerly regarded as strictly male occupational territory, but this is lessening as men become accustomed to women in these jobs. Distance may lend enchantment, but it also leads to stereotyping: as the distance between male and female working lives narrows, the stereotype too is waning, and women are appearing less and less as a "foreign country" to their male colleagues.

Of course, we can hardly expect that a magnetic force as powerful as sexuality will ever entirely vanish from the workplace, nor is this necessarily desirable. Phil Randall, a Chicago management consultant, sees sexual attraction as inevitable in a more humane workplace: "The fact that people who work together can have affairs is something that companies have to allow for. I hope they'll look carefully at teams of men and women whose love—or whatever relationship they have outside the office—makes them more creative at work." At the same time, a few men are learning to develop nonsexual relationships with sexually attractive peers, observes Anthony Astrachan, author of *How Men Feel,* "disentangling competence from sexuality, rather than denying either one. It is neither easy nor traditional, but some men are learning (with some pain) how to do it."

Those men who succeed in developing nonsexual friendships with their female colleagues—and their number increases daily—are experiencing a gratifying sense of personal growth, an ability to look beyond gender at individual competency and accomplishment. Several men who have made this transition report that it has enriched not only their relationships at work but also their personal lives. "I'm finding it easier to make friends, with men as well as women," said one. "Women seem to have some sort of special talent for friendship, and it's rubbing off on me."

The morale-boosting, performance-improving impact of the feminine presence has not escaped the notice of corporate personnel managers. Jane Evans, an executive vice-president of General Mills, reports that corporations are searching for women who know how to help men open up, share their feelings, become comfortable with women. Executive search firms agree, adding that one of the major barriers to the promotion of women is the male executive who does not understand women and can only look on them in such supportive roles as wives, mothers, daughters, and secretaries. This musty attitude is as much a problem for the male executive, whose narrow perspective denies him the productive abilities of qualified women, as it is for the women whose progress he attempts to stall.

As women in so-called traditional male jobs cease to be a novelty, men are beginning to recognize the benefits that women bring to the workplace. A survey of male CEOs in Fortune 500 companies on the effects of women in executive positions yielded a generally positive reaction, with a substantial percentage stating that women bring a humanizing quality to the corporate world and are also improving business. The growth of an information/service economy calls for the kind of skills and problem-solving approaches that are essentially feminine. Information and service are, like women's historic culture, processual; and there is a developing awareness in business and industry of the linkage between productivity and what is usually referred to as "human resources," or the relationships among people at work.

Mary Bradley, a former teacher in adult education and now a corporate training director, has this to say on the subject of the feminine influence on technology: "Formerly, my experience and that of most women has consisted of learning how to function in a male system. But in my present work environment, which combines computer technology with education, the situation is reversed: men have to move into what has always been a female system—education, helping people develop new skills, which is what a high-technology economy is all about—and when it comes to education, men whose training has been exclusively in business and industry are totally lost. They understand equipment, marketing, the good old bottom line, but they don't know what goes into the development of a human being. They've never before paid much attention to human needs in their enterprises—they thought that was for social workers. But now they have to pay attention because it means money and expansion and business opportunities."

In the "improving business" area, women's interpersonal skills receive a consistently high rating among employers. The ability to convey warmth and empathy goes a long way, in everything from selling stocks and bonds to winning cases in court. The once solidly male world of Wall Street acknowledges that female brokers are making a special contribution to the field because of their tendency to pay more attention to a client's needs. Moreover, women are better at selling because of their superior verbal talents. "In this business we sell products that are very ephemeral," says Gail Winslow, who is with a brokerage firm in Washington. "Women have an edge because we tend to paint pictures with our words."[6]

In the tough, combative legal arena, Patricia Bobb, a Chicago attorney, finds an advantage for women in their extra "verbal sensitivity to jurors," a quality that Judge Jerry Pacht of Los Angeles has observed in his courtroom and which he believes gives female attorneys an edge in jury selection. An attorney and professor of law, Grace Blumberg, describes the process through which a group of female lawyers developed a brief on a divorce case dealing with a woman's right to community property as "communitarian and communicative, full of feeling and interpersonal experience. . . . They created an atmosphere of social intimacy between relative strangers." With women approaching 50 percent of law school graduates as compared with 10 percent twenty to thirty years ago, legal scholars and other specialists are looking forward to long-overdue changes in the legal system. Says Derek Bok, president of Harvard University, "Over the next generation, I predict society's greatest opportunities will lie in tapping human inclinations toward collaboration and compromise rather than stirring our proclivities for competition and rivalry."

For many women in influential positions, changing the workplace is at the heart of their commitment to feminism. For Donna Shalala, the practice of feminism is not limited to serving as a role model; it encompasses "thinking of ways in which I can humanize the institution." She believes that women's issues should be integrated into a larger, humanistic agenda. "My single professional focus is to make institutions act better than they ever thought they could act." An assistant secretary at the Department of Housing and Urban Development during the Carter administration, she called the department heads together to conduct a "women's impact study," as a result of which shelters for battered women became eligible for community development grants, and housing units to accommodate large families headed by a woman were included in planning.

Humanizing the institution does not always take the form of large-scale social advances; it often manifests itself in more subtle ways, such as the softening of the sterile ambience of the workplace in an effort to make it more homelike. Sue Bohle, president of her own public relations firm with offices in Los Angeles and San Francisco, lets her supervisors choose the type of furniture they want. "I like antique reproductions and lots of plants, and my walls are done in a rose brocaded print. But if you go next door, you'll see an office done in contemporary furnishings—teak and beige. Everyone gets to select her own colors and designs; it's highly individualized." Bohle encourages her staff to develop their social skills and to consult her about any problems, personal or professional. "It's important for me to feel that they're happy at their work. That may have something to do with me personally, but I think it also has something to do with my being a woman. I'm willing to take the time to listen and talk to them about their problem, even when I'm under great pressure.''

The willingness to listen and the quality of caring and comforting that exists in many women comes through in their work, sometimes without their being aware of it, as they go about their daily tasks in the business and professional world. The cumulative effect of such empathic behavior does not show up in organizational blueprints or financial statements; but in building small, often imperceptible bridges between home and work, this aspect of feminization is performing a function essential to the health of the American workplace.

You Can Go Home Again

A trend that reflects most vividly the attempt to bring home and work together is the rise of the home-based business, a form of entrepreneurship that includes among its growing number of adherents many dropouts from the corporate rat-race. Starting a home-based business is a risky venture, and there are numerous failures, recalling the fate of the small entrepreneurs in the late nineteenth century. But the payoffs are attractive enough to lure a growing number of people who prefer a residential work setting and control over their working lives to the security, such as it is, of a nine-to-five job.

Working at home has always been a preferred option for women; for some women, during the early child-care years, it has been the only possible income-producing option available to them. At the turn of the century, women ran boardinghouses, did dressmaking and other types of sewing, and turned out piecework in their homes for sweat shops. Today, an estimated one million women in the United States operate businesses from their homes. They work part-time and full-time, earning salaries ranging from pin money to hundreds of thousands of dollars a year, and their businesses cover all kinds of professional services as well as products developed from homemaking skills. They have their own network, a national association that performs educational and informational services for women with home-based businesses.

Today, working at home is attracting men as well as women, in small-town and rural areas as well as in large cities. In Los Angeles,

Elaine Carlson baked cookies in her kitchen and sold them out of her home before going into national distribution. In New York, Carlos Echegaray creates painted wooden sculptures of cats and sells them worldwide to galleries and museums. In rural Wisconsin, Jean Ellison hand-looms cloth and sells it as fast as it is woven to neighbors and local shops. Columnist Jim Sanderson quotes a man he identifies as Roger: "Not every man is gung ho about the corporate world. I've always wanted to run my own shop. For three years my wife helped me develop a mail-order business out of our home. Now she's gone to work full-time, which she loves, and I stay home with the kids and still make a modest living. It's terrific; everybody gets what they want."

Other home-based businesses include aerobics exercise, yoga and karate classes, catering services, hairstyling, copy editing, jewelry design, not to mention an ever-expanding variety of consulting services, some of them, like those offered by computer consultants, spawned by high tech. And a number of organizations, among them universities, government agencies, and business corporations, are encouraging some of their employees to work at home by having them plug in the modems of their computers to the organization's computer technology.

The working-at-home trend is being accelerated by several recent developments, especially the growing popularity of mail-order shopping as a time and money saver, and the availability of home computers, which make it possible to run a small business with little or no clerical help. These practical considerations are bolstered by a changing set of personal priorities that are motivating men and women to reexamine such concepts as "success" and "achievement" and to weigh them against the costs of following traditional paths to these goals. Recent studies of masculine and feminine attitudes toward success suggest a growing disenchantment among both sexes with the prevailing standards by which success is defined: the relentless striving, the ruthless competitiveness, the tensions and conflicts endemic to the hyper, all-against-all environment in which the game of success is played.

REEVALUATING SUCCESS

The idea of success has always carried different nuances for women than for men. Traditionally, a woman's success was measured by the achievements of her husband and children. But today's high-salaried women executives or self-made entrepreneurs are still in many cases ambivalent about applying the term *successful* to themselves, unless they are also enjoying a satisfying personal life. Tinka Streibert, who gave up an executive job in television to run a child-care center, defines success as "knowing in your gut that what you're doing is right for you." For Karen Szurek, a New York public relations executive, success is two-sided: one side is material, the other concerns the quality of one's personal life: both are equally important. Younger women starting their own businesses say that they are not interested primarily in making money but rather in doing things they enjoy that fit in with their lives.

As the workplace becomes feminized, the feminine definition of success is being adopted by younger men who, disenchanted by the remorseless pressures of their fathers' lives, are attracted to the feminine model of a balance between work and family. Betty Friedan writes of a man in Rhode Island who quit his job at a bank to take care of the house and kids and to paint at home, while his wife, sick of being a housewife, was happy to get a lesser job at the same bank. "I think you're going to see a great wave of men dropping out," he told Friedan. "All we've been hearing for years now is, What does it mean to be a woman? and How can she fulfill herself? But what does it mean to be a man? What do we have but our jobs? Let her support the family for a while, and let me find myself...."[7] The increasing tendency for these younger men to reject corporate transfers when they conflict with their personal and family life has been reported by Yankelovich, among others. In a recent survey among four hundred economics students at Stanford University, both men and women rated a happy marriage as more important than a successful career in attaining the good life.

"We have a large number of students who are turned off on the corporate bullshit," said Dr. Richard Buskirk, director of the Entrepreneur Program at the University of Southern California's School of Business Administration. "They realize that they want control over their own destinies." Social theoretician and futurist Willis Harman adds that work is enhanced when performed in the environment of home and community. "The best solution to having sufficient and satisfactory work roles is found not in some form of job enrichment in the main market economy but in the multitudinous activities involved in a learning and consciously evolving society."[8]

For the majority of working people, who must depend on the mainstream market economy for their economic survival, the good news is that feminization is enriching not only working life but family life as well. Contrary to the conventional wisdom and the gloomy pronouncements of fundamentatlists on the subject, it appears that, in families in which both parents work and share breadwinning and caretaking responsibilities, the family bonds and values—human as opposed to material—are strengthened. According to Professor Sheila B. Kamerman of Columbia University, who has studied such families, working mothers and their husbands place more importance and rely more on these bonds, not only with each other and their children but with their parents and other relatives, than do comparable families conforming to the more traditional configuration of housewife-breadwinner.

The feminization of the workplace is making it possible for both sexes to enjoy a greater range of work options, and a more human, more livable working environment; by reintegrating work and home, both men and women can experience these two worlds with a sense of wholeness, "not as tearing their lives apart," says Emily Stoper, "but as weaving them together, as reuniting two halves." Combining work and love, Freud's prescription for the good life, is our best hope for avoiding stress and burnout and restoring meaning and purpose to our personal and working lives.

Notes

1. Rosabeth Moss Kanter, "Women and the Structure of Organizations," in *Another Voice*, ed. Marcia Millman and R. B. Kanter.
2. Karen Pennar and Edward Mervosh, "Women at Work," *Business Week*, January 28, 1985.
3. Emily Stoper, "Alternative Work Patterns and the Double Life," in *Women, Power and Policy*, ed. Ellen Boneparth.
4. Lionel Tiger and Heather T. Fowler, eds., *Female Hierarchies*.
5. Kathleen Hendrix, "Influx of Women Changing the Workplace," *Los Angeles Times*, September 14, 1984.
6. Hilary Rosenberg, "Ms. Broker Comes into Her Own," *Financial World*, August 31, 1983.
7. Betty Friedan, "Feminism Takes a New Turn," *New York Times Magazine*, November 18, 1982.
8. Willis Harman, "Work," in *Millenium*, ed. Alberto Villoldo and Ken Dychtwald.

Arlie Hochschild with Ann Machung

from *The Second Shift: Working Parents and
the Revolution at Home*
"The Cultural Cover-up"

Sociology professor (at the University of California at
Berkeley) Arlie Hochschild spent eight years observing families from inside the home to see how responsibility for the
second shift (cooking, cleaning, child care) was negotiated
by husbands and wives who both worked. Hochschild has
also published *The Managed Heart*.

In the apartment across from the little study where I work there is a large bay window that never fails to catch my eye. Peering out from inside, wide-eyed and still, is a life-sized female mannequin in an apron. Her arms are folded and have been for years. She's there guarding the place, waiting. She reminds me and other passersby that no one is home. Maybe she's a spoof on the nostalgia for the 1950s "mom," waiting with milk and cookies for the kids to come home in the era before the two-job family.

Perhaps the mannequin mom is the occupant's joke about the darker reality obscured by the image of the woman with the flying hair—briefcase in one hand and child in the other. "There's really no one home," it seems to say, "only a false mother." She invites us to look again at the more common image of the working mother, at what that image hides. The front cover of the *New York Times Magazine* for September 9, 1984, features a working mother walking home with her daughter. The woman is young. She is good-looking. She is smiling. The daughter is smiling as she lugs her mother's briefcase. The role model is taking, the child is a mini-supermon already. If images could talk, this image would say, "*Women* can combine career and children." It would say nothing about the "extra month a year"; nothing about men; that would be covered up.

There is no trace of stress, no suggestion that the mother needs help from others. She isn't harassed. She's busy, and it's glamorous to be busy. Indeed, the image of the on-the-go working mother is very like the glamorous image of the busy top executive. The scarcity of the working mother's time seems like the scarcity of the top executive's time. Yet their situations are totally different. The busy top executive is in a hurry at work because his (or her) time is worth so much. He is in a hurry at home because he works long hours at the office. In contrast, the working mother is in a hurry because her time at work is worth so little, and because she has no help at home. The imagistic analogy between the busy working mother and the busy top executive obscures the wage gap between them at work, and their different amounts of backstage support at home.

The *Times* article gives the impression that the working mother is doing so well because she is *personally* competent, not because she has a sound *social* arrangement. Indeed the image of her *private* characteristics obscures all that is missing in *public* support for the working parent. In this respect, the image of the working mother today shares something with that of the black single mother of the 1960s. In celebrating such an image of personal strength our culture creates an ironic heroism. It extends to middle-class white women a version of womanhood a bit like that offered to low-class women of color.

In speaking of the black single mother, commentators and scholars have sometimes used the term "matriarch," a derogatory term in American culture, and a term brought to popular attention by Daniel Patrick Moynihan's controversial government report *The Negro Family: The Case for National Action.* In a section of the report titled "Tangle of Pathology," Moynihan cited figures showing that black girls scored higher on school tests than black boys. He also showed that 25 percent of black wives in two-job families earned more than their husbands, while only 18 percent of white wives did. In a section of his report titled "Matriarchy," Moynihan quotes social scientist Duncan MacIntyre: ". . . the underemployment among Negro men and compensating higher labor force propensity among Nego women . . . both operate to enlarge the mother's role, undercutting the status of the male and making many Negro families essentially matriarchal."[1] The implication was that black women should aspire to the standards of white women: perform more poorly on educational tests and earn less than their mates. Reading this, black social scientists such as Elaine Kaplan point out that black women are "damned if they worked to support their families and damned if they didn't." Black women were cautioned against being so "matriarchal." But as working mothers in low-paid jobs without much male support, they also legitimately felt themselves the victims of male underemployment. While at the bottom of the social totem pole, they were described as if they were at the top, as "matriarchs." These women pointed out that they "took charge" of their families not because they wanted to "dominate," but because if they didn't pay the rent, buy the food, cook it, and look after the children, no one else would. Black women would have been delighted to share the work and the decision-making with a man. But in Moynihan's report, the black woman's "dominance" came to seem like the problem itself rather than the result of the problem.

Similarly, the common portrayal of the supermom working mother suggests that she is "energetic" and "competent" because these are her *personal* characteristics, not because she has been forced to adapt to an overly demanding schedule. What is hidden in both cases is the extra burden on women. The difference between Moynihan's portrayal of the black working mother as matriarch and the modern portrayal of the white supermom is an unconscious racism. The supermom has come to seem heroic and good, whereas the matriarch seems deviant and bad.

This same extra burden on women is also disguised in the Soviet Union, a large industrial nation that has long employed over 80 percent of its women, and who ... work the extra month a year. In a now legendary short story, titled "A Week Like Any Other," by Natalya Baranskaya, Olga, twenty-six, is a technician in a plastics testing laboratory in Moscow and a wife and mother of two. Olga's supervisor praises her for being a *"real* Soviet Woman"—a supermom. But when Olga is asked on a questionnaire sent out to working mothers to list her hobbies, she answers, "Personally my hobby is running, running here, running there. . . ." Like the black "matriarch," and the multiracial supermom, the image of the "real Soviet woman" confines a *social* problem to the realm of personal character.

Missing from the image of the supermom is the day-care worker, the baby-sitter, the maid—a woman usually in a lower-class position to whom some upper- and middle-class couples pass much, although not all, of the work of the second shift. In the image, the supermom is almost always white and at least middle class. In reality, of course, day-care workers, baby-sitters, au pairs, maids, and housekeepers are often part of two-job couples as well. This growing army of women are taking over the parts of a "mother's work" that employed women relinquish. Most maids and baby-sitters also stay in their occupations for life. When we consider that 46 percent of all working women earn less than $10,000 a year, and a fifth of full-time working women earn less than $7,000 a year, and that the vast majority of women doing this "second shift" work for pay are among them, we can see that most such women can't afford to hire others to clean their homes. Yet the middle-class working mother is held out as a role model to this woman as much as to any other.

In the world of advertising images, the maid is often replaced by a machine. In television ads, for example, we see an elegant woman lightly touching her new refrigerator or microwave oven. Her husband may not be helping her at home, but her *machine* is. She and *it* are a team.² In the real world, however, machines don't always save time. As the sociologist Joan Vanek pointed out in her comparative study of homemakers of the 1920s and 1960s, even with more labor-saving appliances, the later homemakers spent as much time on housework as the earlier ones. The 1960s homemakers spent less time cleaning and washing the house; machines helped with that. But they spent more time shopping, getting appliances repaired, washing clothes (as standards of cleanliness rose), and doing the family bookkeeping. Eighty-five percent of the working couples I interviewed did not employ regular household help; it was up to them and their "mechanical helpmates." Since these took time they didn't have, many dropped their standards of housekeeping.

The image of the woman with the flying hair is missing someone else too: her husband. In the absence of a maid, and with household appliances that help but still take time, a husband's hand becomes important. Yet in the popular culture the image of the working father is still largely missing, and with it the very issue of *sharing*. With the disappearance of this issue, ideas of struggle and marital tension over the lack of sharing are also smuggled out of view. One advertising image shows us a woman just home from work fixing a quick meal with Uncle Ben's rice; the person shown eating it with great enjoyment is a man. In a 1978 study of television advertising, Olive Courtney and Thomas Whipple found that men are shown *demonstrating* products that help with domestic chores, but usually not shown *using* them. Women are often shown serving men and boys, but men and boys are seldom shown serving women or girls.

In the world of print as well, the male of the two-job couple is often invisible. There are dozens of advice books for working mothers, telling them how to "get organized," "make lists," "prioritize," but I found no such books for working fathers. In her book *Having It All,* Helen Gurley Brown, inventor of the "Cosmo Girl" and the author of *Sex and the Single Girl,* tells readers in a chatty, "girl-to-girl" voice how to rise from clerical work to stardom, and how to combine this career success with being "feminine" and married. She offers women flamboyant advice on how to combine "being sexy" with being a career success, but goes light and thin on how to be a good mother too. Women can have fame and fortune, office affairs, silicon injections, and dazzling designer clothes, she says. But the one thing they can't have, apparently, is a man who shares the work at home. Referring to her own husband, Brown writes: "Whether a man will help in the kitchen depends on his mother, says Carol (a friend). Mine *doesn't.* You also can't send him to market ... he comes back with tiny ears of corn vinaigrette, olives and pâté—but it's no good banging your head against the stove because he hasn't got a cassoulet simmering on top of it. Usually they do something to make up for household imbecility ... like love you and pay a lot of bills."[3]

In another advice book to women, *The Superwoman Syndrome,* Marjorie Hansen Shaevitz more candidly admits to losing a struggle to get her husband to share housework: "I spent a lot of time smoldering internally over his apparent recalcitrance [about housework]. I took it one step further by judging that if he really loved me, he would see how hard I was working, how tired I was and would come to my rescue with cheerful resourcefulness. Need I tell you this never happened?"[4]

Shaevitz tells us she became overworked, overwhelmed, and out of control. The problem? She should learn to make lists, to prioritize. She should hire a maid. Shaevitz suggests having few children, having them late, and close together because "this leaves more time in which the parents may pursue careers or other activities." She remarks that "some relief is available if you have a child-oriented spouse" but cautions "many women don't have that luxury...." What changes would help the working mother? She should ask for more favors from friends and she should do fewer. Shaevitz suggests that for the working woman the very principle of reciprocity is a "problem." Shaevitz explains, "the Superwoman not only has some anxiety about asking people for help, but the internal 'catch 22' is that she probably feels she's going to have to repay that help in some multiple way. *And that is also losing control of your life.*"[5] So she should not do such things as "agree to pick up your friend's child for a school play ..." or "listen to a friend's laundry list of problems with her husband and kids."

Shaevitz doesn't feel sharing is wrong; only that women can't get it. Her only vignette concerning a woman who wanted to share is titled "The Instant Equal-Sharing Model" and features the story of Helen, a secretary for a large travel agency, who did "all the housework," decided this was unfair, brought the subject up with her husband, and got him "very upset." In the end, "He stormed out of the house and that was the end of it. [She] never mentioned the subject again."[6] In a four-page epilogue to *The Superwoman Syndrome,* the dread issue of sharing resurfaces in a curious dialogue between Shaevitz and her husband, Mort:

MARJORIE: ... Right now I think we're in for some rough times between men and women, unless men begin participating a little more (you notice I say a *little* more) in the household and with their children. I don't think bright, competent, educated women are going to put up with men who are unwilling to participate in a sharing kind of relationship. You notice I say "sharing," not "equal sharing." Many women tell me they want to have a man in their life, but they are no longer willing to be the only person giving in the relationship. They don't want to be with a man who needs to be taken care of. In that case, it's easier and more pleasant to be without a man.

MORT: Marjorie, that's really infuriating to most men. It's quite clear that men are doing more and that this trend is likely to increase. What men find difficult to accept is that they get little credit for what they do, and an incredible list of complaints about what they don't do. Men and women may give in different ways. Women continue to set ground rules for what they expect, what they want, and how they want it delivered. I can tell you that most highly competent, successful men—the kind of men most women look for—simply will not respond to a behavioral checklist.

MARJORIE: ... The consequence of letting your wife do it all is that she is likely to get angry, resentful and maybe even sick.

MORT: Couples need to take a look at what this situation is behind the wife's pointing a finger at the husband. You know that doesn't work either. I think many men will probably be happy to "let her go"—they'll find someone else to take care of them.[7]

Marjorie talks about "many women" and Mort talks about "most men," but the dialogue seems strangely animated by their own struggle. In the end, Mort Shaevitz refers obscurely to the idea of a woman "getting help from *everyone*—her husband, her children, and society,'' a faceless crowd through which the Superwoman once again strides alone. *Having It All* and *The Superwoman Syndrome* advise women on how to do without a change in men, how to be a woman who is different from her mother, married to a man not much different from her father. By adding ''super'' before ''woman'' and substracting meaning from the word *all,* these authors tell women how to gracefully accommodate to the stalled revolution.

There have been two cultural responses that counter the supermom: one is making fun of her and one is proposing an alternative to her— ''the new man.'' The humorous response is to be found in the joke books, memo pads, key chains, ashtrays, cocktail napkins, and coffee mugs sold in novelty shops year round and in gift shops around Mother's Day. It critiques the supermom by making her look ridiculous. One joke book by Barbara and Jim Dale, titled the *Working Woman Book,* advises, ''The first step in a good relationship with your children is memorizing their names.'' (In a section called ''What You Can Do'' in a chapter on raising children, *The Superwoman Syndrome seriously* advises: ''A. Talk with your child, B. Play a game, C. Go to a sports event . . .'' and under ''Demonstrate Your Affection By'' it helpfully notes, ''A. Hugging, B. Kissing. . . .'')[8]

Or again: ''The famous Flying Wallendas were renowned for their feat of balancing seven Wallendas on a thin shaft of wood supported only by four Wallendas beneath whom was but one, strong, reliable, determined Wallenda . . . undoubtedly *Mrs.* Wallenda.''

One mug portrays a working mother with the familiar briefcase in one hand and baby in the other. But there is no striding, no smile, no backswept hair. The woman's mouth is a wiggly line. Her hair is unkempt. One shoe is red, one blue. Papers cascade out of her briefcase. In one hand she holds a wailing baby, in the other she holds a broom. Beneath her it says, ''I am a working mother. I am nuts.'' There is nothing glamorous about being time-poor; the mug seems to say, ''I'm not happy. I'm not fine.'' Implicitly the cup critiques the frazzled supermom herself, not her inflexible work schedule, not the crisis in day care, not the glacial pace of change in our idea of ''a real man.'' Her options were fine; what was crazy— and funny—was her *decision* to work. That's what makes the extra month a year a joke. In this way the commercial vision of the working mother incorporates a watered-down criticism of itself, has a good laugh, and continues on.

A serious critique of the supermom parallels the humorous one, and in the popular journalism of the late 1980s, this serious approach seems to be crowding out many other journalistic approaches to the woman question. In *Woman on a Seesaw: The Ups and Downs of Making It,* for example, Hilary Cosell bitterly rues her single-minded focus on career, which barely made time for a husband and precluded having children. For example:

There I was, coming home from ten or twelve or sometimes more hours at work, pretty much shot after the day, and I'd do this simply marvelous imitation of all the successful fathers I remembered from childhood. All the men I swore I'd never grow up and marry, let alone be like ... The men who would come home from the office, grab a drink or two, collapse on the couch, shovel in a meal and be utterly useless for anything beyond the most mundane and desultory conversation. And there I'd be, swilling a vodka on the rocks or two, shoving a Stouffer's into my mouth and staggering off to take a bath, watch "Hill Street Blues" and fade away with Ted Koppel. To get up and do it all again.[9]

Like the frazzled coffee-mug mom, Cosell admits her stress. Like the coffee-mug mom, she deplores her "wrong decision" to enter the rat race, but does not question the unwritten rules of that race. She seems to accept the status quo—the inner ticking of that career system and the way the men in it live. Both the humorous and the serious critiques of the supermom tell us "things are not fine," but like the image of the working mother they criticize, they convey a fatalism about alternatives: They say, "That's just how it is."

A second cultural trend tacitly critiques the supermom image by proposing an alternative—the new man. Increasingly, books, articles, films, and comics celebrate the man who feels that time with his child and sharing housework are compatible with being "a real man." Above a series of articles in his syndicated newspaper column about his first year as a father, a series which later became a popular book titled *Good Morning, Merry Sunshine,* Bob Greene is pictured holding his baby daughter Amanda. Greene is not in transit between home and work. He is sitting down, apparently at home, where he works as a writer. He is in a short-sleeved shirt instead of a coat and tie—no need to address the professional world outside. He is smiling contentedly. In his arms, his daughter faces the camera, laughing. He is successful—he is writing this column, this book. He writes on "male" topics like the Chicago mayoral election. He's an involved father. But he's not a house husband, like the man in the movie *Mr. Mom,* who for a disastrous, funny period—role reversal is an ancient, always humorous theme in literature—exchanges roles with his wife. Greene's wife, Susan, is *also* home with Amanda; he joins, but doesn't replace, his wife at home. As he writes in his journal:

> Started early this morning. I worked hard on a column about the upcoming Chicago mayoral election. I had to go to the far north side of town to interview a man; then once I got back downtown I had several hours of phone checking to do. There were some changes to be made after I had finished writing. It was well after dark before I was finished. I was still buzzing from the nonstop reporting and writing, when I got home, all of the elements of the story were still knocking around my head. Susan said, "Amanda learned how to drink from a cup today." I went into the kitchen and watched her. I watched Amanda drink from the cup, and nothing else mattered.[10]

The new man "has it all" in the same way the supermom has it all. He is a male version of the woman with the flying hair. Bob Greene is an involved father and also successful in a competitive field. In writing only about his own highly atypical experience, though, Greene unintentionally conveys the idea that *men face no conflict* between doing a job and raising a child.

In fact, most working fathers who fully share the emotional responsibility and physical care of children and do half the housework face great difficulty. As long as the "woman's work" that some men do is socially devalued, as long as it is defined as woman's work, as long as it's tacked onto a "regular" work day, men who share it are likely to develop the same jagged mouth and frazzled hair as the coffee-mug mom. The image of the new man is like the image of the supermom: it obscures the strain.

The image of the supermom and, to a far less extent, the image of the new man enter a curious cultural circle. First, more men and women become working couples. Spotting these men and women as a market, advertisers surround them with images—on billboards, on magazine covers, in television commercials—mainly of the do-it-all woman. Then journalists write articles about her. Advice books follow, and finally, more slowly and ponderously, the scientific word gets out about "changes in the family." As a result of this chain of interpretations, the two-job couple, the new object of attention, looks down the hall of mirrors to see "themselves."

What working mothers find in the mirror of culture has much to do with what the dilemmas in their lives make them look for. When the working mothers I talked with considered the image of the supermom, they imagined a woman who was unusually efficient, organized, energetic, bright, and confident. To be a supermom seemed like a good thing. To be called one was a compliment. She wasn't real, but she was ideal. Nancy Holt, a social worker and the mother of a son named Joey, found the idea of a supermom curiously *useful*. She was to face a terrible choice between having a stable marriage and an equal one, and she was to choose the stable marriage. She was to struggle hard to suppress her conflict with her husband and to perform an emotional cover-up. The supermom image appealed to her because it offered her a cultural cover-up to go with her emotional one. It clothed her compromise with an aura of inevitability. It obscured the crisis she and her husband faced over the second shift, her conflict with her husband over it, and her attempts to suppress the conflict to preserve their marriage—leaving in their place the illusive, light, almost-winking image of that woman with the flying hair.

Notes

1. Lee Rainwater and W. L. Yancey, *The Moynihan Report and the Politics of Controversy* (Cambridge, Mass.: M.I.T. Press, 1967), p. 32.
2. In her book *Redesigning the American Dream* (New York: W. W. Norton, 1984), p. 91, Delores Hayden describes how, in 1935, General Electric and *Architectural Forum* jointly sponsored a competition for who could design the best house for "Mr. and Mrs. Bliss"—the model couple of the period (Mr. Bliss was an engineer, Mrs. Bliss was a housewife with a college degree in home economics. They had one boy, one girl). The winner proposed a home using 322 electrical appliances. Electricity, the contest organizers proposed, was Mrs. Bliss's "servant."
3. Helen Gurley Brown, *Having it All* (New York: Simon and Schuster, 1982), p. 67.
4. Shaevitz, Marjorie H., *The Superwoman Syndrome* (New York: Warner, 1984), p. xvii.
5. Ibid., p. 112. All quotes within this paragraph are from ibid.
6. Ibid., p. 53.
7. Ibid., pp. 205–206.
8. Ibid., pp. 100–101.
9. Hilary Cosell, *Woman on a Seesaw: The Ups and Downs of Making It* (New York: G. P. Putnam's Sons, 1985), p. 30.
10. Bob Greene, "Trying to Keep Up with Amanda," *San Francisco Chronicle,* June 16, 1984, "People" section.

Kathleen Gerson

---

from *Hard Choices*
How Women Decide about Work, Career and Motherhood
"The Politics of Parenthood"

Kathleen Gerson, a professor of Sociology at New York University, states in her preface to *Hard Choices* that "by identifying constraints [to human freedom] and by illuminating the points at which meaningful human choice is possible, [she] seeks to expand the range of human action." In the excerpt that follows she argues that the state should play a significant role in ensuring gender equality in such areas as income and occupational opportunity so as to broaden the range of options possible for women both at work and at home.

The diversity of women's perceived interests makes the formulation of social policy on issues of gender inherently problematic. Policies aimed at achieving gender equality and diminishing the obstacles to combining work and parenthood will threaten those women, and men, who stand to lose from the erosion of traditional arrangements. Similarly, policies that promote female domesticity and make nontraditional options harder to implement will please the domestic group but provoke strenuous protest from those who have chosen or been forced to leave the domestic sphere. These conflicting stances make it difficult, if not impossible, to construct a coherent set of policies for women that meet the needs of all groups. Most policies, whatever their content, will face opposition from one group or another.

Political conflict between opposing interest groups forms the context in which change takes place. Opposition to change limits the degree and type of change possible, but it cannot stifle change in some form. For a variety of reasons far beyond anyone's control, the emerging diversity among women is here to stay. Because some type of change appears inevitable, public policy becomes a critical ingredient in determining whether social change reduces or exacerbates the problems women experience. We must ask at this point which social policies would be more effective in easing the contradictions women face.

Although women's interests diverge in the short run, in the long run, gender equality in income, occupational opportunities, and domestic options would lessen the contradictions all women face and expand the range of choices open to women and men alike. Children, moreover, would be the ultimate beneficiaries of policies that mandate sexual equality at work and in the home.

POLICY GOALS

Inequality at the workplace inhibits equality in the sexual division of parenting responsibilities; inequality in parenting inhibits occupational and economic equality.[1] Effective social policy must thus address sexual inequality on both fronts.

In the public sphere, the fundamental underpinning of workplace inequality is job segregation by sex. This system facilitates other forms of occupational inequality, such as the lower earnings and blocked mobility routes that characterize female-dominated occupations. Reducing workplace inequality requires diminishing job segregation by sex, providing equal pay for jobs of comparable worth, and restructuring female-dominated occupations to provide upward mobility over time as well as the social and financial rewards associated with a career.

This study shows that upward mobility and the associated benefits it provides are essential aspects of a satisfying work experience. Women, no less than men, are increasingly unwilling to settle for anything less. But improvements in women's work prospects and conditions are not likely to occur unless employers face political pressure not simply from women as individuals but, more important, from state policies. These women's lives show that affirmative action does make a difference, especially for working-class women who lack the economic freedom and educational resources to force change from below or look elsewhere for nourishing work.

Equality at work would have a number of consequences for women and men. First, it would reduce income disparity between them. This in turn would give women greater leverage to draw men more fully into household and parenting responsibilities and also improve the economic position of female-headed households.

Second, making female-dominated occupations more socially and economically attractive would lessen the devaluation of women's work and might ultimately draw more men into female-dominated jobs. Genuine workplace equality requires not only that women have access to traditionally male positions, but also that men become better integrated into traditionally female ones. Stasz (1982) points out that, despite the influx of women into male-dominated fields, a significant decrease in sex segregation depends upon a parallel movement of men into female-dominated job categories. Current efforts to secure equal pay for jobs of comparable worth may facilitate this process by narrowing the earnings gap between male-dominated and female-dominated occupations. If these efforts do not succeed in reducing occupational sex segregation by attracting more men into female-dominated occupations, however, the problem of gender asymmetry at the workplace will remain. History has shown that separate usually leads to unequal and that identifiably "women's work" will tend to be undervalued no matter what its content (Rosaldo, 1974; Treiman and Hartmann, 1981). Because much of the work women do is associated with children, providing increased social and economic rewards for women's work might have the added benefit of increasing the quality of care available for children.

Finally, if jobs became more sexually integrated and the disparity between male and female earnings narrowed, women and men would find it more economically rational to share equally in parenting. They would at least have a wider range of choice in deciding who would be the primary breadwinner. The increased time made available to fathers to care for their children would offset the loss of caretaking time available to work-committed mothers. Changes in workplace organization should reverberate into the private sphere, where inequality in the household could more easily diminish. Reducing domestic inequality would, in turn, give women greater freedom to pursue nondomestic goals.

Occupational equality will have a limited impact, however, unless the obstacles to integrating work and child rearing are reduced for both sexes. As long as employers penalize workers who are responsible for the care of children, male breadwinners will find it difficult to become involved fathers and mothers will find it difficult to become successful workers. Traditional households and childless workers will retain an advantage over those who would try to combine committed work with involved parenthood until parenthood is defined as a right and not just a privilege of all workers, regardless of gender.

Two types of social policies would reduce the barriers working parents face. First, legislation requiring employers to offer paid parental leave to both men and women on request (much as employers are now required to offer sick leave) would increase the options open to dual-earner households, help women workers who wish to bear children to remain in or rejoin the labor force, and make it easier for childless couples to opt for parenthood without endangering their financial solvency or occupational goals. Of no less importance, such policies would improve the chances that children of working parents will receive the care they need in the crucial first months of life. Such policies are not without precedent. Sweden, for example, guarantees the right to parental leave with job protection for up to eighteen months for parents of either sex.

Similarly, the development of a wide range of child-care services, programs, and facilities would help mothers and fathers better integrate their work and family lives. This range could, and should, include tax incentives to promote private sector alternatives such as neighborhood and workplace-based day care as well as publicly funded programs. The European example is also instructive here, for most northern European countries provide public day-care programs to the poor and nonpoor alike as a matter of course. The United States lags far behind European nations in providing government-supported child-care services. Indeed, this country stands in a minority among the rich, industrial nations in its failure to construct a coherent family policy that recognizes the rights and needs of working parents throughout the class structure. (See Kahn and Kamerman, 1975; Kamerman and Kahn, 1981; Wilensky, 1975, for overviews of welfare policies among the advanced industrial nations.)

In addition to promoting gender equality, these measures would increase the range of choice for working and child rearing open to both women and men. They would also help alleviate the dilemmas faced by nondomestic women of all social classes. Although social programs are important, legislative efforts to promote affirmative action, to secure equal pay for jobs of comparable worth, to prohibit discrimination against parents of either sex, and to provide new means of child care for overburdened parents are equally critical. Innumerable other policies might be added to this agenda, but those outlined here go to the roots of gender inequality and deserve central attention.

THE STATE AND SOCIAL CHANGE

Given the existing diversity among women and men, no consistent set of policies can meet the various, often conflicting interests of differently situated groups. Those who continue to follow traditional patterns are especially likely to oppose the social arrangements the policies outlined here would promote.

The various groups who oppose state efforts to support gender equality and the development of alternative family forms offer three arguments to support their position: that such policies would bestow an unfair advantage on women and nontraditional arrangements; that state intervention in family life will hasten the "decline" of the family; and that children will suffer from women's movement out of the home. Each of these arguments has serious flaws.

First, affirmative action and other policies that mandate equal opportunity at the workplace do not discriminate against men. Rather, they redress a former imbalance by giving women some of the rights and privileges men have historically enjoyed. Because men have had the privilege of not having to compete with qualified women, they will experience these changes as unfair. In the long run, however, the seuxal integration of occupations in the better rewarded sectors of the economy will remove the undeserved advantage now given to mediocre men and render the system more, not less, meritocratic.

Similarly, policies that ease the conflicts between work and family do not outlaw traditional arrangements or even make them significantly harder to implement. Rather, they acknowledge the fact of irreversible social change and address the problems thus created. To this extent, they challenge the social and economic advantages traditional forms have been afforded and compel them to compete on fairer terms with other alternatives.

Second, some maintain that, if women forsake the home for the workplace, they will usher in increased state and expert intrusion into family affairs, a sphere of life better left to parents (read: women) alone. Even some New Left critics (for example, Lasch, 1977, 1980) find themselves uncharacteristically aligned with conservatives who bemoan the dangers of state interference in private life and the unwarranted injection of experts into the process of child rearing. Although Lasch claims he has been misunderstood, he has become an influential spokesman in defense of the patriarchal family. He argues that the rise of child-rearing experts and public programs has undermined the paternal authority of which the modern nuclear family was built. As a result, the father is no longer able to provide the strong figure around which children can form oedipal struggles and conflicts. This robs children of the opportunity to rebel and resolve their oedipal conflicts as they mature, leading to destructive psychodynamic consequences.

This is, indeed, a contorted and curious defense of the privatized, bourgeois family *and* female subjugation. Lasch fails to discuss the cornerstone of this system of paternalism: women at home caring for children and families. Lasch thus appears to fear the destructive impact of socially based efforts to ease the plight of women on *men's* authority and *men's* psychodynamic development. But the consequences of these efforts, even in his argument, are likely to be liberating for women.

This argument against state support for nontraditional families also contains a logical flaw. The rise of the state and the rise of experts are both by-products of advanced industrialism (or postindustrialism): they are outcomes of the same social forces, but they are not caused by one another and are not the same phenomenon. Experts in the "helping professions," in particular, are an endemic aspect of postindustrial society, with or without a coherent family policy.

State policies that promote gender equality and provide support services for child rearing will not hasten the so-called decline of the family, lower the quality of family life, or destroy family privacy and independence. To the contrary, such policies are likely to have the opposite effect. Given current realities, policies that recognize the irreversibility of women's movement out of the home and provide needed support services are more likely to improve family life than to harm it. (See Joffe, 1977, for a well-reasoned discussion of these issues.)

It is, moreover, erroneous to equate weak or hidden state policy with the absence of policy. When the state fails to intervene on behalf of social justice, it is implementing policy as surely as when it does so. This is the fallacy of "benign neglect." The very reluctance of the American state to provide universally available child care or mandate female equality at work has been as much a form of state policy as any so-called interventionist or strong family policy might be. For better or for worse, the state will shape private life in some way. The issue is not the degree of state involvement, but rather the form it takes.

Ruggie's (1982:10) contrast between policies toward women in Sweden and England shows that the state's efforts or failure to promote "a universal framework" of family and work policies can make a critical difference. There are, however, those who believe that, whether or not a coherent state policy regarding the family is desirable, its formulation is impossible. Steiner (1981) argues that there are too many different types of state policies affecting the family—

from taxation to education—to make it either possible or desirable to coordinate them toward one goal or end. This argument is probably correct, but it is beside the point. The difficulty in coordinating all state policies does not preclude a concerted state effort to redress the grievances of women. Moreover, policies that take account of the diverse needs of a variety of households (without discriminating against or in favor of any one type) should be directed at providing a range of options, not consistently promoting only one option. Surely our traditional national commitment to tolerance and diversity requires no less from us.

There is no evidence to support the argument that state participation per se weakens the fabric of family ties or contributes to the family's demise. The forces that are changing private life as we have known it will have their impact regardless of the state's response. Policies can either ease these changes or make them more difficult to live with, but they cannot prevent some type of change from occurring. Families in some form will always be with us; no known society, past or present, has been without them. The question concerns their form and quality. Policies that recognize and address the new constraints and dilemmas many families face can inject new vitality into our private lives.

Finally, perhaps the most widespread fear, even among those most disposed to support and follow new paths, is the danger to children posed by women who work. Concern over the welfare of the nation's children is justified, but the blame for children's plight is misplaced. It is not women's equality that threatens children's welfare, but rather the social and economic devaluation of children and those who would care for them. Until we value our children enough to provide them with the services they need and reward those entrusted with their care, we cannot expect women to shoulder the burden our political and economic systems refuse to accept. The new vulnerabilities children face because of changing family structures have not ultimately been caused by women, and they cannot ultimately be solved by women alone. For reasons far beyond their individual control, working mothers cannot and will not return to the home; decreeing that women belong at home and refusing to ease their movement out of it will not stem the tide of women, with and without children, moving into the world of work.

Indeed, in the face of this massive social change, female inequality is the greatest threat to children's welfare. As long as we undervalue those who care for children, we will undervalue children and their needs. If we are committed to improving the quality of children's lives, we will increase the rewards to those who provide both paid and unpaid care to children, provide supportive structures and services for families with children, and promote economic equality for women, who increasingly must support children without the aid of men.

Of equal importance are policies that allow and promote participatory fatherhood. Such policies increase the number of parents available to the child and the number of options available to families. A child thus stands a better chance of receiving care from a concerned, committed, and competent caretaker—rather than one who has been forced into the job. Mothers and fathers might both approach the job of child rearing with greater enthusiasm if they felt they had more choice concerning how to go about it. And whatever losses children might incur from a decrease in time spent with their mothers would be more than offset by the benefits they gained from an accompanying decline in "paternal deprivation."[2]

The reproduction and regeneration of a society through its offspring is inherently a social, and not merely a female, task. Social policy must recognize that parenthood is a shared endeavor and that children are ultimately a social as well as a private responsibility. Because men and women will increasingly share in the economic responsibilities of rearing children, it is appropriate that they more equitably share in the emotional and nurturing responsibilities as well. At the most fundamental level, we must move beyond outdated concepts that define "mothering" as a specific style of interpersonal caring and "fathering" as limited to the acts of procreation and breadwinning. These gender-biased definitions do not accurately describe what fathers and mothers can and often do give their children, nor do they fit the circumstances facing growing numbers of parents. We would do well to recognize that both genders possess the human capacities to nurture and to work.

We need not fear a world in which men and women shoulder equal burdens in the home as well as at work. The range of human cultures makes clear that beliefs about the proper place of women and the proper way to rear children result more from social circumstances than from scientific fact. Throughout human history, societies have constructed their family lives, reared their children, and even defined childhood in a variety of ways without high levels of social disorganization or mental breakdown (see, for example, Ariès, 1962; Badinter, 1981; Gordon, 1978; Kagen, 1976; Laslett, 1972). These variations confirm that there is no one "correct" family form and attest to the resilience of women, men, and children.

We should fear, however, the consequences of *not* moving toward gender equality. Although the economic and political costs of such policies are likely to be high, the costs of ignoring, punishing, or trying to prevent the changes now under way are likely to be even higher. If we fail to approach current changes in women's position with a respect for diversity and a concern for women's plight, the individual and social problems spawned by these inevitable changes will surely grow more severe.

The conflicts and dilemmas women face will not diminish, despite women's changing social position, until the costs and rewards of working and parenting are more equally distributed by gender. As long as the social costs of parenting fall more heavily on women than men, women with good workplace prospects will continue to resist full-time motherhood. Similarly, as long as women are denied equal access to the rewards of working, those with poor prospects will cling to economic dependence within marriage as their only protection from alienating work. A growing number, however, will be forced to combine work with child rearing, despite the obstacles that lie in their path. The biggest losers, of course, are those who lose their economic, social, and emotional base at home and cannot offset this loss with genuine opportunities for rewarding work.

In the absence of a social policy that respects the variety of paths a woman can take and recognizes that this diversity is here to stay, women will remain ambivalent about their choices, whether for work, motherhood, or some combination of the two. Many will be forced to opt for childlessness or less parenting, despite the negative sanctions opponents of social change would like to attach to these outcomes. Others, choosing domestic paths, will find these equally conflict-laden. The level of conflict among women and between women, men, and the institutions of government and work will surely persist and will likely rise.

However appealing past patterns may appear, they are simply not viable alternatives for many, for their structural underpinnings are eroding. The most humane and sensible choice, then, is to take the difficult, conflict-laden steps toward gender equality at work and in the home. To do so will not ensure human liberation, but the failure to do so will promote increasing personal and social discontent, and not for women alone.[3]

Those who would mourn the past we have lost would do well to recognize that social change is an inherently ambivalent process in which some things are lost and some things are gained. As Hirschhorn (1977: 448–49) notes: "Yet we know that each time people resolve the ambivalence they are the richer for it; . . . that, just as they experience losses, so they develop the capacities to cope with those losses." The women we have met in these pages testify to this human capacity to prevail over and not just survive the challenge of change. It is appropriate to ask our political and social institutions to do so as well.

Notes

1. Polatnik (1973) analyzes the circular nature of gender inequality. In her explanation of why men do not rear children, she argues that male dominance is perpetuated and reinforced by the interaction between male advantages at work and women's responsibilities for rearing the young.

2. For still rare, but increasingly frequent discussions of paternal deprivation and the role of the father in child development, see Fein (1978), Lamb (1982), Lynn (1974), Parke (1981), Pedersen (1980), and Rapoport et al. (1977).

3. There are those who argue that gender equality, especially in parenting, would bring with it genuine human liberation as psychodynamic asymmetry was eradicated or "feminine" and "masculine" personalities became integrated. (See, for example, Dinnerstein, 1976.) It is, however, possible to imagine a world in which women are equal that is still unequal, unjust, and inhumane in other ways. Unfortunately, there is little evidence to suggest either that women with power behave more morally than male power holders or that the human race would be psychologically transformed by gender equality. Nevertheless, even if equality between the sexes is unlikely to create utopia, it is surely a worthy goal in itself.

Gloria Steinem

"Life After Backlash: Our Women in Washington"
&
"Creating Jobs We *Can't* Be Fired From"

Gloria Steinem is a founder of the National Women's Political Caucus and of *Ms.* magazine, where she serves as a consulting editor. She is the author of several books, including the best-selling *Revolution From Within: A Book of Self-Esteem* and most recently *Moving Beyond Words.*

LIFE AFTER BACKLASH
OUR WOMEN IN WASHINGTON

Let's make one thing clear. This isn't the Year of the Woman. That won't happen until we have half the U.S. Congress and every other decision-making body, a president once in a while, women leaders who are as diverse as we are, fathers who are as responsible as mothers for bringing up children, and much, much more.

Nonetheless, 1992 *was* the year when feminist effort to represent women's lives in the electoral system—an issue-driven movement built by millions of women over twenty years—made a quantum leap forward. Women turned out to vote in larger and more self-respecting numbers than ever before. The number of women U.S. senators tripled and women in the House of Representatives increased by one third. Issues of special concern to the female half of this country became pivotal to male candidates' success. And the antiequality Reagan/Bush era finally gave way to the insurgency of Clinton, a new generation of leader who may be more knowledgeable and supportive of equality, and far more at ease in an equal partnership, than any other male presidential candidate in U.S. history.

So how are we going to turn this new critical mass of understanding into positive change in the lives of most women? First, we must not overestimate the automatic power this new platform gives us. Second, we must not underestimate a right wing that, having lost power at the top, is stepping up pressures outside, from efforts to elect extremists at lower levels to anti-abortion terrorism. Third, we must understand that success in Washington, D.C., like life itself, is an organizing problem. As Franklin Roosevelt supposedly told a group of concerned citizens, ''You've convinced me, now go out and force me to do it.''

To figure out what we must do in these first crucial months, I talked to veteran activists both above and below the poverty line, spokeswomen for major constituencies, staffers on Capitol Hill, lobbyists for women's issues, and old and new members of Congress. I asked them two questions: "What can we expect of our women representatives in the House and the Senate, on both the domestic and international fronts, in the first 100 days? What do congress-women and senators need from us in order to be effective?" These are the shared themes of their replies, plus a few suggestions of my own.

MAKE OUR MANDATE CLEAR—OVER AND OVER

As one Capitol Hill staffer put it, "Credit may go where it's due, but not unless it's claimed." To ensure that we get our due, we must know and let others know the decisive role played by women's votes and issues in this election. Our women in the House and the Senate can do this in their statements on the floor, in the media, and to government agencies for which they have oversight powers. We can do it by writing to and lobbying their recalcitrant colleagues, by getting any groups of which we are a part to make statements, by writing letters to the editor, and in any other messages we can get into local media.

For instance, we can make it clear that in spite of the Bush/Quayle efforts to obscure their unpopular positions, the anti-Bush margin among women voters of all races remained 16 percent; more than enough to decide the election. Bush campaign spokespeople cited the defection of white Republican women in the suburbs, particularly on the issue of abortion, as a key to their defeat, and so should we. We can also detail that women (of all races) who are employed outside the home preferred Clinton to Bush or Perot by a margin of 12 percent, that 74 percent of lesbian and gay voters went for Clinton, as did nearly half of all Catholic women voters, and almost three quarters of single parents cast their ballots against Bush (a sweet victory for Murphy Brown).

Finally, we must build on this momentum to assure still better future results. We can do this by planning and publicizing women's candidacies against unsupportive members of Congress, vulnerable or not. (There's nothing like the thought of being unseated to make politicians rethink issues.) We can build war chests for important campaigns even before there is a candidate—feminists in Minnesota have already begun a $1 million fund to support a woman in the next U.S. Senate race. And we can increase future voter turnout by making registration and issue-education an automatic part of every group we are part of, whether it's a battered women's shelter or a professional network.

WHAT'S AT STAKE RIGHT NOW

The first few weeks after inauguration may seem like a gift. Executive orders can be changed with the stroke of a pen. Those Clinton has pledged to sign include: rescinding the "gag rule" that forbids discussing abortion in Title X funded clinics; allowing the use of fetal tissue in medical research; removing the ban on importing the abortion pill RU 486 for personal use; and allowing lesbian women and gay men to serve openly in the military. On the international front, Clinton has promised to rescind the Mexico City policy that, in forbidding recipients of U.S. foreign aid to counsel, refer, or perform abortions, has contributed to an abortion-related death rate of one woman every three minutes.

But we cannot assume these orders are as simple as their signing. Groups in opposition have already been lobbying Clinton intensely. For example, within weeks of the election, Colin Powell and other military leaders were publicly pressing him to reverse his stand on lesbians and gays. We need to be the force on the other side—offering both pressure and reward.

After monitoring the removal of those roadblocks, congresswomen and constituency groups must make sure the administration takes affirmative steps as well. For instance, the French manufacturers of RU 486 must be encouraged to submit the drug for testing in this country. And to make those executive orders meaningful, Congress must be asked to do the following: Remove the Title X language restricting abortion as "a family planning method," which has been used to keep abortion out of reproductive health care programs, and restore Title X funds for contraceptive services. Repeal the Hyde and Helms amendments that forbid using federal funds for abortion-related services (unless the woman's life is endangered) for Medicaid recipients in the U.S. and women abroad. And expand funding for family planning programs here and internationally.

The reality or threat of a presidential veto stopped a number of bills; as a result our reps have ready-to-go legislation. For example:

There's the Family and Medical Leave Act that Bush killed just before the election. The National Institutes of Health Revitalization Act, which includes funds for research on reproductive cancers and older women's health, plus a permanent authorization of the Office of Research on Women's Health to ensure women's inclusion in all health trials. The Freedom of Choice Act restores *Roe* v. *Wade,* though the current version still allows states to discriminate against minors and poor women. The Striker Replacement Act helps safeguard the right to strike by preventing employers from permanently hiring strikebreakers (thus helping women to organize, and strengthening women who are already union members). An Equal Remedies Act removes the cap on damages now imposed on sex discrimination cases. And the Economic Growth Incentives and Families Tax Relief Act benefits urban areas in which poor women and children are concentrated.

Of course, there will be arguments. For instance, whether to reinstate Congresswoman Pat Schroeder's original version of the Family and Medical Leave Act that included more employers and longer leave. And whether this election's mandate on abortion supports a minor's access—thus striking down parental notification—and if it prevents the coercion implicit in Medicaid funding for childbirth but not abortion.

Because less time need be spent on philosophical wars with a hostile White House, our women can get down to the nitty-gritty of eligibility and funding levels. Several already mandated but wounded programs like Head Start, and the Title IX regulations against sex discrimination in schools (including sexual harassment and pregnancy discrimination), need fast reinforcement. So does the Equal Employment Opportunity Commission, now no safer than any other henhouse run by a fox.

Clinton's top three priorities for the first 100 days are job creation, work force training, and health care reform. As for the first, we need our congresswomen to include such already proven innovations as the women's communally owned microenterprises that have created thousands of new jobs (see "Up the Down Economy," *Ms.,* March/April 1992). But women must also be included in the $20 billion windfall in business contracts and hiring that Clinton has slated for public works programs. Using their congressional oversight powers, our reps must enforce affirmative action policies within government agencies. When it comes to work force training, everything from nontraditional jobs to providing child care for trainees must be addressed. Given that women's health needs require our using the system more than men do, we should have more say.

What about events likely to come after this first 100 days? We need to begin planning for the reintroduction of the Equal Rights Amendment, and strategizing to ensure that this time it is coordinated with state ratification. We must prepare for phasing in a national system of child care by developing impact statements that explain the long-term financial benefits. Also on the horizon are Clinton's promised proposals to reform welfare. Because of his overemphasis on workfare, we must be geared up for a major struggle. As welfare activist Theresa Funiciello says, "Women legislators must inject some sanity into the immensely misogynistic debate by holding on to the principle that mothering is work."

Finally, we need to encourage our senators and congresswomen to develop a foreign policy *as if women mattered,* by routinely including the female half of the world, and broadening the definition of human rights to encompass women's rights. This would mean, among other things, protesting women's special suffering in armed conflicts (for instance, the mass rapes reported in Bosnia), taking a key role in disarmament treaties, and challenging the "debt crisis" imposed on "developing" countries. With our lobbying letters to support them, our women on the Hill can ensure U.S. implementation of the agreements reached at the Earth Summit, especially the provisions affecting women in Agenda 21.

GETTING OUR ACT TOGETHER

In "the U.S.'s most exclusive men's club," only by uniting as a bloc vote will the five Democratic women senators have clout, keep themselves from being picked off one at a time, and produce clear positions that colleagues ignore at their peril. Unity may also help Republican Senator Nancy Kassebaum withstand her party's pressure. Most important, it will force majority leader George Mitchell to come up with support for issues that the women put forward. He'll need their bloc to break filibusters (which require sixty votes) or, given his promise to change the rules to limit filibustering, to achieve simple majorities on even more issues.

In the House, the Congressional Caucus for Women's Issues is already in place. Composed of almost all the congresswomen, plus proequality congressmen (only women serve on its executive committee), the caucus is in need of stronger leadership, and action by simple majority. There's no reason for this body to be mainly a clearinghouse—especially since anti-choice and otherwise problematic Republican congresswomen are unlikely to join it anyway. As an engine of change, the caucus could write, introduce, and negotiate its own legislative packages, plot the tactics of their passage (as the Black Congressional Caucus has done), build coalitions with other caucuses, and negotiate with congressional and administration leadership.

Speaking of leadership, congresswomen need to make it clear that they won't wait twenty years to chair a committee. That means taking on the grandest dragon of them all—congressional rules. "We have to change the process," said one incumbent, "and challenge those glazed-over obstructionists who think that they're chairmen for life."

If you're reading this outside Washington, you're probably wondering: How do I plug into all this? That's exactly what our senators and congresswomen need us to do, by providing lots of backup and support. As Senator Barbara Mikulski says, "We need women to organize on the grass-roots level to make their voices heard. We need women to write to all of their elected representatives, not just the ones who are already on their side."

Knowing about issues and timely action is of paramount importance. Women who belong to groups that put out legislative alerts (like the National Organization for Women) may feel well informed, but what of all the others? A few learn about a specific bill due to membership in a specialized group, but almost none have ways to support the broad agenda. Gone are the umbrella groups, like the Women's Lobby, where one could tap into all congressional actions, like one-stop shopping; the increased number of complex issues has created diverse coalitions built around each major piece of legislation.

Former Congresswoman Bella Abzug proposes a federally funded free-standing National Commission on Equality for Women. It should be authorized to hold public hearings, conduct investigations, propose legislation, and monitor gender balance in all policy-making posts of the executive departments and agencies. As a matter of fact, a federally funded body will be needed to do an overview of women's status in this country anyway, in keeping with the United Nations' mandate that each country prepare a report for the 1995 U.N. Conference on Women in Beijing.

After seeing the depth and breadth of upcoming actions, I believe we also need an independent umbrella network that gets information out—and fast. What technology could now give us is a sophisticated 900 number that provides a menu when we call: For a list of legislation coming up next week, press One. For the positions of representatives from your state, press Two. And so on. Unlike our past 800 numbers, this wouldn't be free. But not only could a properly publicized service pay for itself, right-wingers would be less inclined to tie up the line (as they've done with our 800 numbers). If there is disagreement on a bill, that, too, could be reported.

Until such a 900 number can be organized, we must search out the timing and tactics of the issues dearest to our hearts, and write our opponents to tell them they risk defeat in the next election. We can call our representatives' district offices to find out about upcoming important votes, and write or visit them to lobby. We can ask the groups we belong to for a commitment to a general agenda or at least one major issue. With our friends or within our organizations, we can start an adopt-a-representative program—each person who signs on is responsible for monitoring the actions of just one politician. And on every trip we make to Washington, we can include at least one lobbying call. Democracy can only be sustained by everyday small actions. As Virginia Woolf said, we have to develop "the habit of freedom."

Creating Jobs We *Can't* be Fired From

For the last decade, there has been a new, innovative, and growing part of the women's movement that the press hasn't caught onto at all. Indeed, neither have the majority of us who are Bush-blinded and stuck in the mainstream—which is too bad because they would be greatly cheered by this grass-roots flowering. Part of the problem is language. This loose network describes its work as "economic development," a term that could mean anything from job training to hydroelectric dams. I often describe it as "economic empowerment"—also too inexact. What's growing up here is nothing less than the first economic base for the women's movement. If we're going to agitate freely for out rights we desperately need an economic base of jobs we can't be fired from.

It is also an economic paradigm that is neither capitalist nor socialist. Unlike the example of women business owners who are climbing the ladder Horatio Alger-style, these enterprises tend to be communal. The "Small is Beautiful" or Gandhian village-level socialist economy most resembles this paradigm, which incorporates women's everyday needs and values. Some are small businesses that begin with a little capital created by several women who pool their savings, others are groups of pink-collar workers who take over their own management and profits, and still others are handicraft or other cooperatives that expand production and eliminate the marketing middleman with the help of revolving loan funds and other expertise supplied by feminist groups organized for the purpose.

In all, these groups of women have already created hundreds, perhaps thousands, of jobs exactly where they are needed most—often among women who are getting off welfare or out of battered women's shelters, or laboring in poorly paid jobs that have been making unfair profit for someone else. Since the much-admired Fortune 500 companies of the U.S. have actually cut back jobs since the 1960s, this should be hopeful news; yet you won't read about these job creators in the *Wall Street Journal*.

Until there are organic phrases to describe this growing feminist economics, think of it this way: since women are like a "Third World" country wherever we are—low on capital, low on technology, and labor-intensive—it's not surprising that this most resembles a "Third World" paradigm. There is a growing exchange of information between women's economic development groups in the U.S. and those in the "Third World," with women of the North acknowledging and accepting expertise and encouragement from women of the South for a change. Or those with a scholarly bent might think of this formula: it's the local production model of old-fashioned anarchist theory, but with women's cultural values added.

Even without the right terminology, however, we can already see characteristics of these local groups: small but bright examples of what one day may become patches of a new national and international quilt of economic activity:

1. These groups tend to arise first among women at the very bottom of the larger economy, as if the view from there were more clear, and the absence of temptation toward old versions of women's

economic roles were a blessing in disguise. Washington, D.C., bu-
reaucrats never imagined that women could get off welfare by starting their own businesses, for example, but that's what's happening.
Pioneering feminist groups like the original Women's Economic Development Corporation in St. Paul, Minnesota, act as go-betweens
that help change restrictive welfare regulations, intercede with local
banks or offer small revolving loan funds themselves, and provide
continuing services so that a woman who's out there on the edge of
personal and economic history has some support. In these alliances
between feminists with economic expertise and grass-roots economic
adventurers, it's the women doing the work who are calling the shots.

2. These new groups integrate economic techniques like job training, job creation, marketing, and management with such innovative
techniques as flexible schedules, child care, language workshops for
new immigrants, assertiveness training, help in getting a driver's license, a link to political activity in the larger community, and even
songs, poems, and ceremonies that fill a deeper need than the usual
work life. Like some of the labor organizing groups of the 1930s,
these groups tend to see living as a whole, with work and family,
economics, and culture united.

3. The groups put a premium on autonomy and independence.
Whether they are Native American craftswomen for whom preserving
nature and principles of reciprocity are the bottom line (like the
Ramah Navajo women weavers in New Mexico, they may already
have a skill and a product, and just need help with bypassing the
profiteering middlemen), or the 240 African-American and Latina
workers who own and govern the Cooperative Homecare Associates
of the South Bronx (thus assuring benefits and career opportunities
to each other while giving better service to the homebound ill and
elderly), the point is: the people who do the work should also make
the decisions.

4. These grass-roots groups are also gaining the confidence and
expertise to analyze and challenge the economic mainstream. After
the challenge made by ''Third World'' women's development groups
to economic policies at the 1985 United Nations World Women's
Conference in Nairobi, Kenya, U.S. women began to realize they
could and must understand and take on their own economy. Since
then, an effort to demystify economics and promote ''economic literacy'' has sprung up at the grass roots.

Since this new economic paradigm strives to value what is important in our lives, from humane work patterns and child-rearing to personal self-esteem and economic independence, perhaps the best definition of it comes from Rebecca Adamson of First Nations Financial Project, which has redefined economics to include the viewpoint of indigenous people: "The science of dealing with the production, distribution, and consumption of wealth in a naturally holistic, reciprocal manner that respects humankind, fellow species, and the ecobalance of life."

Or perhaps we just need the words of Alice Walker's poem, "We Alone":

> This could be our revolution:
> To love what is plentiful
> as much as
> what is scarce.

Karen Johnson and Charlea Massion

"Why a Women's Medical Specialty?"

Psychiatrist Karen Johnson and family physician Charlea Massion show why more money needs to be spent on women's health care in America. The author of *Trusting Ourselves: The Complete Guide to Emotional Well-being for Women,* Karen Johnson is a clinical professor of psychiatry at the University of California at San Francisco. Massion has a private practice in Santa Cruz.

No existing medical specialty devotes itself exclusively to the comprehensive physical and emotional care of women. We believe this is a deficiency that can be corrected through the development of a new multidisciplinary specialty in women's health.

Currently, when a woman seeks medical care her body is arbitrarily divided among specialists. Obstetrician-gynecologists, traditionally considered "women's doctors," are delegated reproductive organs, but rarely know how to evaluate the most frequent problems women experience. For example, should we develop cardio-vascular disease, the number one killer of U.S. women, we must be referred to an internist.

Considered primary care physicians for *adults,* internists often unknowingly make clinical recommendations to women based on research done primarily with men. It is an enormous leap of faith to assume that what is well documented in male patients applies equally to women. In spite of their training in the emotional as well as the physical aspects of health, family physicians are no further ahead of their colleagues in internal medicine when it comes to women's health. And because these practitioners also care for children and men, they simply cannot concentrate on the health needs of women.

No matter what the area of specialty, when a physician can find no demonstrable explanation for a woman's abdominal distress or aching temples or relentless chest pain, she is sent to a psychiatrist. The implication that "it's all in your head" may reflect the reality that medical science has yet to commit adequate research attention to many of women's most pressing health problems.

Certain health problems are not integrated by the expertise of a single specialty—for example, domestic violence, which is a serious health threat to women. Depending on how the injured woman enters the health system, she may be treated by an emergency room physician for fractures, an ob-gyn for vaginal lacerations and repeated infections, or a psychiatrist for panic attacks and depression. Each clinician sees only a fragment of the overall problem and may have neither the knowledge nor resources to intervene effectively. This is just one of many problems women face that would be better treated by an integrated approach.

In addition, the tendency to use men as research subjects has delayed our understanding of how drugs may be metabolized differently in the more complicated hormonal environment of women's bodies. And while many medical problems are common for both women and men, the incidence of some is far more frequent among women. Thyroid disease, rheumatoid arthritis, adult-type diabetes, osteoporosis, and depression all appear more often in women—and we really don't know why.

The failure to study women as a distinct subset of the adult population, much as geriatricians focus on the elderly, has contributed to many misconceptions about women's health. For example, women were not included in a major study that recommends aspirin as preventive therapy for coronary disease, or in any of the large clinical trials on cholesterol-lowering drugs.

It is true that numerous medical problems experienced only by women are covered by current specialties, but there is no multidisciplinary approach. Anyone who understands women would not be surprised to learn that participating in a mutual support group may double the life expectancy of a woman with breast cancer. Women's physical wellness and emotional well-being are intimately entwined. Yet no one in medicine is trained to offer this kind of comprehensive service based upon research and clinical experience with women.

Not surprisingly, there is considerable resistance to this proposal from organized medicine. Some medical leaders argue that if internal medicine and ob-gyn simply expand their training programs to incorporate the new knowledge and clinical expertise with women, there would be no need to create another specialty. We applaud these efforts, but they are no substitute for a well-trained group of physicians who focus exclusively on the physical and emotional health concerns of women.

There may also be another reason for resistance by organized medicine: this is the first medical specialty proposed by women, for women. It signals a shift in power within the medical hierarchy.

Audre Lorde

from *The Cancer Journals*
"Breast Cancer: Power vs. Prosthesis"

In this excerpt from her diary Audre Lorde reflects upon her personal encounter with breast cancer, her survival of a mastectomy, and the cultural images of womanhood that made the experience only more painful and arduous. Among Lorde's published works are her autobiography, *Zami: A New Spelling of My Name*; the nonfiction titles *Sister Outsider: Essays and Speeches* and *Uses of the Erotic: The Erotic as Power*; and the volumes of poetry *Undersong* and *Chosen Poems Old and New*. Audre Lorde died in December 1992.

On Labor Day, 1978, during my regular monthly self-examination, I discovered a lump in my right breast which later proved to be malignant. During my following hospitalization, my mastectomy and its aftermath, I passed through many stages of pain, despair, fury, sadness, and growth. I moved through these stages, sometimes feeling as if I had no choice, other times recognizing that I could choose oblivion—or a passivity that is very close to oblivion—but did not want to. As I slowly began to feel more equal to processing and examining the different parts of this experience, I also began to feel that in the process of losing a breast I had become a more whole person.

After a mastectomy, for many women including myself, there is a feeling of wanting to go back, of not wanting to persevere through this experience to whatever enlightenment might be at the core of it. And it is this feeling, this nostalgia, which is encouraged by most of the post-surgical counseling for women with breast cancer. This regressive tie to the past is emphasized by the concentration upon breast cancer as a cosmetic problem, one which can be solved by a prosthetic pretense. The American Cancer Society's Reach For Recovery Program, while doing a valuable service in contacting women immediately after surgery and letting them know they are not alone, nonetheless encourages this false and dangerous nostalgia in the mistaken belief that women are too weak to deal directly and courageously with the realities of our lives.

The woman from Reach For Recovery who came to see me in the hospital, while quite admirable and even impressive in her own right, certainly did not speak to my experience nor my concerns. As a forty-four-year-old black lesbian feminist, I knew there were very few role models around for me in this situation, but my primary concerns two days after mastectomy were hardly about what man I could capture in the future, whether or not my old boyfriend would still find me attractive enough, and even less about whether my two children would be embarrassed by me around their friends.

My concerns were about my chances for survival, the effects of a possibly shortened life upon my work and my priorities. Could this cancer have been prevented, and what could I do in the future to prevent its recurrence? Would I be able to maintain the control over my life that I had always taken for granted? A lifetime of loving women had taught me that when women love each other, physical change does not alter that love. It did not occur to me that anyone who really loved me would love me any less because I had one breast instead of two, although it did occur to me to wonder if they would be able to love and deal with the new me. So my concerns were quite different from those spoken to me by the Reach For Recovery volunteer, but not one bit less crucial nor less poignant.

Yet every attempt I made to examine or question the possibility of a real integration of this experience into the totality of my life and my loving and my work, was ignored by this woman, or uneasily glossed over by her as not looking on "the bright side of things." I felt outraged and insulted, and weak as I was, this left me feeling even more isolated than before.

In the critical and vulnerable period following surgery, self-examination and self-evaluation are positive steps. To imply to a woman that yes, she can be the "same" as before surgery, with the skillful application of a little puff of lambs-wool, and/or silicone gel, is to place an emphasis upon prosthesis which encourages her not to deal with herself as physically and emotionally real, even though altered and traumatized. This emphasis upon the cosmetic after surgery reinforces this society's stereotype of women, that we are only what we look or appear, so this is the only aspect of our existence we need to address. Any woman who has had a breast removed because of cancer knows she does not feel the same. But we are allowed no psychic time or space to examine what our true feelings are, to make them our own. With quick cosmetic reassurance, we are told that our feelings are not important, our appearance is all, the sum total of self.

I did not have to look down at the bandages on my chest to know that I did not feel the same as before surgery. But I still felt like myself, like Audre, and that encompassed so much more than simply the way my chest appeared.

The emphasis upon physical pretense at this crucial point in a woman's reclaiming of her self and her body-image has two negative effects:

1. It encourages women to dwell in the past rather than a future. This prevents a woman from assessing herself in the present, and from coming to terms with the changed planes of her own body. Since these then remain alien to her, buried under prosthetic devices, she must mourn the loss of her breast in secret, as if it were the result of some crime of which she were guilty.

2. It encourages a woman to focus her energies upon the mastectomy as a cosmetic occurrence, to the exclusion of other factors in a constellation that could include her own death. It removes her from what that constellation means in terms of her living, and from developing priorities of usage for whatever time she has before her. It encourages her to ignore the necessity for nutritional vigilance and psychic armament that can help prevent recurrence.

I am talking here about the need for every woman to live a considered life. The necessity for that consideration grows and deepens as one faces directly one's own mortality and death. Self scrutiny and an evaluation of our lives, while painful, can be rewarding and strengthening journeys toward a deeper self. For as we open ourselves more and more to the genuine conditions of our lives, women become less and less willing to tolerate those conditions unaltered, or to passively accept external and destructive controls over our lives and our identities. Any short-circuiting of this quest for self-definition and power, however well-meaning and under whatever guise, must be seen as damaging, for it keeps the post-mastectomy woman in a position of perpetual and secret insufficiency, infantilized and dependent for her identity upon an external definition by appearance. In this way women are kept from expressing the power of our knowledge and experience, and through that expression, developing strengths that challenge those structures within our lives that support the cancer establishment. For instance, why hasn't the American Cancer Society publicized the connections between animal fat and breast cancer for our daughters the way it has publicized the connection between cigarette smoke and lung cancer? These links between animal fat, hormone production and breast cancer are not secret. (See G. Hems, in *British Journal of Cancer,* vol. 37, no. 6, 1978.)

Ten days after having my breast removed, I went to my doctor's office to have the stitches taken out. This was my first journey out since coming home from the hospital, and I was truly looking forward to it. A friend had washed my hair for me and it was black and shining, with my new grey hairs glistening in the sun. Color was starting to come back into my face and around my eyes. I wore the most opalescent of my moonstones, and a single floating bird dangling from my right ear in the name of grand assymmetry. With an African kentecloth tunic and new leather boots, I knew I looked fine, with that brave new-born security of a beautiful woman having come through a very hard time and being very glad to be alive.

I felt really good, within the limits of that grey mush that still persisted in my brain from the effects of the anesthesia.

When I walked into the doctor's office, I was really rather pleased with myself, all things considered, pleased with the way I felt, with my own flair, with my own style. The doctor's nurse, a charmingly bright and steady woman of about my own age who had always given me a feeling of quiet no-nonsense support on my other visits, called me into the examining room. On the way, she asked me how I was feeling.

"Pretty good," I said, half-expecting her to make some comment about how good I looked.

"You're not wearing a prosthesis," she said, a little anxiously, and not at all like a question.

"No," I said, thrown off my guard for a minute. "It really doesn't feel right," referring to the lambswool puff given to me by the Reach For Recovery volunteer in the hospital.

Usually supportive and understanding, the nurse now looked at me urgently and disapprovingly as she told me that even if it didn't look exactly right, it was "better than nothing," and that as soon as my stitches were out I could be fitted for a "real form."

"You will feel so much better with it on," she said. "And besides, we really like you to wear something, at least when you come in. Otherwise it's bad for the morale of the office."

I could hardly believe my ears! I was too outraged to speak then, but this was to be only the first such assault on my right to define and to claim my own body.

Here we were, in the offices of one of the top breast cancer surgeons in New York City. Every woman there either had a breast removed, might have to have a breast removed, or was afraid of having to have a breast removed. And every woman there could have used a reminder that having one breast did not mean her life was over, nor that she was less a woman, nor that she was condemned to the use of a placebo in order to feel good about herself and the way she looked.

Yet a woman who has one breast and refuses to hide that fact behind a pathetic puff of lambswool which has no relationship nor likeness to her own breasts, a woman who is attempting to come to terms with her changed landscape and changed timetable of life and with her own body and pain and beauty and strength, that woman is seen as a threat to the "morale" of a breast surgeon's office!

Yet when Moishe Dayan, the Prime Minister of Israel, stands up in front of parliament or on TV with an eyepatch over his empty eyesocket, nobody tells him to go get a glass eye, or that he is bad for the morale of the office. The world sees him as a warrior with an honorable wound, and a loss of a piece of himself which he has marked, and mourned, and moved beyond. And if you have trouble dealing with Moishe Dayan's empty eye socket, everyone recognizes that it is your problem to solve, not his.

Well, women with breast cancer are warriors, also. I have been to war, and still am. So has every woman who has had one or both breasts amputated because of the cancer that is becoming the primary physical scourge of our time. For me, my scars are an honorable reminder that I may be a casualty in the cosmic war against radiation, animal fat, air pollution, McDonald's hamburgers, and Red Dye No. 2, but the fight is still going on, and I am still a part of it. I refuse to have my scars hidden or trivialized behind lambswool or silicone gel. I refuse to be reduced in my own eyes or in the eyes of others from warrior to mere victim, simply because it might render me a fraction more acceptable or less dangerous to the still complacent, those who believe if you cover up a problem it ceases to exist. I refuse to hide my body simply because it might make a woman-phobic world more comfortable.

As I sat in my doctor's office trying to order my perceptions of what had just occurred, I realized that the attitude towards prosthesis after breast cancer is an index of this society's attitudes toward women in general as decoration and externally defined sex object.

Two days later I wrote in my journal:

I cannot wear a prosthesis right now because it feels like a lie more than merely a costume, and I have already placed this, my body under threat, seeking new ways of strength and trying to find the courage to tell the truth.

For me, the primary challenge at the core of mastectomy was the stark look at my own mortality, hinged upon the fear of a life-threatening cancer. This event called upon me to re-examine the quality and texture of my entire life, its priorities and commitments, as well as the possible alterations that might be required in the light of that re-examination. I had already faced my own death, whether or not I acknowledged it, and I needed now to develop that strength which survival had given me.

Prosthesis offers the empty comfort of "Nobody will know the difference." But it is that very difference which I wish to affirm, because I have lived it, and survived it, and wish to share that strength with other women. If we are to translate the silence surrounding breast cancer into language and action against this scourge, then the first step is that women with mastectomies must become visible to each other.* For silence and invisibility go hand in hand with powerlessness. By accepting the mask of prosthesis, one-breasted women proclaim ourselves as insufficients dependent upon pretense. We reinforce our own isolation and invisibility from each other, as well as the false complacency of a society which would rather not face the results of its own insanities. In addition, we withhold that visibility and support from one another which is such an aid to perspective and self-acceptance. Surrounded by other women day by day, all of whom appear to have two breasts, it is very difficult sometimes to remember that I AM NOT ALONE. Yet once I face death as a life process, what is there possibly left for me to fear? Who can ever really have power over me again?

As women, we cannot afford to look the other way, nor to consider the incidence of breast cancer as a private or secret personal problem. It is no secret that breast cancer is on the increase among women in America. According to the American Cancer Society's own statistics on breast cancer survival, of the women stricken, only 50 percent are still alive after three years. This figure drops to 30 percent if you are poor, or black, or in any other way part of the underside of this society. We cannot ignore these facts, nor their implications, nor their effect upon our lives, individually and collectively. Early detection and early treatment is crucial in the management of breast cancer

---

*particular thanks to Maureen Brady for the conversation which developed this insight.

if those sorry statistics of survival are to improve. But for the incidence of early detection and early treatment to increase, American
women must become free enough from social stereotypes concerning
their appearance to realize that losing a breast is infinitely preferable
to losing one's life. (Or one's eyes, or one's hand. . . .)

Although breast self-examination does not reduce the incidence of
breast cancer, it does markedly reduce the rate of mortality, since
most early tumors are found by women themselves. I discovered my
own tumor upon a monthly breast exam, and so report most of the
other women I know with a good prognosis for survival. With our
alert awareness making such a difference in the survival rate for
breast cancer, women need to face the possibility and the actuality
of breast cancer as a reality rather than as myth, or retribution, or
terror in the night, or a bad dream that will disappear if ignored. After
surgery, there is a need for women to be aware of the possibility of
bilateral recurrence, with vigilance rather than terror. This is not a
spread of cancer, but a new occurrence in the other breast. Each
woman must be aware that an honest acquaintanceship with and
evaluation of her own body is the best tool of detection.

Yet there still appears to be a conspiracy on the part of Cancer
Inc. to insist to every woman who has lost a breast that she is no
different from before, if with a little skillful pretense and a few
ounces of silicone gel she can pretend to herself and the watching
world—the only orientation toward the world that women are supposed to have—that nothing has happened to challenge her. With
this orientation a woman after surgery is allowed no time or space
within which to weep, rage, internalize, and transcend her own loss.
She is left no space to come to terms with her altered life, not to
transform it into another level of dynamic existence.

The greatest incidence of breast cancer in American women appears
within the ages of forty to fifty-five. These are the very years when
women are portrayed in the popular media as fading and desexualized
figures. Contrary to the media picture, I find myself as a woman of
insight ascending into my highest powers, my greatest psychic strengths,
and my fullest satisfactions. I am freer of the constraints and fears and
indecisions of my younger years, and survival throughout these years
has taught me how to value my own beauty, and how to look closely
into the beauty of others. It has also taught me to value the lessons of
survival, as well as my own perceptions. I feel more deeply, value those
feelings more, and can put those feelings together with what I know in

order to fashion a vision of and pathway toward true change. Within this time of assertion and growth, even the advent of a life-threatening cancer and the trauma of a mastectomy can be integrated into the life-force as knowledge and eventual strength, fuel for a more dynamic and focussed existence. Since the supposed threat of self-actualized women is one that our society seeks constantly to protect itself against, it is not coincidental that the sharing of this knowledge among women is diverted, in this case by the invisibility imposed by an insistence upon prosthesis as a norm for post-mastectomy women.

There is nothing wrong, per se, with the use of prostheses, if they can be chosen freely, for whatever reason, after a woman has had a chance to accept her new body. But usually prostheses serve a real function, to approximate the performance of a missing physical part. In other amputations and with other prosthetic devices, function is the main point of their existence. Artificial limbs perform specific tasks, allowing us to manipulate or to walk. Dentures allow us to chew our food. Only false breasts are designed for appearance only, as if the only real function of women's breasts were to appear in a certain shape and size and symmetry to onlookers, or to yield to external pressure. For no woman wearing a prosthesis can even for one moment believe it is her own breast, any more than a woman wearing falsies can.

Yet breast prostheses are offered to women after surgery in much the same way that candy is offered to babies after an injection, never mind that the end effect may be destructive. Their comfort is illusory; a transitional period can be provided by any loose-fitting blouse. After surgery, I most certainly did not feel better with a lambswool puff stuck in the front of my bra. The real truth is that certain other people feel better with that lump stuck into my bra, because they do not have to deal with me nor themselves in terms of mortality nor in terms of difference.

Attitudes toward the necessity for prostheses after breast surgery are merely a reflection of those attitudes within our society toward women in general as objectified and depersonalized sexual conveniences. Women have been programmed to view our bodies only in terms of how they look and feel to others, rather than how they feel to ourselves, and how we wish to use them. We are surrounded by media images portraying women as essentially decorative machines of consumer function, constantly doing battle with rampant decay. (Take your vitamins every day and he *might* keep you, if you don't forget to whiten your teeth, cover up your smells, color your grey hair and iron out your wrinkles. . . .) As women, we fight this depersonalization every day, this pressure toward the conversion of one's own self-image into a media expectation of what might satisfy male demand. The insistence upon breast prostheses as "decent" rather than functional is an additional example of that wipe-out of self in which women are constantly encouraged to take part. I am personally affronted by the message that I am only acceptable if I look "right" or "normal," where those norms have nothing to do with my own perceptions of who I am. Where "normal" means the "right" color, shape, size, or number of breasts, a woman's perception of her own body and the strengths that come from that perception are discouraged, trivialized, and ignored. When I mourn my right breast, it is not the appearance of it I mourn, but the feeling and the fact. But where the superficial is supreme, the idea that a woman can be beautiful and one-breasted is considered depraved, or at best, bizarre, a threat to "morale."

In order to keep me available to myself, and able to concentrate my energies upon the challenges of those worlds through which I move, I must consider what my body means to me. I must also separate those external demands about how I look and feel to others, from what I really want for my own body, and how I feel to my selves. As women we have been taught to respond with a guilty twitch at any mention of the particulars of our own oppression, as if we are ultimately guilty of whatever has been done to us. The rape victim is accused of enticing the rapist. The battered wife is accused of having angered her husband. A mastectomy is not a guilty act that must be hidden in order for me to regain acceptance or protect the sensibilities of others. Pretense has never brought about lasting change or progress.

Every woman has a right to define her own desires, make her own choices. But prostheses are often chosen, not from desire, but in default. Some women complain it is too much effort to fight the concerted pressure exerted by the fashion industry. Being one-breasted does not mean being unfashionable; it means giving some time and energy to choosing or constructing the proper clothes. In some cases, it means making or remaking clothing or jewelry. The fact that the fashion needs of one-breasted women are not currently being met doesn't mean that the concerted pressure of our demands cannot change that.*

---

*particular thanks to Frances Clayton for the conversations that developed this insight.

There was a time in America not long ago when pregnant women were supposed to hide their physical realities. The pregnant woman who ventured forth into public had to design and construct her own clothing to be comfortable and attractive. With the increased demands of pregnant women who are no longer content to pretend non-existence, maternity fashion is now an established, flourishing, and particular sector of the clothing field.

The design and marketing of items of wear for one-breasted women is only a question of time, and we who are now designing and wearing our own asymmetrical patterns and New Landscape jewelry are certainly in the vanguard of a new fashion!

Some women believe that a breast prosthesis is necessary to preserve correct posture and physical balance. But the weight of each breast is never the same to begin with, nor is the human body ever exactly the same on both sides. With a minimum of exercises to develop the habit of straight posture, the body can accommodate to one-breastedness quite easily, even when the breasts were quite heavy.

Women in public and private employment have reported the loss of jobs and promotions upon their return to work after a mastectomy, without regard to whether or not they wore prostheses. The social and economic discrimination practiced against women who have breast cancer is not diminished by pretending that mastectomies do not exist. Where a woman's job is at risk because of her health history, employment discrimination cannot be fought with a sack of silicone gel, nor with the constant fear and anxiety to which such subterfuge gives rise. Suggesting prosthesis as a solution to employment discrimination is like saying that the way to fight race prejudice is for black people to pretend to be white. Employment discrimination against post-mastectomy women can only be fought in the open, with head-on attacks by strong and self-accepting women who refuse to be relegated to an inferior position, or to cower in a corner because they have one breast.

When post-mastectomy women are dissuaded from any realistic evaluation of themselves, they spend large amounts of time, energy, and money in following any will-o-wisp that seems to promise a more skillful pretense of normality. Without the acceptance of difference as part of our lives, and in a guilty search for illusion, these women fall easy prey to any shabby confidence scheme that happens along. The terror and silent loneliness of women attempting to replace the ghost of a breast leads to yet another victimization. . . .

Ellen Lewin

"Claims to Motherhood: Custody Disputes and Maternal Strategies"

The "good mothering roles" currently expected of women seeking to maintain custody of their children stand at painful odds with the movement toward gender equality, argues Ellen Lewin in this paper which was originally published in a volume of essays edited by Faye Ginsburg and Anna Lowenhaupt Tsing under the title *Uncertain Terms: Negotiating Gender in American Culture*. Lewin, who teaches anthropology at the University of California at Berkeley, is the author of *Mothers and Children*.

This custody thing traumatized me, maybe more than the children. It was like the most frightening experience of my life. And I'm afraid to have another child. I'm afraid someone's going to try and take them away from me.

—Thirty-four-year-old-mother of two

Custody battles between mothers and fathers are increasingly routine features of divorce negotiations. Despite the proliferation of "no-fault" divorce laws, the incidence of divorce-related litigation has grown in recent years, with a substantial proportion of these disputes centering on child custody. Until children reach majority, or the disputing parties exhaust their financial resources, nearly any change in the situation of either parent may be viewed as a "material change of circumstances" worthy of renewed legal inquiry.[1]

Although only a small percentage of men actually seek custody in court, as many as one-third of divorced women report custody litigation threats being raised in the course of divorce negotiations.[2] The outcome of negotiations once custody threats have been instituted (or even hinted at) shows that, father's stated motivations notwithstanding, the threat of a custody action serves to enforce compliance with other paternal demands—for low child and spousal support awards,[3] for a larger share of the marital property, or for visitation arrangements that are convenient for the father.[4]

Even when they feel that they are "good mothers," women tend to capitulate to husbands' demands when custody becomes an issue. There are a number of reasons for this. First, mothers know—or are advised to this effect by their attorneys—that the traditional judicial preference for maternal custody has been breaking down in recent years. Although the absolute number of fathers who actually become custodial parents remains small, this is because so few fathers attempt to win custody. Once a father brings a custody matter to trial, his chances of winning are about equal to those of his former wife.[5]

Women are at a disadvantage in custody litigation because their post-divorce employment may be seen as being in conflict with their maternal obligations, because they have less to offer their children economically, or because their behavior may be more carefully scrutinized for evidence of immorality. Second, custody litigation is expensive, and women are more likely to agree to a compromise, or even to give up custody, because they cannot afford a long court battle. Finally, disputed custody can take a terrible toll on children, and mothers are apt to compromise to spare their children a potentially traumatic ordeal.

Lesbian mothers are particularly vulnerable to such litigation. Judges tend to view them as unsuitable custodial parents solely because of their sexual orientation, even in the absence of any direct evidence of improper parental behavior.[6] Because they are aware of their poor chances in a court of law, lesbian mothers are even more concerned about custody challenges than are other formerly married mothers. Lesbian mothers thus tend to develop careful and consciously crafted strategies aimed at protecting themselves from custody litigation. More frequently than heterosexual mothers, lesbians may perceive a threat to exist even when no direct challenge has been made.[7]

MOTHERHOOD AND GENDER

Being a mother has generally been viewed as a sort of default option—as the natural, essential outcome of being a woman, as a status ascribed, not achieved, and as the "cause," in one way or another, of women's predicament in the world.[8] Threats to custody, however, compel women to define and codify the qualities that make them suitable parents, to be self-conscious and reflective in ways otherwise rarely required. Ties assumed to be based on sentiment become basic elements of strategies that will help avoid custody litigation, or when litigation does occur, facilitate a successful outcome.

Courtroom battles over custody and the other legal machinations, which may accompany, precede, or substitute for them can arise only in a context in which motherhood has come to be viewed as an achieved characteristic. The courts no longer assume that there is something essential about being the female biological parent that destines a woman for custody of her children.[9] Rather, parenthood is seen, though not always explicitly, as a set of skills and resources, and, in the case of women, moral entitlements, which insure adequate care of minor children. Custody disputes, then, depend on contradicting the notion that motherhood, and therefore gender itself, is natural; claimants to custody must display their skills, prove to others what would otherwise be assumed to emanate from biology.[10]

As already mentioned, when lesbianism is raised in a custody situation, other factors tend to slip into the background. It is difficult enough to prove one's maternal capabilities, but to do so under conditions that view two aspects of one's identity as inherently opposed is even more difficult. Judges and others who make decisions about family policy tend to assume that homosexuality cannot be compatible with parenthood under any conditions.[11] The assumption that homosexuality and parenthood cannot be harmoniously or morally combined emerges, of course, not only in custody determinations but in decisions about adoption and foster family policy, visitation rights for gay fathers, and even concerns about homosexuals working in such fields as teaching and child care.[12]

The increase of custody challenges by fathers would seem to indicate greater paternal interest in childrearing and increasing social recognition of the importance of fathers as caretaking parents, a goal which has been at the heart of some feminist recommendations.[13] I will argue, however, that the strategies mothers employ to protect themselves from custody threats, and the social organization that evolves in the context of these threats, act instead to strengthen a matrifocal emphasis in families facing custody challenges. When the possibility of custody litigation throws its shadow over the divorced mother and her children, mothers tend to define parenthood as a solitary maternal venture, with little room for paternal contributions.

Ironically, this outcome differs little from the picture that continues to emerge of two-parent families even in "post-feminist" times. Despite much celebration of the growing importance of fathers as primary parents and caretakers, studies reveal that maternal employment notwithstanding, fathers spend only marginally more time caring for children and doing housework than they did in earlier times.[14] Thus, custody challenges have converged with other factors which produce family patterns in which mothers serve as primary, if not sole, caretakers of children.

MATERNAL STRATEGIES

In this paper, I will describe some of the strategies[15] divorced mothers, both lesbian and heterosexual, devise for managing the threat of custody litigation.[16] Central to most mothers' efforts to protect themselves from custody challenges are what we might call strategies of appeasement. Strategies of appeasement describe efforts made by mothers to influence fathers not to bring custody actions. Mothers who fear such litigation typically keep a "low profile" (particularly if they are lesbians or have a co-resident lover), abandon claims to marital property, child and spousal support, and make compromises on issues like visitation.

Strategies of appeasement are fundamental to most mothers' efforts to avoid custody litigation. No matter how respectable a woman may be, and no matter how much she really needs the economic or interactional involvement of her former husband to manage her childrearing obligations, she tends to become extremely fearful when custody is raised as a point of contention, regardless of how oblique the possibility of legal action may be. Mothers who confront custody challenges often feel that they have to defend their very being, that their essential value as persons is somehow under scrutiny.

Lesbians' fears of being totally vulnerable to custody litigation are even more intense, as most lesbian mothers are familiar with cases of mothers who have lost their children solely because of their sexual orientation. Ironically, accusations about lesbianism are quite common in custody litigation, even, as we shall see below, when there is no foundation for them. Thus, it is not unusual for a heterosexual mother to have to confront charges of lesbianism when her husband seeks custody, charges which can be quite difficult to disprove once they have been introduced.

As appeasement requires abandoning or reducing claims not only to paternal involvement but to financial support, it can be difficult to achieve without tapping other network resources. Mothers' ability to maintain strategies of appeasement when they face custody challenges can be enhanced by the availability of strategies of support, that is, by access to female friends or kin who can offer affective and instrumental support.

However, in the absence of a strong, effective network, particularly one which can cushion economic uncertainty, mothers may come to believe that they can depend only on themselves. Self-reliance, competence, and individual ingenuity become key elements of their approach to adversity—a strategy of autonomy. Like many other aspects of the marriage-divorce system as it is emerging in American culture, maternal self-reliance has paradoxical benefits. At the same time that divorce represents the breakdown of the family and a personal failure for women, it provides an important opportunity to establish one's self-reliance, to avoid the expected, but morally ambiguous, dependence marital life implies for women. At the same time that marriage and motherhood represent entry into adult status,[17] the independence gained at divorce may be seen as further progress toward the cultural ideal of achieving individual autonomy.[18]

In the examples that follow I will indicate the ways in which mothers who face actual or potential custody challenges use strategies of appeasement, support, and autonomy in the course of protecting the integrity of their families. These data illustrate the ways in which these three strategic emphases intersect, producing, in many instances, unintended consequences for mother, father, and child. In particular, the claim to being a "good mother," a key element of female gender identity in American culture, is transformed from a natural attribute into the product of self-conscious achievement. This occurs at the same time that assumptions and behaviors displayed by these mothers are, in fact, drawn from elements and oppositions already in place in two-parent families.

STRATEGIES OF APPEASEMENT

Interviews with mothers who had experienced actual custody litigation or who regarded themselves as having been threatened with it at some point before or after their divorces consistently indicate that the mere mention of a custody challenge can dominate the proceedings. Most are aware that avoiding a battle during the divorce does not provide a permanent resolution, as a husband can return to court at any time in the future to seek a new custody ruling. This means that strategies for avoiding litigation must remain in operation at least until children turn eighteen.

Although Linda, a law student at the time of her divorce, is not a lesbian and has no specific reason to fear being declared "unfit," she was intimidated by the threat of a custody battle. Her psychologist husband raised the possibility of a custody suit during their settlement negotiations.

> When I said you're not giving me enough money . . . he said, "Well, if we have to have a fight over money, we might as well have a fight over custody." So I got real panicked and real scared, and I didn't want to fight a custody battle with him. So I agreed just down the line with his financial arrangements. I was real scared. Although he didn't file a custody suit at that time, I knew it was going to come sooner or later. I hoped I could postpone it until I was out of law school and could fight back.

Linda believed that conciliatory behavior would make her husband less willing to pursue a custody challenge. But for lesbians, conciliation may not be enough. Appeasing a former husband and avoiding a custody suit frequently hinges on secrecy, maintaining strict separation of private and public lives, and, in some cases, deceiving the children. Mothers must weigh the potential damage of their children "letting something slip" to their father or the strain of the children having to keep a secret against the psychological effects on the family of clouding their identities in secrecy.

Shortly before Elaine, a suburban school teacher, filed for divorce, she had become lovers with another married woman. Her husband hired a private detective to observe her activities, and she soon found herself at the center of a custody trial.

> That only got resolved because I lied on the stand, and said it had been a passing phase but it was over. Interestingly enough, the shrink . . . got on the stand and also said he thought it was a passing phase and he thought I was cured. So I got the kids.

Because Elaine lied at the trial, and also because her teaching position could be threatened by disclosure of her sexual orientation, she has had to be extremely cautious in the years since the divorce and has felt unable to challenge any of the financial arrangements which were worked out with her former husband.

> Here I am leading this double life. Publicly I'm a flaming heterosexual, when in truth I'm a lesbian and my kids don't even

really know about it. To go back to court over child support would give my ex-husband the opportunity to bring in the lesbian issue again, so I just figured I'd make it. And I did make it financially. I took in boarders, rented out the garage.

Theresa, the mother of a nine-year-old son, went through a lengthy custody trial, which left her virtually bankrupt. She was not a lesbian at the time of the trial and John, her former husband, was unable to substantiate his accusations that she was. Since the custody dispute, however, she has come out[19] and now feels that she must carefully separate her life as a mother and as a lesbian in order to protect herself from more litigation. She does not perceive her husband's history of psychiatric illness and her own record of social stability and professional accomplishment as improving her chances in any way.

Now that I'm gay, I'd lose. There's just no way in the world I would win, after having my fitness questioned when I was Lady Madonna, let alone now. So I would just simply tell him, no, I won't go to court, if you want custody, take it ... I've done everything to keep my ex-husband or my son from finding out.

The precautions Theresa has taken include living in a middle-class suburban area and arranging her house in a way she considers unimpeachably "bourgeois." The Bay Bridge, which separates her home from San Francisco, where she works and meets lesbian friends, has become a symbol to her of her divided life. She undergoes a transformation as she travels the bridge homeward or toward the city, experiencing the commute as an opportunity to prepare herself for the requirements of her destination. The most vital aspect of her strategy is preventing her son from discovering her lesbianism, not wanting him to bear the burden of keeping her secret.

Ironically, avoidance of her former husband, which would enable Theresa to relax her vigilance a bit, is the very thing that she has not been able to arrange. She considers John, who has a disability which keeps him from regular employment, a model father, and has accepted his offer of childcare in her home while she works. On one level, this arrangement saves her a great deal of money and also insures that her son has regular contact with his father, something she sees as desirable. On another level, the childcare arrangement has eliminated any possibility of privacy for Theresa. She must not only restrict the kinds of friends who visit her home, but must make sure that no compromising material of any sort can be found in the house.

In many instances, the husband only indirectly threatens to bring the mother into court and to use lesbianism as a weapon. Jean, a lesbian mother of two daughters, describes the negotiations surrounding her divorce, which terminated with her sacrificing nearly all of the money she had contributed to the purchase of a house.

> He never brought it into the negotiations directly. But he would like call me and harass me, and by innuendo suggest that there were many issues that he *could* bring up if he wanted to . . . So basically, I traded my equity in the house for that issue not being raised at that time.

Besides the loss of her share of the house, Jean was unable to get Richard to agree to contribute to the children's education or their medical expenses. Although she has considered returning to court to change the agreement, the possibility that her ex-husband would raise the issue of her lesbianism has discouraged her from doing this. Richard nearly always sends his child support payments late and, in a recent dispute, has refused to contribute to the costs of orthodontia for the children. In an effort to improve relations with him, Jean offered to send him a monthly written narrative about the children's activities. He said that he would like her to do this, but refused to consider doing the same thing for the time the children spend with him in the summer.

In another case, Rita, a clerical worker who lives with her woman lover and her eight-year-old son, reports that she has no way to enforce the child support and visitation agreement made at the time of her divorce because of her fear that a custody challenge might arise. Although her ex-husband, Jim, was supposed to pay her $100 a month and see their son every other weekend, he has never made a single payment and has almost never visited the child, failing even to remember his birthday. Despite this history, Rita still thinks that Jim might become interested in custody, perhaps if he were to remarry.

Rita believes, though, that as long as Jim does not pay child support, her position in a possible custody case is strengthened; as a further gesture toward self-protection, Rita has not directly discussed her lesbianism with her son. She lives openly with her lover, sharing a bedroom with her, and explained during the interview that nearly all of their friends are gay. Nevertheless, she feels sure that her son is unaware of the situation and thus protected from having to keep a secret.[20] Rita does not believe that Jim's record of violent behavior toward her (which once resulted in an arrest for battery) would help her in a custody battle.

In some other instances, custody threats are even less explicit, but still serve to affect the way mothers manage their relations with their former husbands. Judy, the mother of a nine-year-old son, left her marriage after she got involved in the women's movement and began a relationship with a woman. Judy works part-time in an office and is active in local feminist organizations.

> I figured I should tell the lawyer I was gay, since he was really pushing to get a lot of money out of my husband ... [but] I was saying no, don't push it, to the lawyer, because I'm gay and I don't want a custody hassle. And the lawyer really got off on that, and started asking me all these questions about did I lust for women, and all that crap. It was really awful.

Judy's son, Michael, spends each summer with Bill, and each summer Bill raises the possibility of having the boy live with him year round. Judy has given some thought to this request, seeing it as evidence of Bill's commitment to their son. However, a lawyer she recently consulted has advised her that allowing such an arrangement, even on a temporary basis, would open the door to a permanent custody change. Judy also perceives any challenge to the existing financial arrangement as too provocative to consider. Since the divorce, Judy's husband has remarried and is doing very well financially. He has never increased his small financial contribution, and has refused to help pay for any unusual expenses, such as music lessons, claiming that this is in line with Judy's feminist principles.

> He's said that since I made this feminist decision to live on my own and not be dependent on a man, why should he give me more money? Which I sort of agree with in a lot of ways. I don't really want to be dependent on him financially.

Bill knows that his son will not be deprived of anything he really needs, because Judy's parents, who are well-to-do, are willing to help her with expenses beyond her means.

The effect of Bill's custody threat, subtle though it has been, is to limit the amount of contact he has with his son and to make quite unlikely any sort of authentically "joint" custody arrangement.[21] Were Judy not fearful, for example, that Bill might launch a custody battle once he had "possession" of Michael during the school year, she might be willing to allow an arrangement that would give her son longer, and more meaningful, exposure to his father. She also might be more aggressive in seeking child support payments that would reflect the actual cost of raising her son and correspond more accurately to her ex-husband's income. In addition, however, to her fear of a custody challenge, Judy's knowledge that she can depend on her parents for assistance mitigates her need to make further financial claims on her former husband. In the same vein, Rita makes no effort to obtain a more significant financial and personal commitment from her former husband while Jean accepts the asymmetrical arrangement she has worked out with her children's father.

IMPACT ON FATHERS

The impact of these strategies is to reinforce the mother's role as the sole support of the household, to limit the contact between father and child, and to accentuate differences between the cultural and economic climates of the maternal and paternal homes. For most mothers, the need to keep distance from their former husbands means that the father is the last person with whom issues affecting the child are discussed; to share real problems with him would be to admit to weakness or error, and the mothers whose custody claims are in doubt cannot risk such exposure. Thus, while the father's interest in custody implies an interest in participating in childrearing, the actual effect of his custody bid is to exclude him from most aspects of parenting.

Carol, a lesbian mother of a son and a daughter, lost custody of her children for several months but finally regained it after a lengthy trial. Although her children visit regularly with their father, she never discusses any of their problems with him.

I do not want to talk with him about any of that kind of stuff because I think he would use it against me. I don't trust him still and I do feel that he would like custody of our son for sure.

Similarly, Linda, the law student described earlier, is conscious of not being able to rely on her ex-husband for any level of material or emotional support. She characterizes her husband as a "spectator" in his approach to fatherhood. He sees himself as doing a good job if he takes the children on excursions, but is unable to manage any of the problems that arise when they make their weekly visits.

If he has a headache, the kids come home. If one of the children has the sniffles, the kids come home. He puts up with the fun, but he doesn't quite know how to handle the inconveniences. In fact, at times he's just dropped them off on the doorstep and pulled away.

Because of the continuing history of custody threats since the end of the marriage, Linda does not feel that she can discuss any parental matters with him.

When I do present problems to him, he points out what I'm doing wrong. And it makes me feel that he's gathering evidence for another custody suit. He will reveal nothing of what he perceives as problems to me. So we don't communicate at all. Luckily, I have friends that I can talk to about my concerns about the kids. The man that I'm involved with, I talk to about them. My happiness I want to share as much as the problems, and it makes me sad that I can't share that with him. But there's too much of a wall of bitterness to talk about us sharing the good things about our kids. And there's not trust enough to share the problems, so there's just no communication around that.

While paternal interest in gaining custody would seem to indicate that fathers are eager to play a fuller role in their children's formative years, not only actual threats of custody litigation but even expressions of interest in spending more time with children can cause mothers to become fearful. On the one hand, mothers often suspect that custody threats are made cynically in order to reduce the amount of child support paid, to negotiate a more favorable property settlement, or to otherwise influence mothers to accept less than adequate economic arrangements. Because custody decisions are never final, the threat of renewed litigation can persist, even after a mother has won custody in court. On the other hand, even fathers who have a sincere interest in their children may find themselves distanced from them, as mothers seek to avoid any kind of contact that might generate evidence usable in a custody challenge.

Sources of Support

When mothers who face custody challenges can use their networks for ongoing material or emotional support, the exclusion of the father from their support system is less likely to leave them either isolated or impaired in their ability to manage unexpected situations.

In Rita's case, for example, the financial difficulties caused by Jim's failure to pay child support are eased by the regular support she receives from her family. Despite the fact that Rita's mother is uneasy with her lesbianism (including being actively hostile toward Rita's lover, Jill), they have developed a daily childcare arrangement, which makes it possible for Rita to manage quite well on a low income.

Rita's relationship with her mother is not one-sided. Her mother depends on her for support when there is a family crisis, and Rita has a strong sense of responsibility toward the entire family. She also has a close relationship with her father, sometimes spending hours talking with him when something bothers her. He helps her with her car and advises her on household repairs. Rita's sister is another source of emotional support. They often talk on the phone, and sometimes care for each other's children for extended periods.

For many mothers, friends, rather than relatives, form the core of the support network. Linda, as mentioned earlier, is able to discuss problems and concerns both with her boyfriend (whom she is planning to marry) and with two close women friends. The emotional support she receives from these friends is supplemented, in the case of her boyfriend, with financial assistance. She describes her women friends as being "like sisters"; both have children close in age to her children and this means that they are ideal people with whom to discuss various parenting dilemmas, the very issues she is afraid to raise with her former husband.

Rosemary, a forty-year-old mother of five, now going through a divorce after twenty years of marriage, often finds herself in need of emotional support. Ironically, though Rosemary is not a lesbian, her husband is gathering evidence about her friendships with other women to allege that she is. No less than women who are lesbians, Rosemary is fearful about defending her "fitness" in court.

> Intellectually, I realize that they're not going to be taken from me. But emotionally, I feel like I'm in a panic, because how the hell do I go around and prove I'm a good parent? You can find a hell of a lot of proof to find you're bad. But you can't find proof that says you're good.

Besides the custody challenge, Rosemary is facing financial disaster in the wake of her husband's departure. The marriage had been quite traditional, so until it was over, Rosemary was not familiar with family finances and the way in which her husband managed his income. Now that she is alone, she has discovered that her husband, Carl, left her in serious debt, forcing her to move from their large house to a small apartment and leaving her unable to obtain credit on her own. The situation is not helped by Carl's hostility when she attempts to communicate with him, nor by his refusal to pay child support until ordered to do so by the court. He has a large income and continues to maintain a comfortable, even luxurious, lifestyle, a contrast Rosemary finds especially painful when her children return from visits and compare her household unfavorably with his.

A number of friendships have helped sustain Rosemary through the difficult period following the collapse of her marriage, but one woman friend has had a particularly central role during this time. Every night at a prearranged time, she and her friend Charlotte (a divorced mother who lost custody of her children) have agreed to talk on the phone. They both discuss their problems, but in recent times Rosemary often cries while Charlotte listens. Rosemary helped Charlotte go through the trauma of her divorce and the loss of her children; now Charlotte is reciprocating. But the support Rosemary receives from this friendship goes beyond these telephone conversations. On occasions when Rosemary feels that she cannot cope with her children alone, she can call Charlotte and ask her to join them for dinner. In addition, without much explicit discussion of Rosemary's serious financial difficulties, Charlotte often arrives at Rosemary's door with a turkey or other food which she "doesn't need."

Strategies of appeasement and strategies of support can dovetail neatly, with support systems enhancing mothers' efforts to appease ex-husbands. But in some instances, these two strategic emphases may conflict, as when the way to appease a litigious father appears to be including him in the day-to-day family routine. Arrangements of this type create particularly stressful situations for mothers, as successful maintenance of a "low profile" is difficult when one's former husband is constantly on the scene.

For example, Theresa's situation, which gives her little choice but to involve her husband as her son's regular caretaker, undermines her efforts to incorporate friends into her support system. The result is a fragmented, highly specialized network. She gets her main emotional support from her friends at work, who accept her as a lesbian and respect her as a skilled professional. But these friends do not cross the bridge into her personal life.

Theresa's lover also provides some needed emotional support, but this is compromised by the secrecy that shrouds their relationship; the relationship itself is as much a source of stress as a support, since it is the most likely point at which secrecy might be breached. Nor can Theresa look to her family for substantial support. She has a warm and affectionate relationship with them, but counts on them for little concrete as they live in an Eastern city and are quite poor. Rather, she is protective toward them, and hesitates to share any information with them that might be alarming.

Similarly, the price of the extensive emotional and economic support Rita receives from her family has been the peripheralization of her tie with her lover, Jill. Her parents refuse to visit her home or to include Jill in family events; at the same time, however, their assistance makes it easier for Rita to maintain a relationship which could discredit her in a custody action.

MAXIMIZING AUTONOMY

For some mothers, insulating themselves from threats to custody depends on self-reliance; these women find it difficult to form supportive networks, particularly when caution restricts their contracts with relatives and with their ex-husbands. As one lesbian mother said:

> I feel like I'm some kind of a spy-agent, or something like that, with a secret assignment that I have to be protecting. Like the state secrets or something. It's a pressure on me.

Similarly, Theresa's inability to maintain sufficient distance from her ex-husband to bring supportive others into her life has essentially pushed her toward a strategy of autonomy. In other instances, women describe disappointments in efforts to sustain supportive networks among friends, perceiving non-mothers as selfish and insensitive to the problems faced by mothers.

Not uncommonly, mothers who describe themselves as sole parents see this as a condition which began during their marriages. For example, Rosemary, now embarking on a custody battle with her husband of twenty years, sees little difference between her circumstances as a married and as a single mother.

> I consider that I was a single parent for twenty years of the marriage. He wasn't there for birthdays, he didn't show up for christenings, it wa. not uncommon for me to stand in the doorway Christmas day and say "Goddamit, mister, it's Christmas, please don't go out sailing today . . ." Going to PTA meetings, getting involved in their Brownies, their Cub Scouts—it was all my job. I did all of that. Discipline, I did all that. I did the cooking, the cleaning, the shopping. I took care of everything. I took the kids to the doctors, I made the appointments. If they had any emergencies, I took care of it. I still do. That's no different.

While for some women, then, self-reliance implies the absence of an effective, reliable support system, for others it reveals competence and skill which they were never able to display before, or which they couldn't acknowledge. Carol, the lesbian mother of two, who won her children back from their father in a lengthy custody suit, described becoming a single mother in terms of personal growth and development.

I felt before that I was in a jar. There were a lot of things cooking around inside, but the lid was on. And now I feel I've had the opportunity to really think for myself, find out what I can do for myself, make the decision myself ... I am the head of the household. I can feel it. That feels good to me. I was the head of the household essentially when he was here, but there was a deference to him ... I feel more grown up [now] than I ever did.

Carol's feelings were echoed by Susan, a heterosexual mother who is cautious in her dealings with her former husband because of oblique threats he has made about custody. Although she has close relationships with her sisters and has several women friends, she does not feel that she can easily depend on any of them for ongoing assistance. She also has established an intimate relationship with a man who gets along well with her son, but she believes that there is a limit to what she can expect from him because he is not, and never can be, the "real father."

Despite an initial period of intense loneliness, a feeling that she was "part of nobody," at the time that she left her marriage, Susan has come to view the end of her marriage and the need for self-reliance it has engendered as the "greatest thing that ever happened to me."

Independence ... As an adult to have control over my own life. To make my own decisions, to not to have to ask anybody to do anything. To do whatever I want without having to consult. In terms of raising my child, to do it the way I see fit, and not to have to fight somebody else over that. My image of that is a flower that's tightened within itself. After the divorce, it opened up like—have you ever seen a slow-motion of a flower opening? That's what I felt like. My personality and my strength just really blossomed.

CONCLUSION

Custody threats tend to eclipse differences among mothers. In the cases discussed here, lesbian and heterosexual mothers coping with potential or actual custody litigation devise strikingly similar strategies for managing threats to family integrity. Whether they bear the additional legal handicap of lesbianism or not, mothers feel able to survive the custody challenge only by bargaining with scarce resources. This generally means both abandoning rights to material benefits that might be obtained from the former husband and peripheralizing him as a parent.

Rather than just "being" mothers, women involved in custody disputes come self-consciously to define their maternal achievements, to break down their roles into specific components and skills which fathers cannot—or will not—perform. Instead of looking to nature to legitimate claims to motherhood, women must depend both on demonstrating competence, as well as on invalidating paternal claims, whether they do this in the formal legal system or through informal negotiation.

The mothers that I interviewed have lost the financial support once available to them from their children's fathers but few suggest that divorce had deprived them of a collaborator in the business of parenting. For those women who face or fear a custody battle, the need to defend their centrality as parents adds a bitter irony to their situations: they know that the custody challenge is, in many instances, a strategy for providing less, rather than more, care for their children. Even when paternal interest in the children is sincere, mothers understand that they will not survive the custody challenge if they offer what their former husbands ostensibly desire—more involvement in the daily business of parenting—as this will only make them more vulnerable to litigation.

Instead, appeasement, accession to paternal demands to an extent that discourages a custody challenge, along with successful use of supporting strategies, marks maternal competence. Being a "good mother" is thus transformed from a state of being, a natural attribute, into evidence of skill, rewarded by preventing fathers from gaining custody or, better yet, by keeping custody disputes from arising.

At the same time, then, that custody threats exacerbate the pressures on these families, they provide a context within which women can demonstrate their competence and achieve not only the status of "good mother" but that of autonomous adult woman. In establishing their claims to motherhood, women facing custody disputes also explicitly negotiate gender, deriving pride from their struggles and defining motherhood as achievement and strength.

Notes

Research for this paper was supported by NIMH Grant MH-30890 and by a grant from the Rockefeller Foundation Gender Roles Program. The author wishes to thank Terrie A. Lyons for her contribution to the research and analysis, and Faye Ginsburg, Carol Shepherd McClain and Anna Tsing for their comments on earlier drafts of this paper.

1. Phyllis Chesler, *Mothers on Trial* (New York: McGraw-Hill, 1986); Nancy D. Polikoff, "Gender and Child-Custody Determinations: Exploding the Myths," in *Families, Politics, and Public Policy: A Feminist Dialogue on Women and the State,* ed. Irene Diamond (New York: Longman, 1983), 183–202; Lenore Weitzman, *The Divorce Revolution* (New York: Free Press, 1985).
2. Weitzman, 310.
3. Single mother families already derive little income from child and spousal awards, as numerous studies have shown. About 40 percent of divorced fathers are not required to make payments, and of the 60 percent who receive support orders, about half do not comply. See B. R. Bergmann and M. D. Roberts, "Income for the Single Parent: Child Support, Work and Welfare," in *Gender in the Workplace,* ed. Clair Brown and Joseph A. Pechman (Washington, DC: Brookings Institute, 1987), 247–270.
4. Terry Arendell, *Mothers and Divorce* (Berkeley: University of California Press, 1986).
5. Polikoff, 184.
6. Nan D. Hunter and Nancy D. Polikoff, "Custody Rights of Lesbian Mothers: Legal Theory and Litigation Strategy," *Buffalo Law Review* 25 (1976): 691–733; Ellen Lewin, "Lesbianism and Motherhood: Implications for Child Custody," *Human Organization* 40, no. 1 (1981): 6–14; Rhonda R. Rivera, "Legal Issues in Gay and Lesbian Parenting," in *Gay and Lesbian Parents,* ed. Frederick W. Bozett (New York: Praeger, 1987), 199–227.
7. Terrie A. Lyons, "Lesbian Mothers' Custody Fears," in *Women Changing Therapy,* ed. Joan H. Robbins and Rachel J. Siegel (New York: Haworth Press, 1983), 231–240.
8. Carole H. Browner and Ellen Lewin, "Female Altruism Reconsidered: The Virgin Mary as Economic Woman," *American Ethnologist 9,* no. 1 (1982): 61–75. See also Judith K. Brown, "A Note on the Division of Labor by Sex," *American Anthropologist 72 (1970): 1073–78; Nancy Chodorow, The Reproduction of Mothering* (Berkeley: University of California Press, 1978) Sherry B. Ortner, "Is Female to Male as Nature is to Culture?" in *Woman, Culture and Society,* ed. Michelle Z. Rosaldo and Louise Lamphere (Stanford: Stanford University Press, 1974), 67–87; Michelle Z.

Rosaldo, "Woman, Culture and Society: A Theoretical Overview," in *Woman, Culture and Society,* ed. Michelle Z. Rosaldo and Louise Lamphere (Stanford: Stanford University Press, 1974), 17–42, for classic interpretations of the impact of motherhood on women's social and cultural status.

9.   Custody law has shifted since the nineteenth century from a primary concern with parental rights (associated with the notion that children are the property of the father), to a maternal preference (by which mothers could only lose custody, particularly of children of "tender years," if they were deemed "unfit"), to the current standard of "best interests of the child," purported to be gender-neutral. See Committee on the Family, Group for the Advancement of Psychiatry, *Divorce, Child Custody and the Family* (San Francisco: Jossey-Bass, 1980); Weitzman, 36.

10.   Along similar lines, it might be noted that the culture increasingly views reproduction itself in this light. The interests of pregnant women and fetuses, for example, are commonly supposed to be separate and antithetical, reflected both in the normalization of a variety of technological interventions during pregnancy and birth and in recent approaches to such matters as "surrogacy." See Barbara Katz Rothman, *The Tentative Pregnancy* (New York: Viking, 1986) and George Annas, "Baby M: Babies (and Justice) for Sale," *Hastings Center Report* 17, no. 3 (1987): 13–15, for discussions of recent developments in these areas. In "Reproductive Technologies and the Deconstruction of Motherhood," her chapter in her edited volume, *Reproductive Technologies: Gender, Motherhood and Medicine* (Minneapolis: University of Minnesota Press, 1987), 10–35, Michelle Stanworth has pointed to the ongoing development of guidelines to insure that women who avail themselves of new conceptive technology are heterosexual and married. Not coincidentally in the same period, the law has come increasingly to resolve custody disputes by making mothers demonstrate their qualifications. Gender, as well as motherhood, must be achieved in all of these contexts.

11.   Lewin, 7.

12.   See Wendell Ricketts and Roberta Achtenberg, "The Adoptive and Foster Gay and Lesbian Parent," in *Gay and Lesbian Parents,* ed. Frederick W. Bozett (New York: Praeger, 1987), 89–111; and Rhonda R. Rivera, "Our Straight-Laced Judges: The Legal Position of Homosexual Persons in the United States," *Hastings Law Journal* 30, no. 4 (1979): 799–956.

13.   See, for example, Chodorow, 211–219; and Dorothy Dinnerstein, *The Mermaid and the Minotaur* (New York: Harper and Row, 1977). Authors representing the perspective of "fathers' rights" generally question what they consider an unwarranted maternal preference in most custody awards, as well as complain about the size of divorce settlements, alimony, and child support payments. Many guides for fathers who wish to seek custody have been published, and the theme of paternal nurturance has been popularized by such films as *Kramer vs. Kramer.* See, for example, Mel Roman and William Haddad, *The Disposable Parent* (New York: Holt, Rinehart, Winston, 1978); and Gerald A. Silver and Myrna Silver, *Weekend Fathers* (Los Angeles: Stratford Press, 1981) for examples of this perspective; see also Polikoff, 183–197 for a critique.

14.   See Heidi I. Hartmann, "The Family as the Locus of Gender, Class, and Political Struggle: The Example of Housework," *Signs* 6, no. 3 (1981): 366–394.

15.   I have spoken elsewhere of the ways in which becoming a mother may be used strategically to enable women to achieve goals with broader cultural significance. Forging links with particular categories of people, notably with children, may be central to maternal agendas in some contexts, as shown by Browner and Lewin, 61–73. In other situations, as for lesbians who use donor insemination, the formation of a particularly valued personal identity appears to define varied approaches to becoming a mother. See Ellen Lewin, "By Design: Reproductive Strategies and the Meaning of Motherhood," in *The Sexual Politics of Reproduction,* ed. Hilary Homans (London: Gower, 1985), 123–38. Maternal strategies are characteristic not only of the process of becoming a mother (with or without a conscious decision) but of subsequent behavior and choices.

16.   Data presented here are excerpted from 135 interviews with lesbian and heterosexual single mothers conducted in the San Francisco Bay Area between 1977 and 1981. Informants' names and some descriptive details have been changed to preserve their anonymity.

17.   See Lois W. Hoffman, "Effects of the First Child on the Woman's Role," in *The First Child and Family Formation*, ed. Warren B. Miller and Lucile F. Newman (Chapel Hill: Carolina Population Center, 1978), 340–67.

18.   See, for example, Robert Bellah, et al., *Habits of the Heart* (Berkeley: University of California Press, 1985).

19.   "Coming out" can refer to one's first homosexual experience, but also describes the point at which one defines oneself as a lesbian or gay and/or acknowledges this identity to others. See, for example, Jeannine Gramick, "Developing a Lesbian Identity," in *Women-Identified Women*, ed. Trudy Darty and Sandee Potter (Palo Alto, CA: Mayfield, 1984), 31–44.

20.   Interestingly, Rita's son was present during most of the interview. She did not appear to censor her remarks or to feel that his presence altered his "unawareness" of her sexual orientation.

21.   See Roman and Haddad, 123–148, 173–174; C. Ware, *Sharing Parenthood After Divorce* (New York: Viking, 1982); Lenore Weitzman and Ruth Dixon, "Child Custody Awards: Legal Standards and Empirical Patterns for Child Custody, Support and Visitation After Divorce," *UC Davis Law Review* 12 (1979): 473–521.

Carolyn G. Heilbrun

from *Writing a Woman's Life*

According to Carolyn G. Heilbrun, biographers writing about women's lives tend often to define them in terms of their roles as wives and mothers rather than as dynamic individuals on exciting professional trajectories (like men). An Avalon Foundation Professor in the Humanities at Columbia University, Heilbrun is the author of *The Garnett Family, Christopher Isherwood* and *Toward a Recognition of Androgyny*. She has also written numerous mystery novels under the pseudonym of Amanda Cross.

Women will starve in silence until new stories are created which confer on them the power of naming themselves.
— SANDRA GILBERT AND SUSAN GUBAR

This is the true story of a woman who was born exactly a century before Freud published *The Psychopathology of Everyday Life.*

At the age of four, living on a large estate with horses and space for vigorous activity, she dressed as a boy in order to be able to play more freely. As she grew up, she dressed as a boy for riding and played the male roles opposite conventionally pretty girls in village productions. She found cross-dressing fun, sometimes going to the village near her estate dressed as a young man with her brother who would dress as a girl.

She was married at eighteen to a man of whom Henry James was to observe that he thought he had married an ordinary woman, and found on his hands a (spiritual) sister of Goethe. A year later her first child was born, six years later her second, who was probably not her husband's. By then she had already taken her first lover, years after her husband had taken many mistresses, including her own maid, and behaved brutally toward her. She left her husband eight years after the marriage began and went to live with a lover and collaborator in the nation's capital. Gaining from her husband a separation and an allowance (from her own money), she published two novels and several novelettes under a male pseudonym. Here is her description of how she dressed when she first came to the city:

> Above all, I hungered for the theater. I had no illusions that a poor woman could indulge such longings. [They] used to say, "You can't be a woman [here] on under twenty-five thousand." And this paradox, that a woman was not really a woman unless she was smartly dressed, was unbearably hampering to the poor woman artist.
>
> Yet I saw that my young male friends—my childhood com-

panions—were living on as little as I, and knew about everything that could possibly interest young people. The literary and political events, the excitements of the theaters and picture salons, of the clubs and of the streets—they saw it all, they were there. I had legs as strong as theirs, and good feet which had learned to walk sturdily in their great clogs upon the rutted roads of [the country]. Yet on the pavement I was like a boat on ice. My delicate shoes cracked open in two days, my pattens sent me spilling, and I always forgot to lift my dress. I was muddy, tired and runny-nosed, and I watched my shoes and my clothes—not to forget my little velvet hats, which the drainpipes watered—go to rack and ruin with alarming rapidity.

Distressed, she consulted her mother, who said: "When I was young and your father was hard up, he hit on the idea of dressing me as a boy. My sister did the same, and we went everywhere with our husbands: to the theater—oh, anywhere we wanted. And it halved our bills." Here, of course, was the perfect solution. "Having been dressed as a boy in my childhood, and having hunted in knee breeches and shirt, such dress was hardly new to me, and I was not shocked to put it on again." She became famous and had many lovers, including one woman, but she loved one man at a time, and these men were usually younger than she and were not married or the lovers of other women. She liked women, and encouraged younger women all her life. She was the lover and friend of some of the outstanding creative men of her day. She ran a comfortable, hospitable home, eventually delighted in her grandchildren, her garden, conversation, and the possibility of social revolution. Her name, of course, was George Sand.*

To describe her further to you I shall borrow the words of the late Ellen Moers, who in turn calls upon descriptions by Sand's contemporaries to compose this portrait: "She has a brilliant, well-stocked mind and a warm heart; she has courage, energy, vitality, generosity, responsibility, good humor, and charm; she has aristocratic distinction combined with bohemian informality; she is a wise,

---

*These passages are drawn from Ellen Moers, "Introduction" to *George Sand: In Her Own Words,* and from *Sand, My Life.* (See Works Cited.)

passionate, down-to-earth human being, and disappointingly sane.''
Moers continues:

> She was a woman who was a great man: that is what her
> admirers most wanted to say about George Sand. But words
> of gender being what they are, suggestions of abnormality and
> monstrosity cling to their portraits of Sand, all unintentionally
> and quite the reverse of what her admirers had in mind. Eliza-
> beth Barrett Browning began a sonnet to Sand with the line
> ''Thou large-brained woman and large-hearted man'' and what
> she intended as a tribute to wholeness came out sounding gro-
> tesque. Similarly Balzac: ''She is boyish, an artist, she is great-
> hearted, generous, devout, and chaste; she has the main charac-
> teristics of a man; ergo, she is not a woman.'' Similarly Tur-
> genev: ''What a brave man she was, and what a good woman.''
> . . . Reading George Sand is to encounter a great man who was
> all woman. [xv]

And, indeed, if we read her life in any available form, we come
again and again to this description of her as both man and woman.
She enacted, through lovers and friends, all relationships from mother
to master (Flaubert called her ''dear master''). She had the power
both to give and to receive, to nurture and to be nurtured. Yet all
who knew and admired her found themselves without language to
describe or address her, without a story, other than her own unique
one, in which to encompass her. Although she played every role,
including conventionally female ones, although she wrote, in her
letters, stereotypically romantic phrases, she did not herself become
the victim of these roles or phrases. In one of her novels, the heroine
lives dressed as a man, though married and spending intervals in
women's clothes; she dies as a man with the word *liberté* on her
lips, having said, ''I have always felt more than a woman,'' meaning,
of course, more than woman as she is defined.

''Oh you, of the third sex,'' Flaubert hailed her, and those words
that would today sound sneering or disturbing were wholly compli-
mentary then. Flaubert, the ultimate master of words, found it impossible to discover any other way to describe the greatest friend of his
life. Henry James, a lifelong admirer of her work, tried many times
to describe Sand, and this artist of language and narrative faltered
again and again in the attempt. George Sand's, he wrote, was ''a

method that may be summed up in a fairly simple, if comprehensive statement: it consisted in her dealing with life exactly as if she had been a man—exactly not being too much to say.'' After her death, James would remark to Flaubert that ''the moral of George Sand's tale, the beauty of what she does for us, is not the extension she gives to the feminine nature, but the richness that she adds to the masculine.'' Flaubert wrote sadly to Turgenev of how at Sand's funeral he had wept ''on seeing the coffin pass by.'' To a woman whose friendship he had shared with Sand, he wrote: ''One had to know her as I knew her to realize how much of the feminine there was in that great man, the immensity of tenderness there was in that genius. She will remain one of the radiant splendors of France, unequaled in her glory'' (quoted in Barry, 384).

If we compare this story with the now famous account of the probable life of Shakespeare's imagined sister in Virginia Woolf's *A Room of One's Own,* we are moved to explain the miracle that was George Sand's life with the failure of Judith Shakespeare and of so many anonymous women poets. It is easy enough to point to Paris and to French mores for an explanation, but this is not what matters. What matters is that lives do not serve as models; only stories do that. And it is a hard thing to make up stories to live by. We can only retell and live by the stories we have read or heard. We live our lives through texts. They may be read, or chanted, or experienced electronically, or come to us, like the murmurings of our mothers, telling us what conventions demand. Whatever their form or medium, these stories have formed us all; they are what we must use to make new fictions, new narratives.

George Eliot, who did in her life what she could never portray in the lives of her heroines, allowed a minor character in *Daniel Deronda* to protest women's storylessness: ''You can never imagine,'' Daniel's mother tells him, ''what it is to have a man's force of genius in you, and yet to suffer at the slavery of being a girl. To have a pattern to cut out . . . a woman's heart must be of such a size and no larger, else it must be pressed small, like Chinese feet; her happiness is to be made as cakes are, by a fixed receipt.''

No careful study of nineteenth century literature can overlook Sand's tremendous effect on the writers of her time. Hers is the work that explains the Brontës, whose passionate novels lay outside the English tradition, and that goes far to explain the work of Dostoyevski, Whitman, Hawthorne, Matthew Arnold, George Eliot, and many others, to mention only writers who did not meet her but were influenced by her work. Yet few courses in Victorian literature, Russian literature, or American literature even mention George Sand. She and her tremendous influence have disappeared from the canons of French and American literature classes with scarcely a trace. Had she not been a woman, such a disappearance would be inconceivable. But, what is most important, the story of her life has not become an available narrative for women to use in making fictions of their lives. The liberating effect of her novels is greater upon male writers than upon women in England and the United States. The narrative she lived is not yet textually embodied. How many new narratives for women enter texts and then other texts and eventually women's lives?

A few years ago, after having read many exciting new biographies of women, I had a shocking experience in going through Peter Ackroyd's biography of T. S. Eliot. I had felt obliged to read it as part of my professional duties, as my special field is modern British literature. And the old sense rushed over me of the ease of male lives, that sense I had so long lived with—for I have been teaching modern British literature for twenty-five years. I fell into this biography like one who hears again the stories of her youth. Here was a life for which there was indeed not only *the* narrative, but so many possible narratives. Despite Eliot's egregious sexual and personal failures, despite professional uncertainties, writing blocks, and frightening social judgments, despite his confused national, religious, and marital loyalties, his story reads as easily, as inevitably, as those of the Hardy boys.

For the first time in years I came to realize how far in my search for women's lives and texts I had moved from this wonderful banquet of possible quests, conceivable stories, available narrations. I settled into this biography—which is very well written, by the way—as easily as women, if one were to believe the advertisements, settle into Harlequin romances. I read the story as romances are read because I knew how it would come out, knew that, of all the choices life might offer him, Eliot would find those that suited. Yet romances, which end when the woman is married at a very young age, are the only stories for women that end with the sense of peace, all passion spent, that we find in the lives of men. I have read many moving lives of women, but they are painful, the price is high, the anxiety is intense, because there is no script to follow, no story portraying how one is to act, let alone any alternative stories.

Ackroyd writes of Eliot that "he could not work easily [on the play *Samson Agonistes*] because there was no literary context for such writing from which to draw energy or inspiration." He had "complained to Virginia Woolf that, in the absence of illustrious models, the contemporary writer was compelled to work on his own." One smiles at what must have passed through her mind as she heard this. Ackroyd continues: "Throughout [Eliot's published work] there is evidence of an imagination which received with full force the impression of others writers' forms and language, and which was then able to assimilate them within an original design. He always needed a safety net, as it were, before he indulged in his own acrobatics" (147). It is precisely such a safety net that is absent from women's lives, let alone their writings. How are they to imagine forms and language they have never heard? How are they to live to write, and to write that other women may live? There was always, Ackroyd tells us, a moment of "despair" during Eliot's creation of a work. For Virginia Woolf, of course, there was all to do from the beginning, and enough despair to have discouraged women for generations.

Ackroyd writes that "only in response to other poetry . . . could Eliot express his deepest feelings" (149). For women, that response has almost always been to the poetry of men, to a point of view not theirs, often, as with Eliot, deliberately excluding them. In *The Wasteland* only the silent hyacinth girl is acceptable, neither loathsome nor destructive—and it is her silence he treasures. Ackroyd says that "the anonymous role of a *Times* reviewer in fact suited [Eliot] very well: it allowed him to adopt the role of the scholar, and thus employ the tone of established authority" (97). Virginia Woolf, who also reviewed for the *Times,* must have liked the anonymous role at first; anonymity eases women's pains, alleviates the anxiety about the appropriateness of gender. As Charlotte Brontë was to write to her publisher, "I am neither a man nor a woman but an author," and Cynthia Ozick and Joyce Carol Oates have said much the same in our day. But had Woolf employed the tone of established authority, she would have denied her life's experience. There is not "objective" or universal tone in literature, for however long we have been told there is. There is only the white, middle-class, male tone.

But the question is not only one of narrative and tone, it is also one of language. How can women create stories of women's lives if they have only male language with which to do it? The question, in

Mary Jacobus's words, is "the nature of women's access to culture and their entry into literary discourse. The demand for education provides the emancipatory thrust of much nineteenth and twentieth century feminism. . . . But this access to a male-dominated culture may equally be felt to bring with it alienation, repression, division—a silencing of the 'feminine,' a loss of women's inheritance. . . . To propose a difference of view, a difference of standard—to begin to ask what the difference might be—is to call in question the very terms which constitute that difference." Jacobus speaks of "the rift experienced by women writers in a patriarchal society, where language itself may reinscribe the structures by which they are oppressed." The "demand for an impossible desire" can condemn women to silence even when their entry to education and the professions seems to have permitted them utterance.

The problem, again in Jacobus's words, is this: "Women's access to discourse involves submission to phallocentricity, to the masculine and the symbolic: refusal, on the other hand, risks reinscribing the feminine as a yet more marginal madness or nonsense." Refusal in this sense for French philosopher Julia Kristeva involves a refusal of the symbolic, the Law of the Father, that would locate women within the realm of the semiotic, "the pre-Oedipal phase of rhythmic onomatopoeic babble which precedes the Symbolic but remains inscribed in those [early] pleasurable and rupturing aspects of language." Woman is thus offered, on the one hand, exclusion from (patriarchal) language itself or, on the other, a circumscription within the feminine domain of language, a domain that "in fact marks the place of women's oppression and confinement." What to do? Jacobus suggests that, "though necessarily working within 'male' discourse," we women "work ceaselessly to deconstruct it: to write what cannot be written" (10–21). As Jimmy Durante put it, thems the conditions that pervail.

What have women done about it? Here is Margaret Homans's summary of where we are: "The French writers who accept the premise that language and experience are coextensive also understand language to be a male construct whose operation depends on women's silence and absence, so that when women write they do not represent themselves as women. In contrast, most recent feminist criticism in this country has pragmatically assumed that experience is separable from language and thus that women are or can be in control of language rather than controlled by it" (186). To put it differently, as Elaine Marks does, American feminist critics see women as *oppressed* by sexism, "their voices unheard within the dominant culture," whereas for French critics, women are *repressed*, equivalent to the unconscious, and therefore not representable in language (55).

What it comes down to is this (in Homans's words): "There is a specifically gender-based alienation from language that is characterized by the special ambiguity of women's simultaneous participation in and exclusion from [the male] hegemonic group." Or (in Jacobus's words): "Can women adapt traditionally male-dominated modes of writing to the articulation of female oppression and desire?" Or (in my words): How can we find narratives of female plots, stories that will affect other stories and, eventually, lives, that will cause us neither to bury Shakespeare's sister nor to throw up our hands in describing George Sand because we are unwilling to call her either a woman (under the old plot) or a man when she isn't one?

In a recent seminar titled "Gender and Literature" offered to Columbia University Master's students, we read, among much else, four stories of women who, feeling trapped in a script they did not write but were slowly beginning to analyze, look about them for a way out, a way on to a different life: "The Awakening" by Kate Chopin, "To Room 19" by Doris Lessing, "A Jury of Her Peers," by Susan Glaspell, and a brilliant but lesser-known story by Jean Stubbs, "Cousin Lewis." What the class came to see was not alone the gender arrangements, the appropriate behavior, that had confined these women in stories that had always been assumed to be intelligent and fair; they also saw the absence of any narrative that could take the women past their moment of revelation and support their bid for freedom from the assigned script. Various dramatic events await these women as they strive to break free, or to satisfy a longing for identity and psychic space: suicide in two cases, murder in one, a more confined marriage in the fourth, "Cousin Lewis," where a woman who donned male clothing to tell her children stories of adventure is declared unfit to raise her children. The class remembered that, in addition, we had read Hawthorne's *The Scarlet Letter* and Cather's *O Pioneers!* In both of these novels the woman had lived through her special destiny but left no path behind her for future women, had lived with no community of women, no sense of bonding with other women. Not only had these women no stories other than their refusal of the plot in which most women lived, and no women with whom to talk of what they had themselves learned, but they would have been hard put to answer the inevitable question asked of unhappy women: What do you want?

If I had to emphasize the lack either of narrative or of language to the formation of new women's lives, I would unquestionably emphasize narrative. Much, of a profound and perceptive nature, has been written about the problem of women coping with male language that will not say what they wish: we remember Woolf's enigmatic statement that Jane Austen was the first to write a woman's sentence. Some part of us responds to this, as to the words of Anne Elliot in *Persuasion*—"Men have had every advantage of us in telling their story. Education has been theirs in so much higher a degree; the pen has been in their hands."—and of Bathsheba in Thomas Hardy's *Far from the Madding Crowd*—"It is difficult for a woman to define her feelings in language which is chiefly made by men to express theirs." But what we speak of here, as I suspect Homans and Jacobus also do, is not so much women's lack of a language as their failure to speak profoundly to one another. As Deborah Cameron has written, "Men do not control meaning at all. Rather women *elect* to use modes of expression men can understand because that is the best way of getting men to listen" (105). The problem, she asserts, is one not of language but of power. And power consists to a large extent in deciding what stories will be told; in Bromwich's (slightly altered) words, male power has made certain stories unthinkable.

As Cameron perceives, women's talk is not inherently or naturally subversive; it becomes so when women begin "to privilege it over their interactions with men (as in consciousness-raising groups). Men trivialize the talk of women not because they are afraid of any such talk, but in order to make women themselves downgrade it." Women's talk will indeed be harmless as long as women consider it trivial compared to talk with men (157–58).

Women must turn to one another for stories; they must share the stories of their lives and their hopes and their unacceptable fantasies. Sartre, in the introduction to his biography of Jean Genet, has defined the story as "freedom confronted by fate, first crushed by misfortunes, then turning against them and gradually controlling them." Genius, he sets out to prove, is "not a gift, but rather the way one invents in desperate situations," and in considering it we must "retrace in detail the history of a liberation" (quoted in Sarde, 8). We have seen that even our women geniuses, and the biographers of women geniuses, do not "retrace in detail the history of a liberation." Rather, even women geniuses do not have their efforts recorded as inventions "in desperate situations." What then of the rest of us?

We must stop reinscribing male words, and rewrite our ideas about what Nancy Miller calls a female impulse to power, as opposed to the erotic impulse which alone is supposed to impel women. We know we are without a text, and must discover one. Virginia Woolf speaks of George Eliot's heroines' "demand for something—they scarcely know what—for something that is perhaps incompatible with the facts of human existence." That is the something women need to reinscribe. As Miller writes, "the plots of women's literature are not about 'life'. . . . They are about the plots of literature itself, about the constraints . . . of rendering a female life in fiction." The reinscriptions of "experience . . . in literature are organizations, when they are not fantasies, of the dominant"—that is, the male—culture. Literature does not write our, women's, "fictions of desire" (43, 44).

How might it do so? In *Alice Doesn't: Feminism, Semiotics, Cinema,* Teresa de Lauretis concludes by identifying "consciousness raising" as a way to appropriate reality: "The fact that today the expression consciousness raising has become dated and more than slightly unpleasant, as any word will that has been appropriated, diluted, digested and spewed out by the media, does not diminish the social and subjective impact of a practice—the collective articulation of one's experience of sexuality and gender—which has produced, and continues to elaborate, a radically new mode of understanding the subject's relation to social-historical reality. Consciousness raising is the original critical instrument that women have developed toward such understanding, the analysis of social reality, and its critical revision." What she is recommending is the "practice of self-consciousness," the "political, theoretical, self-analyzing practice by which the relations of the subject in social reality can be rearticulated from the historical experience of women" (186). To put it simply, we must begin to tell the truth, in groups, to one another. Modern feminism began that way, and we have lost, through shame or fear of ridicule, that important collective phenomenon.

Consciousness raising, as far as it went, revealed to the white, middle-class women who took part in it that, isolated in nuclear families, they suffered individual guilt, each supposing herself a monster when she did not fit the acceptable narrative of a female life. It is questionable how much any individual woman before the women's movement was helped by individual therapy or advice. What became essential was for women to see themselves collectively, not individually, not caught in some individual erotic and familial plot and, inevitably, found wanting. Individual stories from biographies and autobiographies have always been conceived of as individual, eccentric lives. I suspect that female narratives will be found where women exchange stories, where they read and talk collectively of ambitions, and possibilities, and accomplishments.

I do not believe that new stories will find their way into texts if they do not begin in oral exchanges among women in groups hearing and talking to one another. As long as women are isolated one from the other, not allowed to offer other women the most personal accounts of their lives, they will not be part of any narrative of their own. Like Penelope awaiting Ulysses, weaving and unweaving, women will be staving off destiny and not inviting or inventing or controlling it. They will live their lives individually, among the suitors, without a story to be told, wondering whether or when to marry. In the *Odyssey,* it is important that Athena appears to Penelope in a dream as her sister, whom Penelope has not seen since her marriage. What other woman might Athena have impersonated? There were no other women peers in Penelope's life, certainly none near her. One of the reasons Samuel Butler thought the *Odyssey* had been written by a woman was because "when Ulysses and Penelope are in bed and are telling their stories to one another, Penelope tells hers first. I believe a male writer would have made Ulysses's story come first, and Penelope's second" (quoted in Weigle, 204). It does not occur to Butler that Penelope, never the subject, like her husband, of individual narrative, has new stories to tell. But we must note that Penelope has no one other than her husband to whom to tell her stories, and only husbands who have been absent for twenty years could be expected to listen with such attention, and to listen first. Even in more recent literature, we see how alone women are, how without close women friends are Jane Austen's heroines, and Charlotte Brontë's, and George Eliot's.

There will be narratives of female lives only when women no longer live their lives isolated in the houses and the stories of men.

Works Cited

Ackroyd, Peter. *T. S. Eliot.* New York: Simon & Schuster, 1984.

Barry, Joseph, ed. *George Sand: In Her Own Words.* Garden City, NY: Anchor Books, 1979.

Cameron, Deborah. *Feminism and Linguistic Theory.* London: Macmillan, 1985.

De Laurentis, Teresa. *Alice Doesn't: Feminism, Semiotics, Cinema.* Bloomington: Indiana University Press, 1984.

Gilbert, Sandra, and Susan Gubar. *The Madwoman in the Attic.* New Haven: Yale University Press, 1979.

———. No Man's Land. Vol. 1. New Haven: Yale University Press, 1987.

Homans, Margaret. " 'Her Very Own Howl': The Ambiguities of Representation in Recent Fiction." *Signs* 9 (1983): 186–205.

Jacobus, Mary. "The Difference of View." In *Women Writing and Writing About Women,* ed. Mary Jacobus. New York: Barnes and Noble, 1979, pp. 10–21.

James, Henry. *The Notebooks of Henry James,* ed. F. O. Matthiessen and Kenneth B. Murdock. New York: Oxford University Press, 1947.

Marks, Elaine. "Breaking the Bread: Gestures Toward Other Structures, Other Discourses." *Bulletin of the MMLA* 14, no. 1 (Spring 1980): 55.

Miller, Nancy K. *Subject to Change: Reading Feminist Writing.* New York: Columbia University Press, 1988.

Moers, Ellen. "Introduction." In *George Sand: In Her Own Words,* ed. Joseph Barry. Garden City, NY: Anchor Books, 1979, pp. ix-xxii.

Sand, George. *My Life,* trans. and adapted by Dan Hofstadter. New York: Harper Colophon, 1979.

Sarde, Michele. *Colette,* trans. Richard Miller. New York: Morrow, 1980.

Thomson, Patricia. *George Sand and the Victorians.* New York: Columbia University Press, 1976.

Weigle, Marta. *Spiders and Spinsters: Women and Mythology.* Albuquerque: University of New Mexico Press, 1982.

Woolf, Virginia. *A Room of One's Own.* New York: Harcourt, Brace, 1929.

————. "George Eliot." In *Women and Writing,* ed. and with an introduction by Michele Barrett. New York: Harcourt Brace Jovanovich, 1979, pp. 150–160.

Robin Morgan

---

from *The Word of a Woman: Feminist Dispatches
1968–1991*
"The Politics of Silence"

Award-winning poet, political theorist and writer Robin
Morgan is the founder of Sisterhood Is Global, the first international feminist policy institute. Recent among her fourteen
published works are *The Demon Lover: On the Sexuality
of Terrorism, Upstairs in the Garden: Poems Selected and
New* and *The Mer-Child: A Legend for Children and
Other Adults.*

Ms. Morgan's introductory note to "The Politics of Silence" follows.

These notes constitute a further attempt to develop work I began on the subject in "Going Too Far" (1977) and "The Anatomy of Freedom" (1982), and to expand the explorations begun by other feminists on silence. I am especially indebted to Tillie Olsen's "Silences" (Delacorte Press, 1978); Adrienne Rich's "On Lies, Secrets, and Silence" (Norton, 1979) and in particular her essay "Women and Honor: Some Notes on Lying" (1975); Michelle Cliff's "Notes on Speechlessness" and Catherine Nicolson's writing on the "power of deafness" (both in "Sinister Wisdom" No. 5); and Nelle Morton's concept of "hearing each other into speech" ("Beloved Image," paper delivered at the National Conference of the American Academy of Religion, San Francisco, December 1977). Many women, myself included, have written on the silencing committed by the patriarchal structures of sexism and racism, by patriarchal history, culture, language, even modes of perception and definition; some of us have also written on the silences among and between groups of women. The following article focuses instead on the politics of silence between two individual women, in particular between two women in a relationship, as close friends.

Among the Padaung tribes in Burma's Kayah State, there persists a custom of pressing down a girl's collarbones with brass rings; the ritual of "beautification" begins when the female child is five years old, with one ring at a time added during intervals until, as an adult, she may be wearing as many as twenty rings in a tight necklace. Tourists have called the wearers "giraffe women" because of the effect of grossly elongated necks. In fact, the neck muscles tend to atrophy; removal of the rings (said to be a punishment for adultery) can cause suffocation. Padaung men take pride in the thin, "inherently feminine" voices of "soft-spoken" Padaung women.

In London, Paris, or New York, such a practice would be considered barbaric. In London, Paris, or New York, the short necklace now coming back into style for the sophisticated woman is referred to as a collar or choker.

Wherever she waits, and only rarely dares whisper, the silent woman is not to blame. Blame, in addition to being counterproductive and boring, is not the point.

Let us say there are two women. Each is keenly aware of the politics of silence between women and men; each is publicly articulate about the effect (: erasure) of such silencing on women. In private, one is talkative, accustomed to trying to express—on the page or in conversation—thoughts, emotions, and their psychological/political valences. In private, the other woman tends toward silence about such matters, calling herself (as she has heard others do for years) "a silent person," "a private person," or even "shy." These two styles persist and inform the friendship between the two women.

Sometimes the silent one feels under assault by the other's speech. Sometimes the talkative one feels assaulted by the other's silence. (These descriptive terms are themselves only semiarticulations: the talkative one can be taciturn, the silent one can be loquacious.)

There is a politics at work here. It is a politics qualitatively different (albeit related, given the context of patriarchy) from that between a man and a woman. In an androcentric world, male power is power *over,* enactable by a man via whatever mode he chooses: we recognize how the dominant conversationalist male acts from a position of power over women ("Women make such good listeners!"), but so does "the strong silent type" ("*Talk* to me, Herman, *please?*"). Traditionally and cross-culturally, men are accustomed to/expected to pronounce themselves endlessly on matters of "public concern"— for which read the power of running the world—while retreating into inarticulate mumblings in the "womanly" realm of private affairs: emotion.

Between two women, however, another politics is alive, in the engagement of two different kinds of power—power *over* and power *to*—made more complex by the dexterity with which each can be manipulated to masquerade as the other.

For example, the talkative woman has power not only *to* express herself but also power *over* her friend regarding the other's difficulty in/choice in not doing so. Indeed, the common perception (and what perception in patriarchy is common but a patriarchal perception?) is that talkers have privilege and power over nontalkers. This is one truth.

Another truth—the underside to the truth above—is that she who expresses reveals, intentionally or even unintentionally, her thirst to communicate, her vulnerabilities, her willingness to be known, her very self; and longs to inspire a comparable process of revelation, either by response or by the other's initiative, in the silent partner. She spends her power in this place of powerlessness.

Lesbian silence battering at the unhearing ear of heterosexual assumptions.

The silencing of the subjective voice by the myth of objectivity.

Very well, then. Let us say that these two women are not merely friends, but lovers.

Very well, then. Let us say "you" and "I."

Silence creates silence, proselytizing and propagating its message: I fear my talking monopolizes the conversational oxygen between us; I hope fewer words from me will give you the space in which to speak; waiting, I fall silent; my silence comes to have a life of its own.

Or: Communication creates communication: expression as a form of contagion. The contagion can be one of disease, if language is used as a vehicle for lying, control, manipulation, or hypocritical compensation for the absence of other forms of communication (touch, hearing, alternative enriched forms of silence such as an exchange of "knowing" glances). Such an abuse of language is commonplace, truly "sound and fury, signifying nothing," a barrage of words as defense against authentic communication. But if language is valued as a means of understanding, of bridging difference, and of hazarding truth(s), then the contagion is one of health.

As a feminist activist, for instance, I could define myself as an agent of contagion—an instrument for naming, for spreading hitherto unspeakable truths about and between women—in a political attempt to foster an epidemic of human health.

As a lover, it is both simpler and more complicated.

Simpler because every cell of my being aches to talk with, and to hear, the beloved.

More complicated because I fear invading your privacy, bullying your silence. More complicated because you can claim (not without justification) your own respect for words is so great that you use them sparingly. More complicated because your exactitude of speech—when you do speak—is so finely honed it was one of the reasons I first loved you, which means that I must, to be fair, credit your silence as a quality that drew me to you in the first place. More complicated because I fear your anger (often the initial and most accessible means by which your silence overflows into speech) if I prod too much. More complicated because I do not wish to seem probing into your rights to yourself, in an emotional imperialism. More complicated because I fear attributing to you, in a one-sided analysis, objectifying motives projected out of my own enforced so-lipsism, motives that bear no relation to what you really are thinking and feeling.

Both simpler *and* more complicated because you tend to discover what you think and feel in a process of silence and only then, if at all, to share it. Whereas I tend to discover what I have intuited as my thoughts and feelings while in the act of verbalizing or writing them: the word made flesh. This frequently means that I grope aloud, risking the ungainly posture of self-discovery with a witness present, however embarrassing.

So I, ostensibly from a position of (expressive) power, feel actually naked, vulnerable—powerless, as if I used my power in order to set it aside. So you, from a position of ostensible (silent) powerlessness, actually operate with power; power *to* define what is said and not said, heard and not heard (because failing a response from you how can I know that my soundings were heard, much less misunder-stood?), power *over* the entire process of communication between us. You alone know what both of us are thinking.

Knowledge is power. Information is power. The secreting or hoarding of knowledge or information may be an act of tyranny camouflaged as humility.

But: honesty can be a bludgeon disguised as a gift.

Silence accrues slowly, like the minuscule skeletons of a coral reef; it can wear as many colors, take on as many formations; it is just as sharp, but can cut more deeply. Silence can also rise suddenly, at the speed of darkness.

Silence may defend itself by calling its methods "discretion" or "tact." In an erotic context, silence may be defended as a means of preserving mystery, a supposed aphrodisiac (which in itself precludes such glad possibilities as "The more I know you, the more I love you"). It was Colette who wrote, "I do not necessarily respect what I do not understand."

Colette also wrote of the silence between two women intimates as one in which the participants can be utterly at peace in the certainty that out of that quiet fullness anything can be spoken, yet nothing need be. This presumes that the silence is one chosen mutually by both participants. Such a silence vibrates with an equal power *to*. You have introduced me to the speechless pleasures of such a silence, it is true.

A rediscovered clue: the biblical phrase (in the King James version—translated so brilliantly by seventeenth-century English metaphysical poets): *and they knew one another*. To know, to "ken" something, has the same etymological root as the Old English word "cunt." Etymology is political code.

Logos as a concept meant not only the Word, but Creation: breath itself. If Logos is breath as well as utterance, then speaking to your silence is an act of prayer, like arguing with God—whose notorious silence can seem such an indifference as to drive one to atheism.

I yearn to cry out "I am myself, not a ghost of parents or teachers or former lovers who drove you into silence by demanding that you speak in their dialects of possession. I am merely me, and it is you, merely you, I love and hunger to hear!"

You might reply, "I am myself, not a ghost of parents or teachers or former lovers who drove you to performing as the sole way you could get their attention. I am merely me, and it is you, merely you, I hear and love, beneath whatever you say."

But how dare I assume that reply, since it has not been spoken?

It is possible to suffocate in such a silence.

Class plays its part in both articulation and silence, as well as in the different styles of expressing each. (Silence is an expression just as much as being apolitical is a political stance.) Accepted wisdom has it that verbal ease is a privilege of education and class (and what wisdom is accepted, in a patriarchy, but patriarchal wisdom?). Yet the candid, direct, metaphor-rich articulations of, for instance, working-class or poor women can throw into high contrast the repressed verbal style of middle-class women. In a group context, it can even intimidate them.

Culture, too, we are told, plays its part. As a European American, an apostate Jew who has lived most of her life in New York City, and as a member of that financially insecure yet educationally enriched class Europeans term "intelligentsia," I acknowledge that my style tends to dramatize events, exaggerate states of being, and delight in conversation for its own sake, almost as an art form. (Sometimes you say you find this highly entertaining.) In another culture—a more Anglo one, for example—such forms of social congress may be judged as vulgar, prying, superficial, clownish, or stereotypically that of the "effusive American." (This ignores the considerable regional, ethnic, and urban/rural differences in the United States—a common error made by those unfamiliar with the laconic Maine "Yup" and "Nope," the Mississippi front-porch yarn, the Chinatown "talk-story," the Harlem street-rap, ad infinitum.) In a classic gesture of psychological reductionism, it can also be labeled "psychobabble"—as if all U.S. residents lived in California granola bins. (That was petty and unfair, I'm sure, to Californians.) Whose, after all, is "the American voice"? Crazy Horse, Thomas Paine, Willa Cather, Zora Neale Hurston, Emily Dickinson, Ralph Ellison, Walt Whitman, Twain, James, Faulkner, Jeffers, Baldwin, Tennessee Williams, Erdrich, Hong Kingston, Morrison?

To me, obversely, such judges may appear in their forms of social communication to be cold, distant, haughty, secretive, and pretentious. My curiosity about an Englishwoman's life, her intellect and emotions, may seem to her rudely intrusive. Her restraint about inquiring into comparable details of my life, while for her an act of respect, may strike me as a mark of disinterest in—even contempt for—me, a lack of curiosity about wishing to know me at all.

Yet if class as well as culture are at this moment in history both constructs of patriarchy, then what would authentic forms of female communication entail? If women, in two different sexist stereotypes, are supposed to be chatterboxes or to remain silent, does that make me a collaborator with one stereotype and you a collaborator with the other? Or are your silence and my speech both facets of our feminist rebellion? Or is your silence male identification, as a survival mode—and is my loquacity male identification, as a means of controlling the expression between us?

What would a feminist silence sound like? What would genuine free speech say?

*　　*　　*

Age plays a part, I am sufficiently older than you to feel the press of time poignantly limiting, moment by moment, the chances for all I would and could say, all I am eager to hear. This particular aspect of human suffering is not attributable solely to patriarchy—which is politically inconvenient.

My tools as an artist are words—with all the inherent dangers thereof. A lifelong vocation addressing the silence of the unknowable reader.

If a pause can be pregnant, so can a phrase be aborted, or an idea brought to term, communicated, and grow to have a life of its own. What, then, would self-determination over one's own reproductive rights be in terms of speech, in terms of living out loud?

It has taken me almost forty years of writing to realize that I live in an age where language is not only cheapened, but where the technology of modern communication has so shrunk patience and shortened attention span as to make my tools perhaps as outmoded for an art form as a lute or virginal would be for a contemporary composer: quaint, possibly touching, perhaps a bit precious.

So I speak toward the beloved—toward you—out of a sensibility already weary with the pain of being a bad joke: "a word person" (so termed, affectionately, by a friend needing help with her electoral campaign literature); "so *poetic,* even in prose" (this, uneasily, from a colleague in publishing); "more of an intellectual than you think you are" (this astoundingly backhanded compliment from a longtime acquaintance tsk-tsking over the use of "big words" in my writing). I have learned to smile good-naturedly over such insults, even to adopt the safe defenses of caveat and self-deprecation in order to co-opt such blithe definitions of my existence.

In the rare moments when I strike back, I am assured that it was well-meant teasing, that the teasers actually love me for (among other things) my words, that I mustn't lose my sense of humor. Yet one early sign of consciousness unfurled when women began to affirm losing our sense of humor over well-meaning jokes about dumb broads, frigid bitches, and mothers-in-law; it was a sign of consciousness when African Americans ceased to pretend shared amusement over watermelon and natural rhythm stories; when Jews and Italians, Poles and Hungarians confronted jokes about kikes and wops, Polacks and Honkies. When we decided to take ourselves ("too") seriously.

We know that humor is deeply political. There are those who claim all humor has an element of cruelty in it. Yet the humor of mutual recognition is not cruel, but revelatory. It resonates a joyful laughter—a communication of freedom. You and I have shared many such moments of humor, laughing until words fell into a happy silence of breathless gasps and aching ribs.

Consequently, I am loathe to censor—even, teasingly, to censor the teasing—into silence. Or to censor your silence into speech.

Meanwhile, the pain continues. To articulate the pain is, of course, to renew the entire process, and to invite more teasing—this time about one's hypersensitivity.

"You find it easy to talk about your feelings. I don't. Yet I feel as deeply as you do. I just don't flaunt it."

This seems to be a statement about powerlessness.

Then there is the infamous heterosexual cliché comment about two same-sex lovers embracing in public (surrounded by heterosexual lovers doing the same thing): "Look, I'm all for gay rights—but why must they flaunt it?"

If the two statements are related, which is a defense of power held (power decidedly *over*)? Are both?

If you say, "I am not given to verbal diarrhea," are you aware that what was merely your defense arrives with me as an offense?— and has the effect of silencing me? Besides, something snide in me wants to answer, the word is "logorrhea." But that would be to risk sounding elitist as a "word person."

If you say, "The difference is that you want me to change, whereas I love you the way you are," this sounds generous, mature, admirable.

(A short short story: a voyeur and an exhibitionist fell in love, moved across the street from one another, and lived happily apart ever after.).

Another truth is that wishing to preserve the status quo—in this case your silence/my speech—is usually the desire of the power holder; it preserves your inviolability and my accessibility.

Truth curls in nested boxes.

Still another truth is that all lovers fall in love with certain qualities of the beloved—which they then, idiotically, proceed to try to change.

Still another truth is that I want both of us to change, to find some third way between your art of silence and mine of speech, between the excess of the hidden and the surfeit of the revealed. Neither of us chose either of these dualities. (The truth is that you want both of us to change, too.)

Still another truth (a tiny box, this one, worn close to the bone) is that I fear being typecast as the repository of articulated emotion, the one who can be relied upon to "raise the issue," hint/pressure/probe/nag/confront. Curiosity is, to me, an act of desire, of trust, all of a piece with what I've termed "erotic intelligence." Since, then, "wanting to talk about it" is to me one central form of loving—albeit the one traditionally and cross-culturally assigned to women—it can mean, in effect, feeling as if one is bearing more than one's share of the burden of emotional responsibility in a relationship. This is bad enough when dealing with a man. It is a delicate, hushed sort of madness when dealing with another woman.

After the Chinese Revolution, female cadres attempted to unwind the foot bindings of some of their sisters. But the tightly knotted, fetid bandages, which had reduced the human foot to the size of three inches, had sometimes rotted and grown into the flesh. Their removal caused insufferable pain, pain that had not been so experienced since the binding, because numbness had replaced sensation over the years. Removal of the Padaung neck rings can cause suffocation.

How do I speak to you then, without violating your silence? How do I learn to believe you when you claim to love my speech? How do I strip myself of unnecessary verbiage so that my plainsong reaches you uncontaminated by my own defenses, manipulations, pretentions, or presumptions? How can I strain to hear you into speech—or hear what you wish your silence to tell me? How can I affirm your means of survival while not denying my own?

How do I speak to you in the act of love?

How do I love you in the act of speech?

These notes are only one side of the story. Which is, unfortunately, the point. It has taken me words to tell you these things, knowing as I do that the writing itself can be seen as an act of power, certainly of *hubris,* possibly even of revenge. But knowing, too, that these words have been brought forth with great care, risking more than a little, and leaving me raw in the process.

For fear.

For fear of being misunderstood. For fear of being misrepresented. For fear of never being answered.

O beloved voice: Have I just proven why you choose silence?